SALT & SOUR

SALT & SOUR

MY RECIPE FOR STARTING OVER

A COOKBOOK MEMOIR BY
YODA OLINYK

SALT & SOUR
COPYRIGHT © 2020 BY YODA OLINYK

All rights reserved

FIRST CANADIAN EDITION

No part of this book may be used or
reproduced in any manner whatsoever
without the prior written permission of the
author, except in the case of brief
quotations embodied in critical articles or
reviews. Some recipes and brief portions
of this book may appear on the author's
website and Instagram

Salt & Sour is a work of nonfiction.
Some names and identifying details have
been changed to protect the privacy of the
individuals involved. See: *A Memoir: A
Note About the Words in this Story*

The recipes in this book are to be
followed exactly as written. The publisher
is not responsible for your specific health
or allergy needs that may require specific
medical attention. The publisher is not
responsible for any adverse reactions to
any of the recipes contained in this book.
See: *A Cookbook: A Note About the Food
in this Story*

The author has quoted Albert Einstein
and Rumi, as well as adapted a quote by
Allyson Proulx

—

Exterior Book Design by:
Katelyn Landry
Interior Book Design and Layout by:
Labour of Love Books
Interior Illustrations by:
Andres Garzon

—

Printed and bound in Victoria, BC
Distributed by: Labour of Love
Books (for inquiries, please email
manager@saltandsourbook.com)

Imprint: Independently published
ISBN: 9798674472889 (paperback)

Humbly dedicated to "Rachel," "Sam," "Nancy," "Charlotte," "Alisa," and all the other women within my own story who prefer not to be named or mentioned. This book is also written for all the women and men who have their own stories that are untold or unheard — I see you. And I honour you.

And, for my family.

Although there are recipes in this book, this is not a cookbook *per se*. This book is a collection of the stories that have impacted my life the most, some of which are followed by a recipe.

In addition, I think it is important to note that this is not a vegan cookbook. For those of you who don't know me personally, or have not been following my journey, I own a vegan catering company in London, Ontario, Canada. This might lead people to expect my book to be entirely plant-based (or at least mention my experiences with veganism at some point). Veganism has been a very important (and complicated) part of my career as a chef, but I have determined that it is a subject far too vast and intricate to include in *this* particular book. In conclusion, I have decided to include all types of recipes from my family heritage, travels and from the entire span of my career as a chef, plant-based or otherwise. I have also included several vegan and gluten-free recipes, which you can identify next to the recipe name. I've used (v) and (gf) to indicate vegan and gluten-free recipes, respectively.

———

As with any set of instructions, it is best to read the recipe in its entirety *before* you pick up your knife or turn on your stove. It is also most efficient to have all your ingredients assembled, and any equipment accessible, before you start the cooking process. You may have noticed on cooking shows that the chef always has his or her ingredients in small bowls on the counter, ready to go. This is called 'mise en place,' and it is a crucial part of any recipe. When using this book, I want you to imagine that each recipe starts with, '*First, gather your ingredients. Prepare them as listed on the recipe.*' For example, if the recipe states, '*medium onion, finely chopped,*' you should have that chopped onion in a small bowl or dish, ready to go, *before* you begin the next step. You can also use this time to look out for any instructions that may require prep to be done hours (or even days) ahead of time. This will not only make your cooking experience easier and more successful, but it will also make you feel like Jamie Oliver or Nigella Lawson as you calmly glide around your kitchen with ease.

It's important to note that everyone's homes/ovens/equipment/tastes are different. Most of these recipes are quite forgiving and have room for interpretation — if your intuition is telling you those cookies don't *look* done, by all means, adjust the cooking time. The same goes for seasoning, mixing times and serving sizes.

For your reference, all temperatures are listed in Fahrenheit. Most ingredients are measured by volume — the ones that are listed by weight are also listed by *approximate volume* in case you don't have a kitchen scale. Unless I've used the words 'packed' (e.g. *'2 cups packed brown sugar'*) or 'heaping,' you should fill your container (cup, tablespoon, etc.) and level it off with the back of a knife or spatula.

For consistency sake, all eggs are large, farm eggs; all flour is all-purpose; all olive oil is extra virgin; all butter is salted, all pepper is black; all salt is kosher — unless otherwise specified. Seasonings like herbs, spices and hot sauce are always optional, however salt and sour are not.

———

Another thing to note about the recipes in this book is that some of them have been dictated to me by their creators. You may find that this collection is more whimsical and rustic than you might find in a traditional cookbook. I have tried my very best to balance classic cooking archetypes with the integrity of the original version. Each and every recipe has been extensively tested for accuracy and deliciousness. (It's a tough job, but someone had to do it!)

This feels like a good place to thank my recipe testers and their families, who donated their time, kitchens and taste buds to make this book possible: Jessica L, Katelyn L, Brad S, Katie M, Carla

C, Anna C, Mariano E, Cheryl and Rick W, Tanner W, Tracey L, Tammy and Paul G, Kelly W, Chloe D, Jude A, Claire C, Kim and Dave H, Jason M, Kathy and Guenter D, Sonya J, Christine C, Shannon T, Becky and Charlie S, Amy T, Lisa S, Kristen N, Vanessa F and Amanda R. Special shout out goes to Danielle G and Karissa V who took on more than I ever expected or could dream of.

Gathering these recipes has been a very special journey into my own family history and the traditions of my loved ones. Developing these recipes has sparked an unmatched sense of nostalgia and has nourished me in ways I never imagined. It is truly an honour to share them with you and I hope that these recipes help create the same solace in your kitchen, and in your heart, as they did in mine.

At the very least, I hope these recipes make you feel full.

A MEMOIR
A NOTE ABOUT THE WORDS IN THIS BOOK

This book contains my complicated experiences with a relationship that involved deep layers of dishonesty, emotional and financial abuse. I've reflected on these experiences thoroughly which has included the excavation and examination of trauma, and many other details I'd rather forget. To wit, this is *my* account of what happened, to the best of my memory. To offer privacy to the people involved in this story, the names and identifying details of characters and places have been changed. Some of the timelines have also been compressed and may be outlined outside of precise chronological order. I have, to the best of my ability, extensively fact-checked every detail in this book, to ensure that this story is the truth — nothing more, nothing less.

There have been many moments during the process of writing this book that I've wanted to give up, so I understand if there are moments as the reader, that provoke you to want to do the same.

If I could tell you just one thing in those moments, it's that all I have ever wanted to do, to get through the saddest thing I've ever faced, is to share my story in the kindest way that I know how, with as much grace as I can muster. Even the people closest to me grappled with this story, so when you read this, you might go through moments of anger or resentment. This story might make you feel helpless or hopeless. You might want to jump into the story to shake me, slap me, hug me or cry with me. Whatever comes up, I ask that you honour it and remember the 10 words that got me through everything you're about to read:

I'm sorry. I forgive you. I love you. Thank you.

This story includes references to heavy subject matter including sexual harassment, suicide and depression. Although this book contains my own approach in processing trauma, it is not meant to be used as a substitute for professional assistance.

Please seek treatment from the appropriate health care professional if you need support with your mental health or processing trauma.

PROLOGUE

It was August 20th, 2017. I woke up without him. My heart felt like it was a burnt pot being scrubbed with steel wool.

There wasn't a single gram in the recipe of my being that didn't acknowledge the empty space beside me. I had shared this bed with the man whom I thought I would someday marry and raise a family with, for the last six years. Loneliness overwhelmed me in a way I'd never known, and it demanded unthinkable effort to accept the bitterness of this moment. I clutched my chest. The sudden movements made by stirring in bed caused the pains all over my body to make themselves known. My back muscles had been ravaged from years of being stretched to their limits. My stomach was in knots from the anxiety that had been mushrooming for months. My jaw was screaming from clenching it tightly and grinding my teeth. My face was stiff from tears and rage. My nerves were tender and raw, as if they were being grated on both ends.

But it was my heart which ached the most … from waking up without him.

I whistled for my two dogs to join me, desperate for comfort and company. They obliged, one nuzzling my side with her snout while the other placed her paw on my leg. Their affection made me shake with both gratitude and sorrow — gratitude for them, and what was left of my life — and sorrow for all the rest.

I knew that once today was over, I'd have to live with what I'd done, and worse, what *he* had done. I could barely stomach it. My guts felt like they were going through a blender on maximum speed. I lay there still, trying to quell my nausea, in complete disbelief. Just two weeks earlier, he and I were slow dancing in the middle of a patch of grass, while the world around us watched. As images and memories flashed in my mind, my eyes began burning with tears begging to come to the surface. There was not enough time to mourn the day ahead. Even if there were time, I wasn't sure that I had enough energy left to produce tears — I was wilted to my very core. I felt like spinach that had been left in the pan on high heat for too long.

The story of how I landed here is surreal and unfair. There are sharp corners. Serrated edges. A metallic taste. A hissing sound. On that day in August, there was no silver lining to the story. There was no phoenix rising from the ashes. There was no sweetness to soothe the bitter taste in my mouth. All I could taste that morning was salt and sour. Blood and sweat. Regret and remorse and rage and ruin.

———

You are holding that story — the story of how I got here.

The story of how and why I woke up alone on August 20th, 2017, and all the mornings that followed, where I was forced to learn the harsh lessons of what sudden solitude and crushing loneliness can teach someone.

This is a story of giving up on my dream to help someone else pursue their own — a decision made out of love, necessity and oppression. This story is about disowning my intuition and confusing dysfunction for love. It catalogues a series of unforgivable actions that went against my identity as a friend, Girl Boss, chef and as a decent human being. This story is about all the people who got hurt, and how those same people ended up saving me from myself, and from a man who wasn't good.

This is the story of how I would come to see the truth about that man. It's about holding all my memories up to the light and seeing them for what they truly are. The story starts with how we fell in love; how he swept me off my feet and kept me there. You'll notice that certain parts of this story sound a bit like a fairy tale — I had to let those moments go, and *so will you*. Moving on from the idea of a happy ending required me to gather all the red flags from over six years and trade them in for my final white flag — to surrender to the truth, and to relinquish a future that I thought was my destiny. This story is about how and why I decided to blow up my entire life, and give up on that future, to do the right thing.

This story is made up of heaping cups of guilt, dashes of failure, a pinch of sabotage. It's overflowing with loss and sprinkled with consequences. My lack of integrity is on full blast, for all the world to see. The shield of lies is baked right in. And yes, there are some recipes too.

These recipes, and the stories behind them, might break your heart. You see, this isn't the story of: Girl meets Boy, Girl falls in love, Boy betrays her. That is what happened, in one way or another, but what I'm going to tell you is about so much more than that. It's about starving myself of the two constants in my life since I was a little girl — *food and words.* It's about how my unwavering joy for cooking was stolen from me, and how I gave up on my passion for writing when the truth became too painful to put into words.

This is the story about falling in and out of love with a man, with my words, with my craft and with myself.

———

You're going to read about all the moments that mattered and see how I missed them. It will not be easy. You'll read about the five days I spent mourning. You'll watch as I unravel, rebel and resist. I'll tell you all about the people who coaxed the truth out; the people who saved my life. I'll explain about how I sat in the quiet with all the chaos and had to pare all the pretty, fleshy fruit away until all that was left was the core. The core was bitter and it wrecked me. It mangled me. It desolated my reality as I knew it. I lost nearly everything because of that single, solitary, painfully un-simple truth and everything that came with it. The rock bottom. The nakedness. The chaos. The doubt. The pain. The discomfort. The panic. The loneliness.

You'll see from my story that the truth didn't just *happen* to me. I begged for it. I pleaded. I even got down on my knees and prayed for it. When the truth finally came for me, it stuck to me like molasses to a wooden spoon. I wasn't ready. I fought back. I winced. I wept. I cried on my bathroom floor with my hands held in fists, punching and shaking and refusing to believe it.

But the truth, in all its pungency, was also responsible for causing the light and love inside of me, to poke through the darkness that was beginning to consume me. The light had always been there, waiting to come out. It's the same light that resides inside of you, as well.

It took a long time, but eventually I gathered all that light and love, and I folded in some resiliency and tenacity and patience (so much patience!) and I wrote this book with it. Writing often felt like I was pouring lemon juice directly on a cut that I desperately wanted to scab over. Have you ever done that? It stings like hell. Now, imagine packing salt into that gaping, infested, lemon rubbed, burning wound.

All it took to get past the salt and the sour was strength and love.

That's all it ever takes.

———

Nothing about this story has been easy, including sharing it with the world. My motivation behind publishing this story, regardless of whatever ramifications I may endure because of it, is because I believe that this is a story that *needs* to be told. For some people, this book might provide some long overdue closure and perhaps some justice. Although I am incredibly proud to be able to offer that to whomever might need it, it's important to know that this story isn't about revenge or getting even. Furthermore, this story is not about being a victim or demonizing anyone. Publishing this book is an acknowledgment of the poignant role I played in a story that is difficult to read, write or even admit out loud. Putting my experience down on paper and sharing it has been an incredibly cathartic experience, but a sobering one as well. I'm not innocent, and I'm not guilty. I'm

4

just here, baring it all. I'm here and I'm honest, and those are two things I felt like I couldn't be, for a very long time.

Many people loved what I will refer to as 'The Restaurant.' Although on paper, it was a successful endeavour — one which fostered many friendships and created lasting memories — it was also the worst thing that has ever happened to me. Somehow, after all of it, I'm still standing. And now I'm here to tell you my account of what happened there and everything that led me here.

This is the first time I have ever publicly shared my story. From the bottom of my heart, I hope that it helps more than it hurts.

From empty plates and blank pages, this is my recipe for starting over in life, love, words and food.

PART ONE

"YOU'RE GOING TO BE SO HAPPY," LIFE SAID.

"... BUT FIRST, I'LL MAKE YOU STRONG."

 Words were my first love and I've loved them ever since.

I've been a writer since I was 10 years old. There is a stack of diaries in my closet that is taller than I am. They're covered in dust and filled with weighty words about boys, love, friendship and adventures. My innermost thoughts, my teenage angst, my darkest secrets and sacred dreams can all be found in that mighty stack of books. Everything that has ever happened to me, I wrote it down. I never told myself I should; I've never put it on my to-do list; writing is just what I've always done. Words are what I love. Writing feels almost as important as breathing.

There have only ever been three stretches of time in my life that I have gone without writing for more than a few days at a time. The first time was when I was just a teenager; a teenager who was growing up too fast.

———

My first word as a child was "Self!"

When I was being taught to tie my shoelaces, I tore the laces from my mother's hands defiantly and shouted, "Self!" When my Dad was teaching me how to ride a bike, I released his grip and sped off, wildly declaring, "Self!" According to my parents, this included eating, bathing, dressing and swimming. My desire to be self-sufficient was mostly harmless, except in rare cases, like the time I refused help getting out of the car. After insisting on doing it by myself, my foot got tangled in the seatbelt and I fell from the car, face first into the gravel and split my lip open. "Self!" was sometimes detrimental. "Self!" sometimes resulted in blood.

Even as a child, far too young to fully understand what autonomy even meant, I begged my parents for agency over my own life. My parents, tired and vulnerable, gave it to me. I was

9

content *enough* when I was playing with other kids and spending time with my sister, but no matter what, I always craved independence and freedom. Doing things by myself made me feel like I was in control of my life. *Love me, but leave me alone*, was something I always felt unable, but desperate, to communicate.

———

I refused to wear anything other than baggy hand-me-downs from my male cousins, except when my parents forced me to. I dressed girly once or twice a year, for Picture Day at school, or when my grandparents were visiting and I was forced to wear one of the designer sweaters my Omi had given me, that I would have rather abandoned. Although I was quite athletic and boyish, I was far too clumsy and awkward to be good at any team sport. My real desire (and the only thing I ever truly thrived at) being activities I could do *alone* — like long distance running and track. "Self!"

I definitely wasn't considered an athlete by any standards, but I didn't fit into any of the other classic school age architypes either. I was considered 'gifted,' but I was too ashamed of my smartness to let myself be considered one of the nerdy kids. I hated wearing glasses and hid my smile that bore braces for almost two years — anything that caused people to label me as 'brainy,' I rebelled against. I even went so far as to get the answers wrong on purpose sometimes, rejecting my natural intellect, because I noticed if I was just another kid who didn't understand, I was more likeable. I was innately a strong leader who loved to learn, but I often forced myself to be more reserved and quiet. All of these things made the boys in my class like me more, but confused my parents and teachers. It was the beginning of a long history of people pleasing and trying to fit in.

Throughout middle school, I was liked but not liked *enough* to be considered popular. I was too scrawny in some parts to be considered curvy, and since my chest had filled in, I was too curvy to be considered one of the 'skinny girls.' I was gifted but often acted clueless. I was a control freak who wanted to appear unflappable. I was a leader who feared being bossy. Basically, I didn't identify with much as a child and I constantly craved the idea of fitting in *somewhere.*

Church gave me my first sense of community and belonging, but even church was done in the unconventional way. I believed in God but no one in my family had a defined religion. My parents allowed me to explore it if I wanted to, so every Sunday for a few years before I hit adolescence, I would bike to the only church in my small town and sit down for the service by myself. Even though I was young, I refused to attend Sunday school with the other children and instead stayed upstairs with the adult congregation. I sat with my mother who was curious and joined me occasionally, but I often sat by myself.

By the time I started high school, I was even more confused. I had crushes on boys but daydreamed of kissing girls. My passions were reading and writing but I still didn't want to be classified as artsy or a bookworm, so I hid my love for books and words. I purposely kept my locker a little untidy so nobody would know what a control freak I actually was. I was so torn between wanting to belong (which meant acting like everyone else) and wanting to be my *own* person. *Love me, but leave me alone!*

Around the age of 15, I figured out the secret of fitting in. The 'bad kids' that I'd been warned about would take me in as one of their own, as long as I acted like them. If I took up smoking and started cutting class and got my eyebrow pierced. If I cursed in class and got sent to the principal's office once a week. If I listened to the same music they liked, if I shoplifted, if I stole my parents' vodka and brought it to the school dance. If I acted like them, I could be *part* of something; I could finally belong. This wasn't a problem until smoking stolen cigarettes turned into daily bong hits. And vodka at the school dance turned into ecstasy on weeknights. And then all of this turned into daily cocaine use.

Cocaine solved two problems for me. First, it made me feel like I *fit in* more than I ever had in my young life. The second thing cocaine offered me was the illusion of complete and utter *control*. Nothing made me feel like I was more in control than when I was high on cocaine. I could snort a small line and sit down to write 20 pages in my diary — my mind moving faster than my hand could scribble my thoughts down. I could paint pictures, write poetry, create music — I could accomplish so much when I was high. Not only that, but I felt like I was a master of my emotions; I was confident in a way I'd never known. Not only did I fit in, but it felt like the world was *mine*, when I was high on cocaine.

I told myself for months that I wasn't addicted. I told myself I wasn't addicted because it wasn't affecting my day-to-day life and I could stop at any time. I told my former circle of friends that I didn't have a 'problem,' when they cornered me, intervention style, after school. "You're only 15," they declared with grave concern. I told them to stay out of my life and promptly went to snort several lines in the bathroom between third and fourth period. I didn't need them — I had new friends now. *Family.*

My new friends and I did cocaine everywhere. In mall bathrooms, in movie theatres, and even once at my home, when my Dad was renovating the hallway outside my bedroom. My friends and I anxiously waited, straws in hand, for him to turn on one of his power tools so he wouldn't hear us, and then *snoooooooooortttttt* — away we went.

This went on for months until I was shaken into seeing that I needed to change. We do not change until we must, after all.

———

I can barely remember getting the life-changing phone call telling me that my friend Louis had tried to kill himself. I barely remember anything about that night, except that he was high out of his mind, when he left the party. I can barely remember visiting him in the hospital, seeing the gunshot wound to the bottom of his chin. I can barely remember lying to his mother when she asked me if I was still using, afraid she would tell me I couldn't visit him, if I wasn't clean. I vaguely remember when he came home from the hospital months later, and we poured a plate of Christmas dinner into a blender so he could drink it with a straw — his jaw still sewn shut.

There's a part of me that wishes I could remember it more clearly. And there's a part of me that is grateful that I can barely remember that time of my life at all.

I don't remember how I felt when I finally decided to quit using drugs. There is no record of it, because I had stopped writing for the first time since I was a child. It was too painful to watch my new friends abandoning me as I got closer to getting clean and as they sank further into addiction. I couldn't judge them, but I couldn't save them either. I was forced to leave the family I had built and it was too hard to write about it.

When I started writing again, I was *different*. I was only 17 and I had not only seen the effects of things far too heavy for a young girl, but I was experiencing real shame for the first time in my life. As I took responsibility for the role I played in my friend's suicide attempt, I dragged that deep, dark shame behind me, like a bulk bag of potatoes, everywhere I went, for years and years. The bag of potatoes slowed me down during recovery. It weighed on my heart. It caused me to want to grow up too fast, so I could escape my small town and get away from those memories.

I had to find a new family now because my chosen family was gone, and my actual family was about to fall apart.

We didn't look like sisters. My sister, two years my senior, takes after our mother with her fair skin and temperament. When we were kids, her hair was as white as vanilla frosting and mine was dark and unruly. She was the shy and well behaved one, where as I, the tomboy, was constantly getting dirty or getting into trouble. I was much more wild and hyper than my sister, only occasionally sinking into an adult-like seriousness, usually when I was writing.

My sister and I had gone through bouts of typical sibling rivalry over the years, but we started to lean on each other more when our parents started drifting apart.

They were never *cruel* to each other, but there was a deafening lack of affection that accumulated as the years went by. When my sister and I were little, we would stay up late and listen to them arguing through cupped hands over closed doors. I can remember wondering if they were ever in love like we saw on the movies. I was so curious in fact, that I once snuck into their bedroom and opened a box of love letters my mother had stashed in the back of a drawer. I read them over and over until they were creased and worn. I touched the lines of pen to paper and could feel my parents' love and passion for each other, bleeding through the words in those letters.

Where that love had gone, I wasn't sure.

———

My childhood was a mostly happy one. Every summer, we went camping. My parents usually invited their closest friends, who we referred to as Aunt Ruby and Uncle Doug, along for our family vacations. We went swimming in the lake for hours, cooked modest camping food like chili and hotdogs, and sang by

15

the fire with our cousins. When we weren't camping, we'd be at home in our pool, or spitting watermelon seeds off the balcony to see who could make them launch the farthest. When summer started turning into fall, we held on. Every fall, my parents would rent a cottage with Ruby and Doug and we'd spend one more glorious week milking the last of the great outdoors. We went foraging for mushrooms and we'd carry as many of them as we could back to the cottage, and sauté them in butter and garlic. We went canoeing in the evenings and even if it rained all week, we didn't mind. Rain meant we stayed inside playing board games and doing crafts for hours on end. My Dad taught us how to play chess and my mother stayed by the stove, cooking pot roast and green beans almondine.

Winters were tough. My mother suffered from seasonal depression and our long driveway out in the countryside meant hours of shovelling for my Dad, sometimes twice a day. We couldn't wait for spring when we would drive to the strawberry farm a few blocks from our home and pick heaping baskets of plump, juicy strawberries. On the car ride home, my parents would let us eat as many as we could, and we'd devour them until we had canker sores and stomach aches. My mother would bring what was left of them inside, quarter them, sprinkle them with white sugar and a tiny bit of lemon zest, and let them sit on the counter for the rest of the day, stewing in their own juices. We'd eat them later that night with vanilla ice cream or yogurt. If there were any left over, my Dad made strawberry wine.

My Dad has always been a bit of a mad-scientist type with lots of hobbies and experiments going on all the time. He split his time between his office, where he made circuit boards, and what we called his 'lab,' — a tiny room in our basement, teeming with chemical concoctions and lined wall-to-wall with textbooks of various subjects. Woodworking, astronomy, cheese making, beer brewing, upcycling just about anything. I grew up believing my Dad was a Jack-of-all-trades, mastering them all.

Sometimes his temper flared and he occasionally took it out on household appliances or his keyboard. When we were kids, our bedroom was directly above his office, so my sister and I could often hear him tinkering on projects. Once in a while, we would hear him pounding on the computer desk with his fists, or throwing something across the room. He was never abusive to any of us but he was quick to anger.

My Dad was always trying to teach us about the things he loved: science, space, poetry, guitar and gardening. He set up his telescope on our back patio one spring and lifted us up so we could see his favourite star. He hummed while he worked, always having something to fix outside, often switching the radio dial between classical music and rock and roll. He was a bit reclusive and didn't hang out with the other Dads in town, but he was always kind to our friends and made my sister and I giggle with glee when he ran outside every winter in bare feet to do what he called 'the snow dance.' He was goofy but reserved; smart and shy. I get the feeling my Dad had a hard time fitting in, too.

———

My mother was a badass, working woman. She was incredibly intelligent and successful, working as a plant manager during our young years, and then becoming a renowned mathematician. I saw how she commanded respect from her colleagues and watched as she rose the ranks in her male dominated industry. She was also very maternal and loved taking care of my sister and me, especially in the form of food. She was an incredible cook, taking much inspiration from her German roots. She rarely made anything extravagant, instead focussing on family favourites and rustic, braised meals that we could eat for days on end. Although my mother was far too busy running the world to bake cupcakes for the school bake sale, if she struggled to balance her work and home life, I rarely noticed. When I did, it didn't bother me. To me, she was the definition of a Girl Boss long before those words had any meaning to me.

On the rare moments when she wasn't working or taking care of the family, my mother was perched on the couch with an iced tea and a book. Both my parents loved books, but my mother

17

loved books so much she used them as a kind of currency. Every time she travelled for work (which was often), she would bring home stacks of books for my sister and me. She used books to show us she loved us and was thinking of us when she was away. I often asked about what she was reading, and we would sit side by side on the couch sometimes, quietly reading to ourselves, sometimes sharing a plate of pickles.

One summer when I was 12 or so, my mother stopped reading. She stopped going to work and didn't leave her room. Ruby came to help my Dad look after us and told us that our mother was sick. "It's like when she gets sad in wintertime," Ruby explained. "But right now, she's sad *all the time.*"

Because both my parents worked and because my mother was sick a lot of the time, my sister and I had no choice but to become self-sufficient when we were very, very young. This is not to say that we weren't taken care of, because we were, but my parents were both so busy, they often didn't watch us closely. This meant we sometimes ate potato chips for dinner. Our childhood friends relished in coming over for sleepovers because it meant we could eat candy all night and watch movies until the sun came up.

It also meant that my sister and I started partying way too much when we were way too young. It meant I got away with doing cocaine and getting into trouble at school and no one really noticing.

————

It wasn't until after my mother left that I started writing about food.

The day she left, I was spending the weekend at my friend Chloe's summer house. We were in the middle of a weekend of unsupervised teenage bliss: board games, taking silly polaroids, floating down the lazy river with a vodka cooler. Although Chloe's parents had left their cupboards and fridge well stocked, Chloe and I preferred simple food that would soak up the vodka coolers. Our favourite dish, which we made several times, was

'Garlic Noo Noos.' It was a simple, borderline unexceptional pasta dish with granulated garlic, dried parsley and powdered parmesan cheese. We slurped it up with great gusto, until our hangovers subsided enough to start drinking again.

Part way through the weekend, during my third or fourth batch of Garlic Noo Noos, I got a frantic phone call from my sister telling me that our mother was gone. I tried to calm my sister's nerves by reminding her that our mother was probably just on one of her long business trips. My sister persisted, "No! The couch is gone … There was a *moving truck*. She. Took. Her. Books. She's gone!"

I rushed home to find my Dad standing in the middle of our living room, where the couch had been, with a blank stare on his face. Just a few hours earlier, I had been floating on the lake with very few cares in the world, and now I was standing in the middle of a broken family.

I was a self-centred teenager at the time, with boy problems and hair problems and a recovering coke problem, so I don't think I fully grasped how unhappy my parents were. They'd never seemed that *solid*, I suppose. I guess I always assumed that my mother might leave someday. She talked about it sometimes. It wasn't a total shock to anyone, which is probably why I refused to believe that her sudden departure would have any real impact on me.

But it *did* impact me. For the second time since I was 10 years old, I stopped writing the day after she left.

I was afraid of the words that might come out if I sat down and thought about it. I didn't want to say how angry I was at her — but I *was* angry. So angry in fact, that I refused to go see her new apartment in the city, avoiding her for several months, which drove a wedge further into my family as a whole. My sister moved out shortly after my mother, to live with her high school sweetheart, while my Dad started to use definitive words like 'divorce.' Everyone was confused and lost and hurting. I don't think I considered the fact that my mother was feeling all those things too, or how much she was struggling with her mental health — I was far too angry for that.

———

Instead of going to college that year, I stayed home with my Dad to save money and heal the gaping wound of my mother's departure. Life with my Dad was relatively easy — we co-habited more like roommates than we did as parent-and-child. Cooking was our biggest practical challenge. For several months after my mother left, we ate store-bought macaroni and cheese and frozen pizzas because we both felt hopeless behind the stove. My mother had cooked nearly every meal I'd ever eaten. Even when she was away on business trips, she would batch cook stir fries and cabbage rolls for us to heat up.

She shined the brightest on Sundays. On Sundays, I would watch my mother glide around the kitchen making one of our favourite meals. I can still smell the rosemary scented baby potatoes wafting through the house. I can taste the perfectly cooked carrots with crunchy bits of caramelized garlic. I can see my mother at the stove, whisking flour into the pan to make the most silky, savoury gravy.

I'd never cooked anything remotely resembling a proper meal, but one night, in an act of desperation, I decided I was going to try to replicate her pot roast, so my Dad and I would be able to enjoy a good meal. I went to the chest freezer in our basement and tried to find something that resembled a roast. Near the bottom, I found a chunk of meat wrapped haphazardly in butcher's paper labelled *'Rump.'* I unwrapped it, poked it for a while, filled a pot with water, and started boiling it. I thought that's what I had seen my mother do over the years. I thought I was *braising.*

After about an hour of boiling, I looked into the pot and saw a grey lump of meat covered in sludgy, slimy water. It didn't look right, and that's when I remembered my mother baking it in the oven. I found her old roasting pan, covered the bottom with some chunked potatoes and carrots, added some of the scummy cooking liquid and put the lump of meat on top. I cranked the oven to 450° and watched carefully through the door as the meat turned from grey, to slightly greyish brown and the house started to smell like potatoes.

When it looked done, I had one more task — *gravy*. "Gravy!" I muttered to myself, "Gravy fixes everything!"

I remembered watching my mother make gravy many times and she always followed the same two steps. First, she would pour a little red wine in the pan. I would find out years later that this is called 'deglazing,' and to do it properly, the way my mother did, you need a hot pan and a small amount of wine to create steam that — when stirred aggressively and constantly — would release the tasty bits stuck to the bottom of the pan. I poured about half a bottle of wine over the grey lump and waited.

Nothing happened, so I followed the next step I'd watched my mother perform over the years — adding flour to thicken the cooking liquid into a smooth, silky gravy. I got a small glass bowl of flour from the cupboard and clumsily dumped it in, skipping the crucial step of first mixing it with some cold water to form a 'slurry.' I whisked with a fork. I whisked and whisked and whisked. This was *not* Pot Roast and gravy. This was a half-brown, half-grey lump of mystery meat with some limp carrots and scorched potatoes and a chunky, pastel-purple coloured 'gravy.' I stared into the pan feeling rather defeated. My stomach growled, so I plopped some on a plate and called my Dad in for dinner.

While I poked and prodded, trying to release some of the meat from the bits that were inedible, my Dad eagerly cleaned his plate. He was hungry too, starving for both a home-cooked meal and some nostalgia perhaps.

———

My roasts got better over time and I started spending my time behind the same stove my mother used for all those years. My Dad would try every one of my experiments, even the ones that turned out black and bitter and burnt.

And that's what we did for the rest of the summer. I cooked and tried to nourish us, while my Dad kept busy in the garden and the yard. By the time that summer came to an end, I started writing again, this time filling my pages with scribbles about sauce techniques, bizarre flavour combinations and doodles of plates I dreamt I would someday prepare. My Dad joined me in the kitchen as he started feeling better, and we spent that winter teaching ourselves to make the classic dishes my mother used to make on Sunday night: Pot Roast, Moussaka, Chicken Parmesan. In the spring, we planted the garden and watched thunderstorms on the balcony. In the summer, when the flowers were blooming and our garden was full of tomatoes, we hosted dinner parties with Ruby and Doug, and other friends. One particularly magical night, my Dad wrote a song called 'The Summer of Love,' and sang it on our front porch while I barbequed chicken slathered in honey and garlic, and some zucchini from the garden.

The summer of love is all around us ... The summer of love and food around us ...

When that summer was over, and a year had passed since my mother left, my Dad and I both knew that it was time for me to leave as well. I had finally decided what I wanted to study, and although it was difficult for me to pack up and move two hours away to college, my Dad and I had forged a bond that summer that would last forever.

So, away I went to Culinary School — I wanted to learn to cook like my mother.

MY MOTHER'S POT ROAST
SERVES A FAMILY OF 4 (WITH LEFTOVERS)

This recipe is almost word-for-word as dictated by my mother. She swears that she never put wine in pot roast and thinks I probably got my memory confused with German Beef Stew or Stroganoff. Although this recipe does not strictly follow the classic cooking techniques I learned about in Culinary school, everything my mother makes is delicious and rustic. This dish is no exception.

To Prepare The Roast
1 kg fresh beef rump roast (or round) — look for well marbled beef that is not too lean. If you're unsure, ask your butcher — they will know.

Into The Pot Goes
1 medium white onion, peeled and sliced
1-2 large carrots, peeled and roughly chunked
4 garlic cloves, peeled and quartered
4-6 medium potatoes, roughly chunked
1 leek, sliced (optional)
Generous pinch of salt and pepper
1 cup beef stock

For The Gravy
3-4 tbsp flour
Cold water

My Mother's Method
Preheat your oven to 350°.

First, sear your roast. Heat some oil in your Dutch oven or heavy bottom pot. Pat the roast dry with paper towel. When the oil is hot, place meat into the pot and brown on all sides. Remove the roast from the pot and set aside.

To the pot, add sliced onions and turn down your heat to medium, cooking until tender, stirring once or twice (about 4-5 minutes). When onions are cooked, place the seared roast on top and arrange the carrots, potatoes, garlic and leeks (if using) around it. Season everything with a very generous pinch of salt and pepper. Place a lid on your roast and put it in the oven for one hour.

After one hour, reduce heat to 300° and bake for an additional two hours. (There is no need to baste or turn the meat.)

When ready, remove the roast from the oven. Carefully lift roast onto a serving platter and let rest for at least 30 minutes — this will prevent it from shredding when you slice it. Remove vegetables with a slotted spoon and place around the roast.

Finally, to make the gravy — place Dutch oven on the stovetop and crank it up to high heat. (If you've used a different roasting pot, save any liquid left in the bottom and scrape into a medium sized pot and follow the same instructions.) Mix 3-4 tablespoons of flour into a small bowl and whisk with enough water to make a lump-free, thick paste. Once the liquid is boiling, slowly whisk flour paste into the liquid, whisking constantly until you have a thick, smooth gravy. Thin out with water if needed and season to taste.

Serve gravy with roast and before you eat, send a little prayer to your mother.

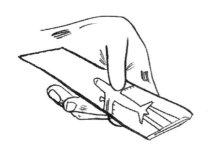

Culinary School consisted of what I would describe as a fairly typical college experience. I spent too much of my student loan on cheap beers at the local pub. I gained the 'freshman fifteen' after eating too many late night curbside fries with gravy. I fought with my roommate over who ate the last of the crackers we co-owned. Overall, college had been a fruitful experience and I was learning a lot about food.

Even though I cooked all day in class, I went back to my dorm each day craving more. I managed to make some pretty elaborate feasts on my $15 hot plate including some authentic spaghetti and meatballs with the cute Italian boy in my class. We rolled fresh pasta dough on my tiny counter top with an empty wine bottle and hung it to dry on a coat hanger. We simmered tomato sauce all day while listening to folk music and drinking boxed wine. We made giant meatballs using his grandmother's recipe, and around 11 p.m., we ate. By that time we were half drunk and it felt like we were half in love. It was such rustic and bewitching food.

Cooking was all I wanted to do, so I was quite happy to spend all my free time peeling potatoes, rolling dough and practising my knife skills. One of my favourite dishes to make was pierogi because it reminded me of my childhood and quelled some of my homesickness. It was also incredibly cheap — after I purchased a few potatoes and a small bag of flour, I could splurge on some really good quality cheese for the filling.

I hoped my paternal grandmother was looking down on me and feeling proud of my authentic Ukrainian pierogi, even though I made them with only one electric burner and one frying pan. I started to gain a reputation in our dorm and often came home to find recipes tacked to my door with notes saying, *"I miss my mother's _____. Can we make it sometime?"* Shepherd's Pie, Lasagna, French Onion Soup ... I had been dubbed 'The Girl

Who Cooks Your Mother's Famous Recipe.' I had learned from my own mother that cooking was about more than just feeding someone's belly and nourishing them. It was about loving someone; while simultaneously *feeding* yourself.

One of my favourite memories of my year at college was during Christmas break. There were three boys from Trinidad who had come to Canada for their renowned landscaping program — they had never seen a snowflake let alone experienced a blizzard. During Christmastime when all the students went home to be with their families, the Trinidadians were stuck in the storm, longing for home. They quickly sunk into sorrow and since I'd seen seasonal depression before, I knew what might help.

I called them down to the patio one evening. They arrived somber and shivering, cursing Canadian winter and their solitude. I opened the communal barbeque lid to reveal grilled pineapple rings and marinated prawns. We hurried inside with our Tropical Feast and devoured it, huddled up by the electric heater in my small kitchen.

We continued to host Tropical Feasts once a week that winter, eventually inviting almost our entire dorm to join, until the sun came out in the spring.

———

I had found my calling! I was eating, breathing, writing and sleeping with food on my mind. I was focussed, passionate and hungry to taste the food of the world. I wanted to work in famous French restaurants. I wanted to teach at a Culinary School. I wanted to write a cookbook. I wanted to travel and taste the food of the world. I wanted to understand bold flavours that were unknown to me. I wanted to step off a plane and feel the heat of a different place. I wanted to pick mangos right from the tree and cook a fish straight from the ocean.

When I wasn't cooking family recipes in my dorm, I spent my spare time dining at places I could barely afford, always bringing my notebook and scribbling down ideas. I often ate alone, sitting at the bar, writing in my diary about the restaurant I wanted to open someday.

My restaurant, I decided, would be quite small. I liked restaurants that felt intimate, when the chef would come into the dining room and explain your meal to you. I wanted less than 30 seats, with a big, bay window in the front with lots of natural light. The walls would be painted forest green and they'd be the home for my antique kitchen tools I had been collecting from yard sales and thrift stores. (They were, for now, collecting dust in my Dad's basement.) The plates would be as flawlessly white as my chef's coat. There would be an open kitchen where customers could look inside and take tours of the kitchen. I would grow a modest garden on our small patio, with herbs and small tomatoes. My employees would shout, *"Yes, Chef!"* like they did on TV. I would pay everyone well and give them a free meal every night. I'd win awards and have newspaper articles written about me. There would always be a lineup out my front door. I fantasized about becoming someone's 'favourite restaurant.'

As my dreams and notebooks overflowed, I graduated from school and moved back home to search for my first kitchen job. I accepted a position at a swanky golf course close to my Dad's house. I plugged away, learning basic skills and how a kitchen operates, all while hosting lavish dinner parties for my friends whenever I had a full day off.

As time went on, my motivation and curiosity grew. I knew if I wanted to be a really successful chef, I would have to get my foot in the door at a fine dining restaurant. My job at the golf course was sufficient for now, but I valiantly tried to get a job at what I considered the best restaurant in the city — The Only on King. I dropped off resume after resume, never getting called back and finally being told by the head chef that I could stop wasting resumes until I got some more experience. "Go see the world," he encouraged.

So, when I was 21 years old, just a few years into my apprenticeship, I took that chef's advice and booked a flight to the farthest place I could possibly go — Australia. I figured when I got home, The Only on King would *have* to hire me.

———

I had only been out of the country once, so travelling across the world, with a little over $2,000 and my knife kit was the scariest thing I'd ever done. I tried my best to be brave. I was fairly anxious leading up to my departure date, so my Dad let me read his old travel journal before I left — the one he brought with him to Europe the first time he backpacked alone. I read all about his anxiety to leave; his reservations; his fears of what was to come. I also read about his adventures; the connections he made and all the strange foods he consumed while travelling France, England and Spain. Reading his journal not only gave me the courage I needed to continue with my travel plans, but also fueled my already burning desire to travel the world even more. *After Australia, I'll go to Europe ... just like Dad* — I thought to myself.

After arriving in Sydney, I backpacked the East coast of Australia for a few months, settling into a few different cities along the way. I stayed in budget hostels most of the time, meeting other travellers just like myself, young and far away from home for their first time. I picked big, juicy mangos straight from the tree. I picked avocados twice the size of my fist and watermelons that were the same colour as the sunset over the Pacific Ocean. I pet kangaroos and koalas at the Steve Irwin Zoo, went to the famous Byron Bay to take surfing lessons and by the time I made my way to Perth, I was more than an amateur fisherwoman. I'd grown experienced enough that I was catching my dinner most nights, sometimes even cooking it over a fire on the beach, with new friends. I lived modestly and earned money doing odd jobs like making peanut brittle in the back of a van in Brisbane and picking macadamia nuts in Adelaide.

I went through hardships and lessons during those months away, figuring out what the word 'homesick' meant for the first time in my young life. I missed my home and all the memories

I'd made that summer with my Dad. I missed visiting my sister and talking about boys and clothes and meaningless things. Even though things with my mother were still a little raw, I missed her and her cooking. I missed my bed with clean sheets, a shower all to myself, my friends, my ex, my big stack of books. I tried to stay present and enjoy my time away, meeting strangers, going on adventures and having very few cares.

I returned home to Canada with my heart full of experiences and a journal filled with recipes and poetry describing sunsets and short love stories. However, to my surprise, my homesickness seemed to linger after I returned home. The life I'd known before I left had changed drastically in just a few short months. My closest friends had moved away — Shannon to Ottawa for her dream job, Sarah to British Columbia with her boyfriend, Chloe to Taiwan to teach English and Jason to backpack the world. The rest of my friends who weren't travelling were starting to settle down, many of them simultaneously announcing pregnancies and engagements. I felt the lack of belonging overtake me like I had when I was young. It seemed everything that was happening was happening *without* me.

I felt like my family was slipping away from me, too. My Dad had started dating again and was spending weekends at his new girlfriend's house. My sister was settling into her new home and relationship. Ruby and Doug were living out their retirement dream on a boat somewhere in the Caribbean. My grandparents lived far away. My mother had been gone for a few years, and although we were on speaking terms now and I'd let some of my anger towards her dissipate, it was still difficult to spend time with her at her new apartment.

I yearned for family and a sense of community, comradery, kinship — anything that made me feel less alone. I kept busy, returning to my job at the golf course, but the loneliness that enveloped me took over my thoughts. I often worried that I was going to be alone forever. I worried that no one would ever want to be with me. I picked myself apart. It's clear when I read back on that time in my life that I was battling my own mental health issues but I was in denial because I didn't want to end up like so many of the women in my family tree.

—

The truth is that I was young and had no idea how to love myself yet. It's not really a surprise that the first words out of my mouth when I met Jeff were: *"Show me who you need me to be, so you'll love me."*

GRANDMA ANNE'S PIEROGI
MAKES 20-30 PIEROGI (DEPENDING ON THE STRENGTH OF YOUR ARMS AND THE SIZE OF YOUR MASON JAR)

My Dad's mother, Anne, died in the 1970s, leaving behind many fond memories and traditional Ukrainian recipes. Her pierogi (or 'Varenyk' as they're called in Ukrainian,) were famous in the Olinyk household. This recipe has been deciphered from the original, very faded hand-written recipe from sometime in the early 1950s. I have made a few edits to the original recipe to make it consistent with the other recipes in this book, but the bones of the recipe are the same as what my grandmother used to make. It is an unconceivable honour to include this recipe in my book.

For The Filling
4-5 medium potatoes, peeled and chunked
1 cup cheddar cheese, grated
Pinch of salt and pepper

For The Dough
2 cups flour
1 egg for dough, 1 egg for "glue"
½ cup whole milk
1 tsp salt

Finish With
Grease (bacon fat, oil, butter, etc.) for frying
1 white onion, peeled and sliced thin

Grandma Olinyk's Method

Boil potatoes in salted water until very tender. Strain, and while warm, mash with cheese, salt and pepper. Chill.

Meanwhile, make the dough by pouring flour onto a clean counter. Make a well in the middle. Drop in one egg, milk and salt. Mix and compact the dough together by hand. If the dough is too crumbly, add another few teaspoons of milk. Knead just until it's smooth. Dust ball with flour, wrap in wax paper, chill at least 30 minutes.

Break the second egg into a bowl and whisk gently. Set it aside. Once your filling and dough are ready and chilled, roll out your ball of dough on a clean counter, dusting with just enough flour to prevent sticking. Roll into a very thin, even layer and then use a round 1.5"/4cm cutter (or lid of a jar) to cut rounds out of the dough. Fill each dough round with a small amount of potato filling (about one tablespoon) and then dip your finger in a bit of beaten egg and use that to seal the pierogi into a half moon. Pinch it firmly or use a fork to seal.

Cook pierogi in boiling salt water until dough packets rise, for just a few minutes. Then, as my Grandma's ancient recipe states, "Fry in grease and onions." Traditional Ukrainian Varenyky are fried in rendered pork scraps ('Shkvarky') or bacon. Onions are fried with pierogi until very lightly browned in spots.

You can also freeze these pierogi after boiling them, on cookie sheets lined with parchment. After they're frozen, put them into a sealed container or bag, and store for up to 3 months in the freezer.

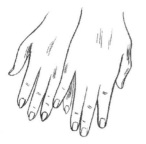

I remember every single detail about the night I fell in love with Jeff Washer.

We were sitting on his couch, at the house I would move into a few months later, wondering who would make the first move. We were both nervous but our hormones were raging, so we spent some time crossing over between certainty and doubt. I remember thinking to myself, as we sat side by side brushing knees and pinkies, accidentally (on purpose), *"This man is everything I've ever wanted."*

Jeff and I began our relationship as co-workers. He was bartender at the golf course I was working at, and I started to look forward to him popping his head into the kitchen every day around 3 p.m. when he would order his staff lunch. We chatted a little bit every day, and as I got to know him, I regarded him as generous and funny. I also learned how much he loved his mother — *swoon!* He was constantly telling me about his big plans for the future. He was handy and artistic and I saw traits in him that reminded me of my own father. He was slightly serious, but still playful and quirky. He was spiritual and he talked about wanting to travel the world with so much passion it made my entire body feel warm.

The night we fell in love, we talked about the science behind human touch as he brushed his hand across my knee, accidentally (on purpose). We talked about food and wine and life and love until the sun came up. We continued our late night hang outs on his couch and went on adventures together, eventually moving to the bedroom where he gave me my very first orgasm and didn't stop.

He was everything I ever wanted in a man, right down to his dark hair and green eyes — matching the description of my future husband I had written about in my diary when I was 10 years old. He had this charming energy about him that everyone around him recognized. I recognized it too, and quite happily let it consume me.

It didn't take long for our lives to become tangled. I'd been in love before, but this … this was *different*. We both felt ready to commit to each other; we were ready to make plans and promises. Or at least, we *wanted* to be ready.

A few weeks into our blooming love, I received the news that I had gotten a job offer at an up and coming restaurant in Whistler. I was over the moon at first, and when I told Jeff the news, he was delighted for me, albeit a little sad that meant I would be moving far away. We both knew right away how much I would regret it if I didn't go, so we agreed to keep dating long-distance.

Early that fall, I flew across the country as planned. I cried for the entire flight. When I arrived in one of the most beautiful places in the world, I didn't stop crying. Even with the breathtaking view of the Rocky Mountains in the background, and an unbelievable job opportunity waiting for me, I was *miserable*. I flew home less than 30 days later, barely giving my adventure in Whistler (or the job) a chance. My friends and parents questioned my decision to come home, since it was out of character for me, but I was convinced it was what I wanted.

I wanted romance, love, family, the fairy tale.

I didn't want "Self!" anymore. I wanted *him*. I wanted to *belong*.

———

After I came home from the coast, things got more serious with Jeff. The night I got home, we stayed up late together talking about our future. We fell asleep in each other's arms, and when we woke in the morning, the sun was beaming down on us through the window, making the white sheets appear blindingly bright. He pulled the comforter over both our heads so we were in a cocoon of warmth and dimness, the bright light turning our skin neon red. He took my face in his hands and said, matter-of-factly, "I'm so in love with you." It wasn't the first time I'd told a boy I loved them back, but it was the first time I said it without flinching.

I moved in with him shortly after that. I met his parents and his mother told me I could call her, 'Mom.' We painted our bedroom light blue. We planted tomatoes in our garden. We settled in. We fucked all over our apartment. I met his friends and they became my friends. We adopted a puppy and named her Gnowee, after an Australian sun goddess. Jeff told a mutual friend that he was going to marry me someday. I told my family that I'd finally met 'The One.' He became my best friend and my family and almost overnight, I *belonged* to someone.

When I read back on my journals from that time, I can't help but touch the pages and wish I could go back to those blissful, carefree first few months, just for a moment. My heart swells when I read about our first real date. He wrapped a blindfold around my eyes and put me in the back of a taxi and asked the driver to go around the block six times. When we stopped, we were back at his house. He had set up our dining room to resemble a mini restaurant. He lit candles and my favourite jazz album was playing in the background. He'd set the table carefully and opened a bottle of expensive wine. It was the sweetest thing I could ever dream up and it was happening *to me.* We spent the evening talking and staring at each other over candlelight and later, in bed, worshipping each other.

It was as if I had summoned him into my life … and perhaps I had. Perhaps all the time I'd spent writing in my diary about how much I wanted someone to belong to, had finally come true. Jeff was my knight in shining armour, here to rescue me from my sorrow and self-loathing. His dark hair, green eyes and huge smile made me melt into him, and just when I thought I couldn't fall any more in love with him, I found out that he and I shared the same dream — to someday open a restaurant. Our shared desire not only deepened our bond, but it made our story even more romantic than it already felt. We started fantasizing about the restaurant we would someday own together. I would cook; he would match wines and create cocktails to go with my creations. It felt like I was living a modern day fairy tale.

———

When I think back to that night on his couch — the night I fell in love — I realize how easy it was to fall for him. He was sitting there, in front of me, talking about marriage someday; of his grand plans to move somewhere sunny and grow lemons. Costa Rica, maybe. We'd have kids and lots of dogs and live a perfect, happy life. I wasn't sure where a *restaurant* fit into all of that … but we were young and it felt like we were unstoppable.

I had found the person I needed to be with in order to feel loved. And he saw that too, and began telling me everything I needed to hear as a lost, lonely, broken and desperate for love 22-year-old girl.

He said all the right things.

Accidentally. On purpose.

As we departed from the honeymoon phase, as couples do, we fought.

It started as bickering over what set of plates we would keep when I moved in. We fought about why I walked beside his friend when we were at the beach instead of beside him. We fought about why he never made an effort to meet any of my friends. I got upset when he would tell me to hush when we were in public together. We would call each other names that started out playful but always hurt in the end. When I would get upset because he was leaning in a little too close to a girl at the bar, he told me I was crazy and just being jealous.

After each fight, we would make up. Riding the highs and lows was like being on a rollercoaster — something I became used to and even *fond of.* The rollercoaster made me dizzy; the dizziness made it easy to miss things.

Soon, our fights became more frequent and intense. After our biggest blowouts, I would slam the bathroom door, curl up into a ball and cry. By the time I realized the fighting had gone too far, I had memorized the details of what every piece of tile and grout looked like in our bathroom. I rationalized all of this as being okay. *My friends don't fight with their partners like this. They obviously don't love each other as much as we do,* I thought to myself each time I peeled myself off the cold bathroom floor.

We were both to blame. We were both carrying trauma from childhood. We were both stubborn. And sometimes, we both forgot to be kind.

There were times during conflict when I thought I felt him slipping away. I was stubborn and headstrong, and I began to see that this "Self!" mentality I had been fostering since I was a child, was destructive to our relationship. I knew that if I was going to prevent myself from being alone again, I would need to protect this man from my own autonomy. So I started to give in. I started to lean on him more, and eventually, I started to develop anxiety about things that didn't scare me before. My friends who lived in faraway cities thought it was out of character when I told them I couldn't visit them as often, because I'd suddenly developed an irrational fear of driving on the highway. I developed a strange anxiety about heights, so flying across the world and backpacking through Europe just like my father had, became a fantasy that faded away into the distance. My brief trip to the West Coast was the last time I would travel alone for six years.

I would of course come to see many years later how classic our codependent dynamic was. I would viscerally understand the terms 'love bombing' and 'gaslighting.' I would slowly but surely catch onto the fact that the lowest lows are not worth a dozen roses or handwritten love notes. I would learn that covering fights up with sprinkles of a fairy tale does not make it okay, just like I had learned that covering a burnt piece of meat in gravy does not make it delicious.

But at this point in the story, I had no understanding of any of these ideas. The only thing I knew was that not wanting to live without him was the most romantic thing I could imagine. For now, it was easier to hold onto that. It was easier for me to give in to what he wanted. Giving in meant ignoring gut feelings. It meant being silent when I wanted to say something. It meant acting small, so he could feel big. It meant doing whatever I had to do to avoid an argument.

———

I eventually got my first sous-chef job at a small hotel, so Jeff and I no longer worked together. We both plugged away at our respective careers around the same pace, while we merged families and settled further into domesticated life.

When conflict arose, I brushed things off quickly, because I was just *so in love* with him and our little life we were creating.

And then something happened that I *couldn't* ignore.

38

I will remember that day forever. It was like that sick feeling you are flooded with when you accidentally send an incriminating text to the wrong person, but you can't press 'undo' fast enough. You just want to go back in time for five seconds, but all you can do is stare at your screen and scream. There's a heat that rises up inside of you. It's that punch-in-the-gut, lose-your-breath, heart-racing, cracked-wide-open kind of feeling that you can only get when you've done something that can't be taken back. It's like the rumble of an angry dog right before it leaps on its prey. It's like the way your heart stops and then jumps after you've plunged into frigid, icy water. It's like that millisecond of calm when you turn a kettle on full blast, right before it starts to hiss. It's the way your stomach flips when you're at the top of a rollercoaster, the moment before you descend. It's that rush — the flood of pain and fear and passion all wrapped up into one. It's trauma. It's stress. It's something you never imagined possible.

I'd felt all of that before. I felt it the moment I got the phone call about Louis's suicide attempt, and I felt it the moment I realized my mother was really gone. This feeling was not unfamiliar — the flutter in your chest, the sweat on your palms, the racing of your heart. The shock of it all. The nervousness of what will come next. The intensity. It felt almost ... a little bit ... like first date butterflies. It felt a little bit like falling in love.

———

It was a day in December that started out like many others. It was the middle of winter and I had gotten up extra early that morning to get started on some emails that were piling up. The smell of coffee flooded the kitchen as I sat eagerly waiting for my computer to power up. It was frigid outside but I was covered in a warm sweater and had a lazy day of writing and cooking to look forward to. I clutched my coffee cup and pulled my sweater closer to me — I was surrounded by warmth and calm.

I scanned through my emails, and that's when I found it. An email from a stranger and an address I didn't recognize. I opened it and my heart immediately started palpitating. The email said:

"Hi there. You don't know me but I need to tell you something. Last week, I saw your boyfriend in his truck, being intimate with someone. I cannot tell you who it was, but I can tell you that I am certain that it was him. I just thought you should know."

My mouth went dry and my lips quivered. My chest felt tight. My head was spinning. My skin felt hot. My jaw clenched. I couldn't even register if it was anger or sadness or grief or jealousy that I was feeling, but I knew it wasn't good.

This wasn't butterflies; this wasn't love.

Without taking much time to collect my thoughts, I ran down the stairs to our bedroom and stood over the bed where Jeff was still asleep. I woke him, and turned my laptop to face him, demanding an explanation. He sat up, still half asleep, and put his head in his hands.

I suppose in the few seconds it took me to get from where I'd first read the email, to where I was now standing, I'd had time to *hope*. I hoped that this was just a mistake. A sabotage. A miscommunication. This person was wrong. They were lying. They were jealous of our happiness. They wanted to destroy us. It couldn't be the truth. I had come up with all of this in the few steps it took for me to get from our kitchen to where I was now, standing beside our bed. I wasn't prepared for what actually happened next. There was an emotion covering his face that I had not seen before, but I would grow to recognize.

It was *guilt.*

"I'm so sorry," he sobbed, remorsefully.

Those words.

I'd heard those words plenty of times; I'd said them plenty of times. But this time, I heard something different. This time, what I heard was, *"You are not enough for me."*

As I demanded details of what happened, Jeff just kept saying he was sorry, over and over. He owned up to the fact that he did kiss one of the servers from the golf course, in his truck, after they'd finished work. It was in the parking lot, while I was waiting for him to get home. This was the place where we had met and courted; where we flirted across the heat lamps; where I made his lunch and wrote love letters on his take out box.

When I left my job there after we started dating, he stayed behind and kept up with his charming persona. I could only imagine how easy it was for him to get attention from his female co-workers. I'd been one of those girls myself, after all. I hadn't even begun to consider the fact that he was a manager and she was an employee, and why that dynamic was unsettling. I wouldn't even begin to question that part of the equation until five years later when I would face the situation all over again.

I couldn't consider any of that, in that moment. All I could do was imagine him in his truck, in the dark parking lot, with beautiful, young, blonde Alisa Burke and imagine how it happened. The flirting, the desire, the touching — accidentally (on purpose).

The 'red flags' that I had missed over the previous weeks and months were also racing through my mind. I thought back to a few months prior when he had left his cell phone at home and I found a flirtatious text from Alisa. When I questioned him about it, he told me it was an innocent inside joke. We fought about it and he condemned me for snooping. In the end, I apologized *to him*.

I thought back to his staff Christmas party a few weeks before. I had seen Alisa in a tight, backless, hot pink dress and felt a rush of jealousy. I saw him talking to her and thought he was standing too close. He was making her laugh and put his hand on her back. It was a fleeting, brief moment that I felt in my gut, and when I asked him about it after the party, it sent him into a fit of rage. He told me I was acting like a crazy, jealous girlfriend. Again, I apologized.

I thought about my friend Charlotte. I heard a rumor that Charlotte had dated Jeff, when they were in high school. When I asked her about it, she confessed that he had cheated her and that

41

was the reason they broke up. When I asked Jeff about it though, he told me I was being nosey and must let it go, which I did, even though it didn't sit right.

As all of these memories tore through my mind, I eventually got up, and stormed out. I drove straight to my Dad's house, where I fell into my childhood bed and wept. I spent the day racking my brain, being paranoid and anxious. I knew that the person who sent me that email went to great lengths to remain anonymous, but I was desperate to figure out who it could be. I asked my Dad to help me perform a search of the IP address from where the email originated, but it didn't give us much information. I emailed the person back, begging them to tell me who it was, to no avail. I combed through Alisa's Facebook page for clues, a hunt that came up fruitless.

I had a choice to make. I could forgive him, move on and try to make things work. Or, I could leave him but that would mean that I would be forced to find a new place to belong.

I thought talking about it would make me feel better, but after I told my sister and my two closest friends, I wanted to wrap up my words, and throw them into the back corner of my closet, where they couldn't hurt me anymore. It hurt so much to admit what he had done, and the only thing that seemed to soothe me was silence. If the secret was mine, no one could judge me and I could still have my fairy tale ending.

I decided to go home and try to make it work (or at least, hear him out). There were several bouquets of flowers waiting for me. Jeff took my hands, looked me in the eyes and apologized again. He told me that he was sorry, but he had been so stressed since I'd moved in, it'd been nothing but changes around the house.

Instead of his apology, I heard, *"You are not enough."*

He explained that since meeting my family and introducing me to his, there was suddenly all of this pressure on us to get married and have our own family.

You are not enough.

42

He told me that sometimes, when I was sad and stressed, he felt so overwhelmed, he would talk to other girls to blow off some steam.

You are not enough.

By the time the sun went down that day, it was me who was apologizing to him, for driving him to be unfaithful. Like an alchemist, he could turn even the bitterest betrayal into an opportunity.

This was the power of his words.

———

Over the next several months, Jeff tried to make things better. Alisa still worked in the same building as him, so if he got home even just a few minutes late from work, I would start spiralling and panicking. He was on his best behaviour for a few months and we even hosted family Christmas that year. From the outside looking in, life was good — we had our first nephew, our friends were getting married, our dog was growing up, our families were becoming one. The world went on despite the scars. I was heartbroken over what had happened but every time I was triggered, he would convince me that I was overreacting. He sat me down and told me that it was *just a kiss*. After a few months of grieving, heavy mood swings and debilitating grief, I started to believe him when he told me I was acting crazy.

The recovery process from this event was the same as after any big fight: apologies, flowers, candlelit dinners, love notes, and lots and lots of make-up sex. This time, he stepped it up a notch and planned a trip to California, where I let the salty shores of Venice Beach wash away his sins.

Towards the end of that vacation, we stopped at an eclectic, fusion tapas bar near Napa Valley. We drank Moscow Mules from copper mugs and ate salty, crispy brussel sprouts with fish sauce and chilies. While a funk band played in the background, he reached across the table for my hand and told me how glad he was that we made it here. He confessed that before we'd taken this trip, he wasn't *sure* if we were going to make it. He told me how sorry he was, again, about Alisa Burke. I recoiled when I heard her name — I didn't want to talk about her. I wanted to stay in that beautiful moment we were creating when I didn't hurt like hell. I wanted to ignore our problems and just be in that happy, little tapas bar where nothing went wrong. I wanted to laugh and make memories. I didn't want to think about him, in his truck, kissing Alisa Burke.

But he had brought me to California for a reason. He brought me there to tell me that he was *inspired* by me. He begged me to keep loving him as much as I did. "I'm so proud of you for forgiving me," he cooed as he kissed my fingers, one by one.

Those words.

I flashed a smile, pulled my hand away and told him to stop hogging all the brussel sprouts. We never spoke of Alisa Burke again.

——

I would continue to hear Jeff's voice in my head, over the course of the next several hours, days, weeks, months and years. *"You are not enough,"* was always on repeat in the back of my mind. I would hear these words when I was walking down the street. I would hear them when I was getting ready to go out with my girlfriends. I would hear them when I was writing poetry; when I was working on menus; when I was cooking. No amount of recognition, awards, friends, success or fame could make me feel any different.

I wasn't enough for him and Alisa Burke was proof. Whenever we were in conflict, I would hear his voice in my head saying, *"I'm so proud of you for forgiving me …"*

It wasn't that his words were salty or sour — it was that they were sweet and made of honey.

SANTA BARBARA BRUSSELS (GF)

CAN SERVE UP TO FOUR, BUT IS BEST EATEN SLOWLY
WITH SOMEONE WHILE SHARING A BOTTLE OF WINE

I've always been a lover of brussel sprouts but never thought of preparing them this way until I had this version in California. This recipe goes fantastically with a California Chardonnay but frankly, this dish is more about the company and conversation you share.

To Prepare The Brussel Sprouts
½ kg brussel sprouts
A good glug of olive oil
Sprinkle of salt and pepper

Marinade
1 tbsp tamari (or soy sauce)
1 tsp fish sauce
1 tsp rice vinegar
1 tsp sesame oil
½ clove of garlic, minced
½ Thai chili, sliced very thin
Juice and zest of half a lime

Method
The trick to this recipe is dressing the brussel sprouts when they are still warm, so the first step is to make sure you have your marinade ready to go. Combine all ingredients for the marinade in a large bowl and set aside. Next, preheat oven to 425°. Prepare a cookie sheet with parchment.

Using a sharp knife, cut the ends of each brussel sprout off, especially if they are browned or dry. Cut any large sprouts in half so they are all relatively the same size. Toss in a bowl with salt, pepper and oil and bake for 12 minutes. Stir once and bake for an additional 7 minutes. By this time, they should be brown and caramelized — a.k.a delicious! Remove from the oven and while still warm, add to the bowl of marinade. Toss. Serve warm, with a bottle of wine, and don't be ashamed to lick your fingers.

I was fresh out of culinary school and like most young cooks, I thought I knew it all. I had done a little travelling, gotten a taste for the industry and was wrapping everything in bacon, just like everyone else. I had a long list of big dreams I was working towards with intense determination and passion. My plan was to pay my dues and then, eventually, to open my own restaurant.

And that was the plan for a long time … until it wasn't.

What really happened was that I entered into an industry that could be incredibly unkind. Cooking is, by definition, a *trade*. And just like any other job that is done primarily with ones' hands and a few tools, cooking is incredibly laborious and requires a specific set of skills if you want to master it. But, unlike most trades, cooking doesn't necessarily mean that one makes more money after they've been through the appropriate training. Regardless of talent, skill, or a degree, most young cooks start earning a living at minimum wage. Cooking is a trade that is treated differently than all the others but there was nothing I could do about it except plug away in the unfair, unkind industry I so desperately wanted to be a part of.

I was a person who was *feeding* everyone, but I often wound up *hungry*. For the first several years of my career, I walked home every night from work, well after midnight, stomach growling, realizing I hadn't eaten anything since breakfast. This was partly due to poor corporate policies that didn't leave enough time for proper breaks and partly because that was just the 'way it is' when you're a line cook. There was some unspoken agreement that when you sign up to be a cook, you will no longer eat food like a civilized person. You will instead shovel in leftover spaghetti noodles or a spoonful of soup often straight from the pot, leaning over the sink or garbage can, more often than not. If you're lucky, there will be an empty milk crate nearby that you can flip over and sit on, but just know, if you do that, you will be behind on your mise en place for the rest of the day. It often wasn't worth being behind, so the strategy became not eating. Hunger, along with working long hours for little pay, was okay with me. I was young and my body had yet to show the signs of breakdown that so many of my colleagues exhibited, from standing on their feet in a hot kitchen for 14 hours a day. Reaching, lifting heavy pots, bending and being stretched to your limit ... I could take it. *This* is where I belonged now.

Working in restaurants is known for being demanding on your psyche as well — long shifts, repetitive tasks, extreme heat, intense pressure and that's not to mention the tempers that tend to run rampant in professional kitchens. To ease the physical pain and the mental stress created by the job, many young chefs turn to their vices. It's no secret that heavy alcohol use and substance abuse are almost standard in the hospitality industry. Joining in was an easy way to form friendships, and camaraderie was crucial in making it through those long, arduous, hot nights in the kitchen. In the early days of my career, this meant taking cigarette breaks even though at the time, I didn't smoke. It also meant guzzling beer with the boys after work, even though I didn't particularly like beer. By the time I made it to the fine dining world, I was drinking heavily every day, chain-smoking whenever I wasn't at work, and it was a constant struggle for me to stay clean. I knew the edge it would give me if I snorted a little coke before service with my kitchen mates. I was committed to staying clean, so I found the edge I needed with other vices: excessive coffee, red wine, perfectionism, control and sometimes even the hunger pangs in my stomach worked as some sort of satirical nourishment, which kept me going.

I was in an industry that was unkind in general, but was especially harsh to women. Most of my colleagues over the years had been respectful, and I made solid friendships with both men and women in the kitchens I'd worked at. But I also faced all kinds of mistreatment ranging from belittling, name calling and sexual harassment. It was often subtle, backhanded compliments like my boss telling me they would be sending me to the dining room to do a live cooking demonstration because I was 'easy on the eyes.' Sometimes it was more direct, like my colleagues talking about the size of my breasts or what I looked like under my chef's coat.

I had to decide daily whether or not I was going to make a big deal about feeling uncomfortable with these comments, or letting them slide, almost always choosing the latter. I wanted to make things easier for myself, so I adopted a sense of humour that was as crude as my comrades. I stayed out late drinking with them so that I would fit in. Life was easier when I was one of them. I may not have been snorting coke in the bathroom, but it felt a little bit like high school all over again.

Life was easier now too, because no matter where I was employed, I knew how to form a family.

———

As I worked away at my career, I was always very grateful to have a partner who understood the restaurant culture I was now so immersed in. Jeff was supportive and compassionate and seemed to truly understand the struggles I faced as a line cook, and as a woman in male dominated kitchens. He would rub my feet after long days when they would ache from standing for too long. He bought me massages as gifts when my hip started bothering me. He talked me through it when I was having trouble with one of my colleagues.

After completing my apprenticeship when I was 23, I landed my first sous-chef job. It wasn't until then that I started to truly understand why all the managers I'd ever worked for were *so* stressed out all the time. I was unprepared for a management position and it quickly had me longing for my old prep job. I missed the days of low responsibility, when I was alone in the kitchen with a long list, working alone in my flow and feeling accomplished at the end of the day. I missed the days when I didn't have to delegate tasks or discipline my comrades.

Management was perhaps, not for me. I wanted to be an invisible part of a team, not the leader of one. *Love me, but leave me alone.*

The chef at the hotel I was working at was kind and mild-mannered, but the man who owned the hotel had a notably short fuse. One night, he threw a pan of burnt butter at the kid who was washing dishes. He screamed loudly and rhetorically asked if any of us had any idea how much butter cost. Everyone stood in shock for a minute while I checked in to make sure the dishwasher was okay. As the dining room started to fill up, we all went into service as if his blow up had never happened. It wasn't uncommon for someone to have a meltdown in that hot, cramped, busy kitchen, but this was next level.

After service, the owner made an insincere apology to all of us, and brought us pitchers of stale beer. "Take a break," he encouraged us, ushering us outside where he sat across from us on a milk crate and chain-smoked. He told us how stressful his day had been, and how he had just gotten out of a meeting with his investors, who wanted to know how much a sprinkle of salt cost, compared to a pinch. After a few glasses of that stale beer, he looked up at us with grim eyes and warned, "Don't ever open your own place ... unless you absolutely hate yourself." By the time we went inside to start cleaning our stations, everyone seemed to have shaken it off. But I couldn't stop thinking about what he had described that night — it stuck with me forever.

The owner's aggression and outbursts continued, causing me to hunt for a new job, and I decided to go back to apply, yet again, for a job at The Only on King. I had experience now and had taken their advice and done some travelling, but I never thought I would actually get hired. When they called me a few weeks later to tell me I had landed the job I'd been seeking for years, I was over the moon and quit my sous-chef job right away.

Working at The Only on King was technically a step down in my career — I left a sous-chef job to become a prep cook again, but I was happy because I worked in solitude for most of the morning each day. I got distracted easily by loud music or yelling, and people asking questions broke my concentration. I was learning how much I enjoyed quiet time in the kitchen, alone in my flow. I loved that kitchen and I was even loving the fact that I had to hustle every day to prove my worth. I was improving and honing my skills; I was filling my resume with knowledge and techniques that most young cooks only dreamed of learning. I worked hard — staying late and starting early, and when I wasn't working, I would often be sitting at the bar writing in my diary. My love for words and food was soaring.

The only problem with my new path was that I wasn't a teenager anymore. I limped at the end of the day. My back hurt constantly. My forearms were a landmine of burns and cuts. My hand screamed at me with early signs of carpal tunnel, even though I was just 24-years-old. More than that, due to my crazy work schedule, I started missing Sunday dinner at my Dad's house. I couldn't attend the birth of my close friend's baby. I was absent for weddings and holidays. I had less time for yoga, walking my dog, seeing my sister and doing the things I truly enjoyed.

I often wondered if there was some way to express all my passion without all this sacrifice. I wondered if loving something *really* did mean compromising things that brought me joy. Was I was compromising too much by being a restaurant chef? Something inside of me wondered if there was more to life than this.

My mind and notebook were full of menu concepts and scribbles, and I wanted to try out some of my own ideas. So when I had a day off, I cooked. My friends started to give me a little bit of money to pay for ingredients and I'd cook up fancy dinner parties for them on my night off. One night, one of them took a picture and posted it to Facebook. Her mother saw it and asked if I would come to her home and cook dinner for her friends. That turned into catering a few Christmas parties and before I knew it, I was taking time off from my dream job to cater various events around the city. It started very slowly, but eventually all these catering requests snowballed into a little catering company. I knew if I pursued my side hustle, my back pain and my 14 hour days would not be *over,* but this felt *different.* Little by little, I found a way to incorporate "Self!" back into my life. I hadn't realized how much I missed her.

I'd never owned a business before or been my own boss. I'd never hired or fired anyone. I essentially had no idea what I was doing. It wasn't always perfect, and it certainly wasn't easy, but it was *my own.* It was an incredibly busy and challenging time in my career — trying to balance my time between my job and my new business. I wasn't the only one struggling to balance my job and my life, though. One night, after a long, sweaty service, my boss at The Only on King told me, "If you open your own place, you'll never have a family. You'll never travel. You'll never see your dog. And you'll be sore and tired and broke forever." He was just *venting* to me — bitter after missing another family barbeque — but part of me knew he was right. His insight had given me the idea to continue pursuing my little catering company, and once I made the decision, things fell into place quickly.

Once I started getting requests for more catering jobs, I started to see how different it was from the restaurant world. I could create all my own menus, have total control and I got to interact with customers more, which is something I didn't even know I was good at. More than that, I got to keep all the profit from each individual catering job in my own pocket and reinvest it in myself. I had never been financially stable before, often finding myself living paycheque to paycheque with minimum wage kitchen work, so this newfound stability felt liberating beyond belief. After several months of successful events, I started looking for a commercial kitchen to turn my weekend catering hobby into a real company. A few months after that, I quit my dream job at The Only on King to pursue catering full time. I couldn't believe it was real.

It started slowly, but my goals to continue working in the fine dining world, and to open my own restaurant someday, began to change.

I opened my first catering kitchen with less than $600 in my bank account and although I struggled for the first year, as most start-ups do, I booked every event I possibly could, and became dedicated to my new lifestyle. I was 'The Little Caterer That Could' — sometimes prepping events for 200 people, out of my tiny 350 square foot kitchen. I worked so hard and I loved it so much. I was proud of myself, and although I had done it with the support of my family and help from my friends, I had done it largely on my own. "Self!"

My bank account started to grow with my business, and eventually I moved into a bigger catering kitchen and even hired part-time staff. Occasionally, I worked too many hours and found myself sick with stress, but as time went on, I learned how to take care of myself. Work-life balance became a theme in my life, and I even left work at lunchtime some days to go for a 90 minute massage. Even if my work and life weren't always balanced, I started thinking about myself in a way I never really had before. *I cared about her.*

My success brought financial stability, so Jeff and I moved to a house a little bit outside the city, adopted a second dog and got new cars. I had enough money coming in that I could afford to take time off when I wanted to, and Jeff and I took lavish vacations every year. We travelled. We christened every room of our new home. We threw dinner parties. We had barbeques on our deck. We fought and made up like clockwork.

I started making time to visit my Dad on Sundays again. I took weekends off to go to my friends' weddings and baby showers. I left work when I wanted to, and made time to walk my dogs in the park. Most nights, I could be home in time for yoga class. My happiness was more than just being a cook now — it meant having freedom to travel, being healthy, spending time with family, cooking for fun and time in nature.

I no longer felt like I was trading my freedom for my work — my work *was* my freedom. I wasn't *giving up* on my dream of someday owning a restaurant — I was *adapting* to my new life that I loved; my new sense of balance and ease. I didn't *need* a restaurant anymore. Instead of searching for more, I felt like I'd *arrived.*

And then, just as quickly as I'd arrived, I departed from that perfect, happy life, when we decided to open The Restaurant.

Sometime in 2014, Jeff and I attended a friend's wedding in Jamaica. We were having a lovely time in our king sized bed just steps away from the crystal, clear waters and flawless, white beach.

Halfway through the week, Jeff booked me an appointment for a hot stone massage to help me de-stress after a tiring Christmas season. I went to my appointment feeling full of love and light as air, gladly receiving his romantic gesture. After I undressed, Jada started rubbing my back with lotion that smelt like coconuts and lavender. Next, she placed a hot stone on my spine. I'd never had a hot stone massage before, and the stone felt a little *too warm* at first, but it quickly mellowed into a pleasant, relaxing heat. She placed larger ones on the back of my calves and thighs while she moved to the front of the table to massage my neck.

The problem was, the stone on my left leg wasn't mellowing. It was hot … like … *really* hot. I tried to adjust my body without her noticing. I squirmed a little as my fists started to involuntarily clench. My jaw tightened as I realized it was burning my skin through the cloth. I stayed in that distress for as long as I physically could before I finally yelped and kicked my leg, throwing the stone on the ground and smashing it.

Jada stared at me in disbelief.

"It was so hot … it was burning me …" I whimpered. She examined my leg and asked the *painfully* simple question, "Why on earth did you wait so long to tell me?"

Why hadn't I admitted to Jada sooner, that the rock was much too hot? Why did I wait *so long* to finally kick that searing stone off of me? I didn't know Jada; I'd never see her again. Plus, it was her job to make me comfortable — I'm sure she didn't *want* me to suffer through what was supposed to be a relaxing massage. I was worried about offending her, so much so, that I was willing to get a second-degree burn and suffer for a week, before speaking my mind to a professional masseuse about my comfort level.

———

Jada was as sweet as that coconut oil. She apologized, refunded me and broke off some aloe from a plant she had behind her desk, with instructions to apply it to the wound later that afternoon.

I left feeling embarrassed about what had happened and by the time I got back to my group, I was limping and in obvious pain. When my friends saw the wound on the fleshy part of my calf, they questioned me. "The masseuse didn't speak English," I lied.

My blistering welt ended up getting infected, and I spent the rest of that week trying to make the best of the fact that I couldn't sit in the sun, swim in the ocean or dance the night away with my friends.

———

There are many instances to reflect on that illustrate how my people pleasing tendencies had gotten out of control, but this one is the loudest, most painful example I have. My lack of emotional fortitude resulted in physical injury. I'd completely lost my words and the ability to speak my mind, and I could no longer stand up for myself even in the simplest of situations.

Boundaries had become non-existent; conflict became my biggest fear. I was terrified of disappointing or upsetting anyone, at all costs.

Foreshadowing? Indeed.

 I'm fairly certain that if you were to survey a room full of young culinary students and ask them what their ultimate, 'End Goal' was, the overwhelming majority of them would tell you it is to open their *own* restaurant. When I was young and hungry, that was my dream too. But at that time, I had no idea what it looked like to work in — let alone own — a restaurant. All I knew was that cooking made me feel alive, so having a restaurant to call my own, made the most sense.

Somewhere along the line, after I left the safe bubble of school, entered into a daunting industry and then launched my own business, my desire to own my own restaurant disappeared. I can say with great certainty that by the time I had the opportunity to do so, every part of my being was telling me not to.

My dream changed, but Jeff's did not.

———

Jeff had always been a bit of an idealist. He had all these big plans which he eagerly shared with anyone who would listen. There was helicopter school, revamping our basement several times, intense workout regimens … I watched over the years as he would give up on plans quickly. The Restaurant, he assured me, was *not* one of those times.

He wanted *more* than the little life we had created for ourselves. He wanted more than staying in bed on Sunday mornings, dinner with our family and saving for our family home. He wanted more than a house on the beach surrounded by lemon trees.

I sometimes wondered what happened to the boy I fell in love with five years earlier. What happened to the boy who told me he wanted to own less than 100 possessions in an effort to become less materialistic? What happened to the boy that found a $20 bill on the ground and rather than putting it in his pocket, gave it to a homeless man a few feet away? Now, he wanted money, fame and recognition. His End Goal was once Costa Rica with me and some lemon trees. But now his End Goal was to *see his name on the side of a building.*

That's what he told me, the night I got the call asking if I wanted to open a restaurant.

———

It was on a warm summer night. Jeff and I were talking over a glass of white wine and Saganaki cheese when I got a phone call. It was a woman named Florine, asking if I might be interested in opening a restaurant as part of a commercial lease that had recently become available. I watched Jeff's eyes light up as I relayed the message to him. And then I watched him deflate a little when he heard me say that I wasn't *really interested.*

The truth is, I wasn't interested *at all,* but Jeff was determined. He convinced me to book an appointment for us to go look at the space. On our way, he told me the story about the moment he realized I was 'The One.' It was that first night on his couch — the night we fell in love — when he found out I wanted to own a restaurant as much as he did. "*That* was the moment," he told me.

I tried to go into that appointment with an open heart — for him. But from the moment I walked into the space it quickly became apparent how much work it would be to go through with his plan. The possibility of actually opening a restaurant wasn't even on my radar, let alone renovating a 90-year-old building with our own two hands and on my own dime. When I told my friends about it, they were shocked that I even went to go *look* at the space. I had voiced, many times, not only how happy I was owning my own catering business, but also the hardships I'd seen in the restaurants I'd worked in over the years. I believe the statement, "I'll never open my own restaurant," crossed my lips more than once.

But Jeff didn't let it go. He was relentless. Before I had agreed to anything, he started drafting plans and scribbling logos. He even presented me with a rough business plan for a restaurant we could own and operate together. He told the story of how we met to anyone who would listen, and made sure to include how our mutual restaurant dream made us a perfect match. He told the story of us opening a restaurant together like it was a romantic fairy tale, and I was prone to getting caught up in romance.

———

I'm not exactly sure when my mind changed.

I'm not sure when I decided to say *yes* to opening a restaurant that I didn't truly want.

I'm not sure how I was convinced to close my catering company and sell most of my equipment without blinking an eye.

I'm not sure when I decided to give up on my own happiness.

I'm not sure why I was willing to sacrifice everything I'd worked so hard for.

I'm not sure how I was convinced to write a cheque for all of my life savings and then when that ran out, to ask our friends and family for money.

I'm not sure when I decided to once again abandon "Self!"

I'm not sure when I made the conscious decision to stop writing for the third time since I was 10 years old.

But I did. Somewhere along the line, I decided to do all of these things. Not only that, but I was convinced I should be happy about it. I smiled when we threw a big party and revealed our name and logo to all our friends on New Year's Eve. I smiled when we clinked glasses and made toasts. Later, the newspapers published the story of how on our first date, we bonded over our shared desire of opening a restaurant — a restaurant that was just like this one. I smiled. I forced a toothy grin for the cameras and I told the story while I tried to stop my cheeks from shaking. I reassured my friends with a smile when we spoke in private, and they would say things like, "We thought you decided that you didn't want to open your own restaurant;" "I thought you said you were really happy with the way catering is going;" "Are you sure you don't want to have kids right now?"

I told them all the things that Jeff had coached me to say. I told them that everything would be fine. I faked excitement hoping that someday it would materialize into something real.

But it didn't, and as our opening date grew closer, I regressed farther into a state of anxiety over my decision. I tried to muster the courage to tell Jeff how I felt but when I did, my words got trapped in my throat — my jaw clenching around them, like an unwilling oyster refusing to be shucked. I let him hug me in the kitchen and tell me that everything was going to be fine. I let him comfort me. I let him wrap my face in his hands and tell me how much he loved me. I let him thank me for giving him his dream.

He reassured me by saying that we would have to work really hard for a while but then we would start taking Sundays off so we could see family — he knew how much that meant to me. He told me that we would hire people to work for us so we could still travel the world. He told me that when we had kids, someone else would be running The Restaurant for us and we could be stay-at-home parents, if that's what we wanted. He held me close while I was having a full blown panic attack and told me that someday, *someday* we'd retire and move to Costa Rica to grow lemons. We'd drink wine all day and pick mint and have siestas and that would be our life.

It was *absurd*. I knew it. Even then, I knew that all of that was impossible. *I knew.*

But it was *so much easier* to believe him.

When we're starving for love, and someone feeds us, it's easy to feel satiated enough that we'll do *anything* for those crumbs. Even if deep down, we know the crumbs are lies.

———

When the day came for us to officially sign the lease on The Restaurant, Jeff and I sat side by side, across from our new landlord and a notary. When I signed my name on the dotted line, my hand was shaking so badly that my signature was practically illegible.

I suppose I should have taken that as a sign, but I was living in a fog, mourning the life I knew was about to be over. This didn't *feel* right.

I wasn't just scared of the unknown. I knew what it felt like to be *scared*. I knew what it meant to work hard for what you wanted. When I quit a secure job to pursue entrepreneurship full time, I was terrified. But it felt *right*, so I pushed past the fear and I did it. When I got clean, I was petrified. But again, it felt right, so I pushed through the pain, and I did it. This. Did. Not. Feel. Right.

But there I was, signing that lease …

———

I wish I could say that Jeff had no idea how much I was struggling. That he didn't know that I cried myself to sleep every night in the weeks before we opened. That he didn't wonder why I had stopped writing, after he'd watched me write every single day since the moment we met. It would be less painful if I could say he had no idea how hard it was on me.

… But he did know.

He watched as I fell apart, mentally and physically. He was there when I crawled into bed, my body sore from crying. Although I put on a brave face for our launch and our opening week, and there certainly were moments of happiness along the way, he knew that opening The Restaurant was the most painful thing I'd ever been through.

… And he just watched. He watched and let me be squeezed like an old dishrag until I was wrung out and worn. He *needed* me to finance it, and he needed me to be his chef.

It was a slow melting of my heart — like ice in a cocktail you're holding too closely. Piece by piece, day by day, my heart melted knowing that he knew how much pain I was in but kept going. The truth is … he didn't love me enough to end it before it began. His dream was coming true before his eyes, and I was the one making it happen for him. He was so willing to let me sacrifice my happiness for his dream.

I can't blame him for that. Because as much as he didn't love me enough to stop it, I didn't love myself enough to insist.

I'm a grown woman. I was 28 years old when we opened The Restaurant. I was a high-functioning, sober-ish, capable adult when I made that decision. I'd already owned a successful business; I knew what we were up against. I knew how much work it was going to take and how many sacrifices were involved. I knew how this was going to change our lives. I can't pretend for a moment that I didn't.

He tried to tell me once that I didn't *have* to do this, but I knew that wasn't true. Walking away just didn't feel like an option — I knew it would break his heart — and that was something I just wasn't willing to do. I loved him far too much and once I saw how happy he was, I couldn't stop it. I wasn't sure he would love me if I did. I guess I believed that if I could just be patient and do this *one thing* for him, that someday things would work out.

He knew all this, of course. And he dangled that in front of my face on a soft, fluffy piece of string: Costa Rica. Lemons. Babies. Dogs. Adventure. Romance. But most of all, *loyalty.*

He didn't love me enough to let me walk away — and I didn't love myself enough to insist.

———

So, I signed the lease. As my pen curled the final stroke on that dotted line, I heard that voice in my ear again. *"Help him get his name on the side of that building,"* she pleaded. *"Maybe then, he will finally be faithful."* This time, the voice wasn't coming from him. This time, it was coming from deep inside of myself. It was coming from that Little Girl who needed to belong. It was telling me, *"You are not enough."*

62

That is what I was thinking when I let my mind be changed. That is what I was thinking when I abandoned "Self!" That is what I was thinking when my hand picked up that pen and signed my name on that dotted line.

And the moment I signed that lease, was the beginning of the end.

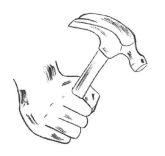 In March 2015, we were given the keys to The Restaurant and we began an intense two-month renovation process. Our budget was incredibly tight, so we did almost all of the work on our own.

Jeff and I were lucky to have so many people believe in us. Both of our fathers came to help us with their handyman skills. My mother sewed us curtains. Our friends came to help sand shelves and paint tables.

My sister was the only one in my family who couldn't help and it broke her heart, I think. She had been feeling unwell for several months — years, even. She had bruises covering her thighs and lower back, from bumping into things, because of her blurry vision and constant dizziness. It had taken two years for the doctors to find her tumour. Perched on her pituitary gland, causing pressure on her optic nerve, which was responsible for her sudden clumsiness. She told our family the news around the same time I announced we were opening The Restaurant. It was a bittersweet time for us all. The Restaurant uplifted us, while simultaneously deflecting our concerns while we waited on the news if her doctor would decide to perform surgery or not.

The next two months were filled with writing business proposals, applying for grants, marketing decisions, painting, scrubbing, scouring thrift stores for affordable décor and building lighting fixtures. My sister's absence was palpable but we had a deadline now and I think I was happy to have a distraction.

———

We spent several weeks interviewing and hiring staff. I brought one cook from my catering company with me to The Restaurant. Brandon was a gentle giant — always smiling, even when he was under a lot of stress, which was often. He was a bit of an old soul — he refused to buy a cell phone, listened to vinyl and bought all his clothes at thrift stores. He had an endearing innocence to him that everyone noticed, and I was incredibly grateful that he was willing to come with me when I told him about The Restaurant.

I also hired Frank who, from the outside, looked a bit aggressive. He was tall, had big arms and a bald head with a scar on it from when he smashed a bottle over his head one night, years ago, during a heavy metal show. He had a rough exterior but was a softie on the inside. His temper flared up every once in a while, but he was also incredibly kind and neighbourly. More than anything though, he had earned my trust and respect, and we became incredibly close friends.

On the front lines, Jeff handled the hiring. Marie, who was timid and sometimes excessively polite but would often say something so funny everyone would be laughing with their heads thrown back. Scarlett was a seasoned server — she was older than the rest of our staff by 20 years, and she had been working in the industry her whole life. Rachel was young, energetic, dramatic and moody. She wore her heart on her sleeve louder than anyone I'd ever met and I remember liking her from the moment she walked through our doors.

If there was anything I was excited about, it was the team we had put together. We all became fast friends and having them be so supportive and ready to work made everything feel easier.

What made things harder, however, was the shoulder pain I had developed, presumably from the physical labour of painting our ceiling and scrubbing years of grease off the kitchen floors. When my pain became unbearable, I left the renovation site early, to attend physiotherapy or get a massage. When I could no longer afford that, I sucked it up and took Aspirin. (A lot of it.)

————

Although we'd cemented our relationship with everything except a ring, Jeff and I still kept our finances fairly separate. I had funded The Restaurant almost entirely by myself, paying for the first and last month's rent from my own personal chequebook and spent almost all of my personal savings by the time renovations were only half done. I signed all the paperwork myself and was the guarantor of our debts because his credit score was so bad. I was forced to put all the cards and accounts in my name which made me feel very uncomfortable. I wished I would have remembered my hot stone burn in those moments but instead I just went along with it.

I tried not to be resentful of Jeff for his shortage of capital. Before we decided to open The Restaurant he was still in school and was working a sales job on commission. He worked hard (there was no denying that) but he was completely irresponsible when it came to his finances. I avoided discussing it with him and when I would see him spending his money frivolously instead of paying his bills, I pushed it farther and farther back in my mind to avoid the confrontation. I'd watched my parents fight about money a lot when I was young, and didn't want to bring any kind of conflict into our relationship. I tried to never make him feel bad about it and congratulated him when he was able to contribute by finding cheap ways to get around a lot of our biggest expenses.

Eventually, my savings ran out so I agreed to put our remaining expenses on my personal credit card. When it was maxed out, we launched a crowdfunding campaign and raised over $12,000. When that money ran out, he suggested we accept a large, interest-free loan to cover the rest of our costs.

When he suggested getting the loan, I was at a point where I couldn't handle the thought of any more debt. He told me it would be a 'cushion' for slower months and that it would be smart of us to accept the zero interest loan. He justified it with the cliché of, "You have to spend money to make money." As a business owner, I knew that was true … but the issue was that *he* wasn't spending any money. Everything fell on me.

A few weeks later, we did a pitch for the loan committee. Jeff spouted numbers from our business plan while I cooked one of the innovative dishes we planned to serve at our new restaurant (a vegan omelette made from chickpeas). In the background of that meeting, while Jeff worked the room, I quietly swirled the pan around as the committee unanimously approved us for the loan. I actually liked public speaking, but for some reason I let him do all the talking while I stayed small and quiet behind him. We were approved for a $10,000 loan and as I signed the forms, I let him remind me, once more, that we were doing this for our *family*.

I probably would have signed up for anything at that point.

By the time we were ready to open, my life savings were completely gone and we were tens of thousands of dollars in debt. The only money I had left to my name was a small stash of cash I kept hidden in the back of my closet for a 'rainy day.' I sensed a rainy day might be coming, so I kept it concealed from Jeff.

———

Each day, for two months, we went to The Restaurant before the sun came up, and we didn't leave until close to midnight. We painted the walls of the dining room deep forest green and hung my antique kitchen tools in the front vestibule. We replaced sinks and installed sump pumps. We polished ancient window trim and repainted the entire kitchen. We built a small prep space in the otherwise unfinished basement because I knew even then, I would need a quiet place to retreat to. We nicknamed the space 'The Dungeon' because it was a windowless, cramped, cold space in the basement. I would end up spending a lot of time there in the coming months.

We tried to make time for each other. We tried to talk before bed and once in a while we would make love in the morning before the renovations began. We ate together in ill-lit corners on piled up boxes or on a drop cloth spread out on the floor. I tried to get excited and stay positive. I tried to open my heart to the idea that even if I wasn't totally resolved with our new lifestyle, it would still be good for us. For our family. For our future.

In May, when The Restaurant was almost ready to open, I had to officially close my catering company. One day, I was quietly cooking in my small but mighty kitchen — the one that I built from scratch and loved so dearly — and the next day *I wasn't*.

There was barely enough time for me to ache.

I hired a few movers to help me get the space cleared out quickly because my shoulder pain had become so debilitating, I couldn't do it alone. I sold everything I didn't have room to store. I washed the floors one last time to prepare for the new tenant. I don't remember much about that day, but I remember standing in my now empty kitchen, and feeling vehemently bitter about having to say goodbye. I was in a fog that day as I watched what felt like my entire identity be packed into boxes and put in the truck.

It was surreal and unfair.

———

When it was time to celebrate our big opening night, we threw a big party for all our friends and family to show off our new space. It was a beautiful, unseasonably warm spring day, so we set the patio for the very first time. I wore a sundress and the night went off without a hitch.

I was under so much pressure to not only be on my game that night, but to smile when we made a toast telling everyone how grateful and excited we were. Faking that much excitement for one night proved to be more exhausting than renovating for two months straight ... but I tried. Damnit, I tried to be grateful that night. I tried to put the pain of closing my catering kitchen a few days earlier aside, so I could recognize how many people were in our corner now. I tried to be grateful for my amazing team that was already making me infinitely proud. I tried to recognize that I was standing in a room, about to open my own restaurant — something that a lot of chefs dream of, but never get to do. I tried to acknowledge the new life I belonged to. *Gratitude must be in there somewhere,* I resigned.

Maybe things would have been different that night if I hadn't just found out about my sister's tumour. Maybe things would have been different if I wasn't icing my shoulder in the bathroom every 15 minutes because I was in agony. Maybe things would have been different if Jeff and I hadn't been in a screaming match earlier that day, or if I didn't feel like there was a 20 litre pail of water resting on my chest.

After our toast and cleaning up, I left the party early to get some sleep for our public grand opening the following day. When I got home, it was all I could do to have a quick shower and go straight to bed. Every person that mattered in my life was still at The Restaurant celebrating, but I was in my shower, trying to scrub the feeling off of me. While I was standing there in the scorching heat, scrubbing my skin raw, tears involuntarily started pouring out of me. I cried thinking about all the sacrifices I'd already made and what was to come. I cried because it didn't add up. I was mourning the loss of "Self"— the "Self" I had been creating and nurturing and growing for the last several years. The force of those tears got stronger and stronger, until I wasn't just crying, I was shaking. Full body heaving.

I cried so hard that I threw up right there in the tub.

I crawled into bed and tried to sleep, but about an hour later, Jeff came home with a bottle of champagne in his hand and asked me to join him to celebrate. I just couldn't bear it.

We were on two separate pages, in two separate worlds, and in that moment, I worried that we might never be on the same page, again.

———

The next day was our first night of service. We were full for both seatings and had a lineup out our door until we ran out of food. It was an evening that *should have* been cherished. I was filled with uncertainty, doubt, and uneasiness for that entire shift. I felt proud too, but it was hard to see in the jumbled mess of emotions. When the night was over and the kitchen was bleached from top to bottom, our staff had gone home and I was sitting on a barstool taking inventory for the following day, I was more exhausted and in pain than I'd ever felt.

I did that night over and over and over, for the next 16 months.

10K EGGLESS OMELETTE (V) (GF)

MAKES ONE OMELETTE

In Latin, the word 'aqua' means water, and 'faba' means bean — so aquafaba is just that — 'Bean Water!' Someone, somewhere discovered that this bean water (typically from cooked chickpeas,) acts as a great egg substitute. Since then, anyone averse to eggs have been using this Miracle Egg Replacer to make all kinds of awesome things!

Not only did this recipe grant me access to a $10,000 loan, but it also has taken me on the road, doing cooking demos and talking aquafaba to the masses for the last few years. I never thought I would say it, but I for one, am incredibly grateful for the humble garbanzo!

For The Omelette
4 tbsp aquafaba (liquid from a can of unsalted chickpeas)
¼ cup chickpea flour
2 tbsp cold water
1 tsp onion powder
¼ tsp salt, or kala namak (black salt) if you have it
⅛ tsp chili powder
⅛ tsp turmeric
Dash of cayenne
Splash of oil or butter, for frying

10K Method
Open a can of chickpeas and strain the liquid into a large bowl. (You can do this every time you open a can of chickpeas and save the aquafaba in a container in the freezer for future recipes!)

Whisk aquafaba in a bowl until it is a bit frothy, about 30 seconds. Add chickpea flour slowly to make a thin batter, followed by the water.

71

Depending on the age of your flour and brand of the chickpeas, this may need to be adjusted with more water or flour. Let the batter sit for about 5 minutes (as it does tend to thicken with time,) and then adjust with more flour or water so it is the consistency of heavy cream or coconut milk. It should be pourable, but thicker than water. Add seasonings and mix well.

When you're ready to cook, heat oil in a small to medium non-stick frying pan (7"/20cm is perfect for 1 omelette). Let the oil get warm first, and when it's hot, stand back and pour your batter in. It will sizzle because of the water content, so be careful not to burn yourself. With your pan on high heat, let the omelette sit for 30 seconds or so. Once you can see the edges setting, gently lift the edge of the omelette with a spatula and tip the pan so the wet batter fills the empty space. Do this a few more times until most of the omelette is cooked. Turn the pan down to medium heat.

Next, use a spatula (or if you're brave, just a flip of the wrist!) to flip the omelette and cook for another minute or two on the other side.

Flip onto a plate and serve with anything you like — hot sauce, green onions, cheese, etc. (But just for the record — the omelette I made that was worth 10K was served plain!)

I chose this.

 This was my mantra now, and I repeated it to myself several times a night during the first few weeks of being open.

I. Chose. This. And. There. Is. No. Going. Back. Now.

The first few weeks were an emulsification of both stress and success. We sabered a bottle of champagne on our patio after getting ranked one of the Top Ten Restaurants in our city. Some nights, after we finished work, the kitchen staff would walk to the bar across the street and we tried to share a meal together when there was time. My kitchen crew motivated me to find contentment and even some joy during what was a stressful launch. I knew I could depend on them and the friendships that grew in that tiny, cramped kitchen were what kept me going.

I missed my old life. I missed "Self!" I missed a life of ease and solitude while I literally sprinted around what was now a hot, frenzied kitchen, crowded with people and problems and stress. I missed being in a big, bright kitchen every day, all by myself, cooking my heart out.

I chose this, I kept repeating. So, I put my head down and tried to make the best of what I had chosen for myself.

————

In early June, a month after we opened, I posted a selfie of Jeff and me on Instagram. Our cheeks were touching and we had big smiles plastered across our faces. We looked a bit tired and sweaty, but it was a gorgeous, hot, sunny day. Plus, we were in good spirits because we'd only been open for one month and we were making money, and had overwhelmingly positive reviews. We were fully booked for the next two months and I welcomed the feeling that washed over me that day. A feeling that told me we *might* make it through all this. I settled into this feeling and clasped onto the hope — *maybe the hard part was over,* I thought to myself, that day on the patio. I captioned our selfie with: *"We survived our first month in business ... and we're still smiling!!"*

I wanted him to stay with me to bask in this newfound feeling, but he told me he had to go inside to get some work done. When he left, I had this strange, little flutter in my gut, but I pushed the feeling aside like I had gotten used to doing. I continued working on my paperwork while I sat alone in a sunbeam, and then went inside to get ready for service. In the kitchen, the team celebrated with frosty beers and got ready for a busy Saturday night. We hammered out food and it was one of the busiest nights we'd ever had. When we went home for the night, I felt the flutter again when I noticed Jeff's insistence on staying up late in our office by himself instead of coming to bed with me. I brushed it off again. Tomorrow was Sunday, and we could sleep in. I couldn't wait!

Sunday mornings were the only time we had to rest. On Mondays and Tuesdays, The Restaurant was closed, but we had shopping, prepping and organizing to do, along with payroll, answering email and catering requests. We served lunch and dinner on Wednesday through Saturday, which usually meant a 12-14 hour day for us both. By Saturday night, we were typically both tired and drained from the week — and that was on weeks where nothing big went wrong. When the sink was leaking, or our sign was vandalized, or someone called in sick, it usually meant I was a wreck by the end of the week. On Sundays, we didn't open until 4 p.m. and it was usually a slower day. I always looked forward to Sunday mornings because we could sleep in a little later than usual, and if the weather was good, we could take our dogs on a long walk. I loved those walks because I felt like we were a real family, with no debt or infidelity or betrayal to speak of. I also loved Sundays when it rained or was too cold for us to go for a walk because we would stay in bed all morning until the very, final moment, when one of us had to go. But we would fight it for as long as we could ... under the covers, safe, warm and in love.

When I was a child, Sundays meant *family*. Sundays meant long baths and my mother combing baby oil into my hair. They meant leisurely afternoons of board games and evenings watching movies. In the summer, Sundays meant my Dad would be outside fixing something or cutting the grass, and my mother would be by the stove. Always by the stove. She would be carefully basting a chicken that was perched on whole bulbs of garlic and leeks from our garden. She would be shaving fennel and steaming potatoes. She would be whisking flour into pan drippings to make gravy. She would be shredding braised meat to cover homemade egg noodles. Sundays were a day of rest, and a day of feasting, and we could always count on my mother making Caesar Salad, almost every single Sunday.

Sunday mornings with Jeff weren't quite like that, but they did remind me of a time when life was simpler.

———

When I woke that Sunday morning, I was actually *smiling*. I was smiling because unlike most mornings when I had to run out the door, I was still in bed relaxing. I was smiling because the love of my life was lying next to me. I was smiling because we'd survived our first month in business.

This particular Sunday was a busy day at The Restaurant so it was no surprise that by 9 a.m., Jeff was already getting ready to leave. I wanted him to stay in bed with me so we could cuddle or make love or at least eat breakfast together. Despite him leaving earlier than I wanted him to, I was smiling, because just for a moment, life didn't feel like it was *messy*. I was overcome with a feeling of calm and was filled with hope — like coming up for air when I hadn't been able to breathe for months.

As I was thinking these thoughts and wondering what I might have for breakfast, I saw Jeff press his forehead against his closet door and I noticed his fists were clenched. I heard him take a deep, deep breath and before I could ask what was wrong, he turned around and I saw he had tears in his eyes.

75

It took only seconds for me to figure out what was going on. I'd seen those eyes before. I knew what his facial expression meant.

Guilt.

My mouth. My heart. My chest. My head. My skin. My jaw.

I've been here before ...

Like the last time, I sat there still and listened. The words that flowed from his mouth next were like hollandaise: smooth, perfectly seasoned, impossible to resist (even though I knew they were bad for me).

He told me that these last few months had been the most stressful time of his life, and that I had grown distant. He felt like he couldn't talk to me anymore, he claimed. He insisted that he came to bed every night feeling so lonely and scared that we weren't going to make it. I was having mood swings ever since I found out about my sister's tumour, and I was constantly stressed and irritated at home. He told me he was just *so lonely* ... he acted out of desperation.

He was up late one night and decided he needed to talk to someone, so instead of waking me, he created a fake email account to remain anonymous and sent a message to a random girl asking if she could talk. He just wanted someone to talk to, and after he got what he needed, he told me he deleted the account and came to bed.

He told me he 'needed his ego stroked.' (These were his exact words.)

"It meant nothing." He was just starving for the affection I had been withholding, he explained.

As I sat there, listening to a story I'd heard before, I was transported back to the first time and was suddenly reminded of how much it stung. Four years ago we sat on the same mattress, in a different bedroom, in a different neighbourhood. It was a different time and a different girl, but it was the same story. He

76

was crying, holding his head in his hands, telling me how ashamed he was.

It felt like I was trussing a chicken, the way I almost involuntarily filled in the gaps for him. Perhaps I had grown distant; perhaps I resented him a little bit and it showed. We *should have* talked more, but we didn't. I was always too tired and I had been avoiding confrontation so much, perhaps I grew cold and pushed him away.

When trussing a chicken, you learn slowly. You do it once, and each time, it gets easier. Pack everything in, tie it up tightly, don't let those threads loosen or everything will come spilling out.

———

Jeff got up from our bed for a moment to blow his nose, and in the short moment that he was gone, I glanced down at my phone. I noticed right away that I had missed several calls from Sam, an acquaintance of mine and a close friend of Chloe. I didn't know her well, but she had come to The Restaurant several times over the two months we spent renovating to lend a hand; painting tables and mudding drywall. She was a sweet girl and although we weren't close, I always liked her and appreciated her kindness.

Why is Sam calling me? I asked myself. By the time I heard Jeff's footsteps coming back towards the bedroom, the pieces came together. "SAM?!!??!" I screamed in his face. I jumped out of bed and started frantically dressing while shaking with rage. Muddled words and excuses were coming out of his mouth which I could not hear. It wasn't a 'stranger' as he had told me — it was young, sweet, innocent Sam whom we both knew and I would have to face someday. It wasn't a 'random girl.' He planned this. He *picked* her.

I fled through our front door and ran, not sure where I was going, until I couldn't run anymore. *I've been here before … I've been here before,* I kept saying to myself.

I collapsed onto the grass at the park not far from our house and rubbed my chest to make sure my heart shreds hadn't spilt out somewhere. I checked my phone again hoping for an explanation and finally finished reading Sam's text: *"You should call Chloe when you get this. She will explain everything."*

Chloe was one of my oldest friends. We met on the playground when we were seven, and had been best friends ever since, save for a few childish fights over the years. We'd been through loss and love and crushes and divorce and pregnancy scares and everything else a girl might go through with her bestie. We had been in fights and lived across oceans, but the one thing that I knew was that Chloe had no reason to lie to me, and she never would.

So, when she told me what she knew, I had no choice but to believe her. Her voice was low and calm. First, she asked if I was okay.

She'd been here before too.

———

Chloe told me that one night, our mutual friend Sam was feeling creeped out by some seemingly random but repetitive emails she'd been receiving for a few days. She tried to ignore them, but they became increasingly aggressive and forward. When the language changed and they progressed to him asking her if they could meet, she realized this wasn't a random stranger, it was possibly someone she *knew*. She enlisted Chloe to help, forwarding her all the messages she'd been sent, and Chloe got to work, trying to solve the mystery of who could be behind these creepy messages.

Chloe tried to log into the account, to look for clues, and after a series of failed attempts to log in, a half blanked out 'recovery phone number' was listed. Only a few of the digits were listed, the rest remained 'X's.' When Chloe entered the exposed digits of the recovery phone number into her phone, Jeff's name popped up on her screen.

78

At first, she refused to believe it was him. She *refused* ... but deep in her heart, she thought it *could have* been him. She recalled the story I told her years prior, about him kissing Alisa Burke, and she knew that over the years there had been times when I worried about his faithfulness. She also recalled the last time she had seen him interact with Sam — how they both found it strange how he tried to touch her hand while he was chatting with her. Chloe knew that if she was going to accuse him, she had to be certain. So, her next move was to take over Sam's email account and try to trick him into revealing his identity. She sent the bait and waited to see if it really was her best friend's partner on the other end of those messages.

She hoped she was wrong. But deep, deep down, *she knew*.

—————

When Chloe confronted Jeff about it, he desperately tried to make her see it as a misunderstanding. At first he was remorseful, and then he became angry at her for catfishing him. Next, he tried to use his usual excuse by telling her I was so distant and he was lonely. Chloe refused to hear him out and told him that he only had one choice — to confess to me. She told him he had until Sunday, and if he didn't tell me by then, she was going to call me and tell me herself. She had all the proof she needed; she'd caught him red-handed. He tried to persuade her differently all weekend long, but his efforts to change her mind were futile. She was much stronger than I.

So on Sunday morning, when his time was up, he waited until the very last moment, and then he confessed. Exactly one month and one day after we opened The Restaurant.

At this point, my heart was so shredded, you could have made a pulled pork sandwich with it.

Sundays would never be the same.

79

SUNDAY CAESAR SALAD (V) (GF)
SERVES 8 APPETIZER SALADS OR 4 ENTREES

I've always had the motto: "You can tell a lot about a place by how they make a Caesar salad." Sometimes a Caesar salad can be incredibly basic and disappointing — store-bought dressing, stale croutons, limp bacon, and browning lettuce. Other times, it can be a whirlwind of flavour that will convince anyone that you CAN make friends with salad. I think this version does just that! It's not quite the version my mother used to make on Sundays, but it is one of my favourite things to eat.

For The Salad
1 large head of romaine lettuce, or 2 small ones, washed and sliced into bite sized pieces
120 grams (approximately 10 large leaves) green, curly kale, stems removed, torn into bite sized pieces
Dash of sea salt
Juice of half a lemon

For The Dressing
¾ cup raw cashews, soaked in warm water for 1 hour minimum
½ cup water
1-2 cloves garlic, peeled, whole (depending on your taste)
¼ cup nutritional yeast
¼ cup lemon juice
1 tbsp capers
1 tbsp Dijon mustard
½ tsp salt
½ tsp pepper

For The "Croutons"
1 cup chickpeas, drained
1 tbsp olive oil
1 tbsp Dijon mustard
1 tbsp nutritional yeast
1 clove garlic, finely minced
Zest of half a lemon
Sprinkle of salt
Dash of pepper

80

For The "Bacon"

100 grams (½ block) extra-firm tofu, pressed and cut into small cubes

2 tbsp tamari (or soy sauce)

2 tbsp sesame oil

2 tbsp balsamic vinegar

2 tbsp maple syrup

1 tsp smoked paprika

Dash of liquid smoke (optional)

A Note About Kale

Most people don't want to eat a bowl of plain kale, so the trick to make this robust green more palatable is to *massage* it. Treat the kale like a friend with a sore back — you want to dig in with some pressure, but not too hard. Massaging the kale helps to break it down so it is more tender and flavourful. You will know the kale is done when it has turned vibrant dark green and feels a little damp to the touch — it should not be soupy or limp.

A Note About Tofu

Tofu is pretty boring on its own — so it's up to you to spice it up! However, keep in mind that a good marinade will be wasted if you don't drain your tofu first. Picture a kitchen sponge. If you try using that sponge to clean up a mess, it won't have any room to absorb anything else if it's full of water. Treat tofu the same way. To remove the water that surrounds a piece of tofu, place it between two tea towels or paper towel and then place a weight (e.g. can of tomato sauce, bag of flour,) on top. Let it sit for 20-30 minutes (or even better, overnight in the fridge). When it's done pressing, it should be dry to the touch — this means it is ready to absorb whatever delicious marinade you put on it! No more boring tofu!

Method

Start with getting the bacon marinating by mixing cubed, pressed tofu with remaining bacon ingredients and stir well. Let this sit for 20 minutes (or better yet, overnight in your fridge!)

In another bowl, mix crouton ingredients. When the oven is heated to 350°, bake tofu and chickpeas on cookie sheets for 20 minutes. Stir them once and then bake for an additional 12-15 minutes and remove from oven to let cool.

Meanwhile, place torn kale in a large mixing bowl. Season with salt and lemon and then massage very well with both hands. *After massaging,* add chopped romaine to the bowl and set aside.

Lastly, make your dressing. Strain cashews that have been soaking and add to a blender. Add everything else (including the fresh water), and blend on high, until you have a thick, creamy, smooth dressing.

Finally, combine cooled tofu bacon, chickpea croutons and cashew dressing with your greens and serve immediately. For extra points, top your salad with nutritional yeast for a parmesan cheese flavour and lemon wedges for anyone who wants an extra zingy salad!

My gut was telling me to *run*. So, I picked myself up off the ground and walked back to our house as far as the driveway, got in my car and drove to my Dad's house. It was where I always went when things were tough. My Dad didn't care if I showed up unannounced, always welcoming me with open arms.

I crawled into my old twin bed that was just barely big enough for me, completely exhausted and cried until I fell asleep. I slept for a while, ignoring phone calls from Jeff and by the time I woke up, it was evening and I had to decide what I was going to do. I thought about it long and hard. I thought about it all night, in fact, barely blinking until the sun rose.

I thought about what it would look like if I left. If I went back to our home, told him I couldn't forgive him a second time, packed my things and ran. The more I thought about it, the more I realized how *impossible* that would be. Every single penny I had was tied up in The Restaurant, except for that small stash of cash in my closet. It was *something,* but it certainly wasn't enough to start over. I was financially tied to The Restaurant through loans and debt, and leaving so suddenly would cost me everything I'd invested. Add to that, The Restaurant was in the height of its momentum and I felt like the entire city and everyone I knew was *looking* at me; watching me; waiting for me to either explode with success, or fail. Leaving The Restaurant after only being open for one month would certainly mean I was a failure. I worried what people would say about me so I let my ego take over as I considered every single "like" on Facebook and Instagram. I also considered how it would look to others if our relationship failed. I didn't want to be like my parents … I wanted to make it work. The more I thought about it, the more it felt like I was trudging through overcooked oatmeal — I was *stuck.*

I thought about all the people who believed in us. My family, our crowdfunders, all the people who donated their time, space or money to help us open. I couldn't let them down.

I thought about our staff — I had three apprentices working under me now, and they all depended on me not only for their paycheques, but for my guidance and friendship. It was immense pressure, and I was shrivelling at the thought of it.

I started to consider everything we had to look forward to — our six month anniversary, our first million dollars, the awards and accolades that would eventually come our way. I thought about all the articles and reviews yet to be written about us.

There was one last factor and when I realized it, the oatmeal I felt I was standing in had become so gummy and gloopy that I couldn't move an inch. Jeff. *I loved him.* Maybe he was right — maybe I really *had* been distant these last few months. My attitude and mood swings had put such a huge weight on our relationship. My struggles wore him down, and that's why he was weak.

By the time Monday morning came, I had made my decision.

… I barely even made it a single day without him.

———

The first time I'd gone through this with Jeff, I had leaned on my friends and family. I told a few close friends about what he'd done with Alisa Burke because I had needed someone to talk to; to share my pain. The memory of that day mirrored this situation so vividly — I could see him, sitting on the edge of the bed, head in his hands, weeping, apologizing profusely. He told me that he would never, ever betray my trust again. He said all the things that cheaters say, but I didn't know it yet. I was young, madly in love and had found the person I thought I was going to marry. I thought nothing bad would ever happen to us. *I should stay … no matter what,* is what I told myself then. There were people in this world who quit when things get hard, but I wasn't going to be one of those people. I was going to fight for the man that I loved.

84

I remember this is what I told my friends when they checked in a few days later to see how I was doing. I regurgitated the speech that Jeff had given me, and they said that they were happy for me out loud. But I could see in their eyes that they didn't really mean it. They felt a little sorry for me, because they knew that Jeff wasn't going to change.

I never wanted to see that look again, when they thought of me.

This time around, I didn't want people looking at me like they didn't *believe* in us. I wanted people to go on thinking we were a perfect couple with a beautiful story. I wanted to stay in the fairy tale, no matter how fake it was. And if anyone found out the truth about him, it would all melt away.

So, I decided to let it go, and I took Jeff back, barely flinching at his mighty transgression. The very next morning, I drove to The Restaurant and got straight to work. We were closed on Mondays, so it was just Frank there getting ready for a long prep day. My eyes were puffy from crying and red from a lack of sleep. I felt like I was in a dizzy fog all morning. I wanted to confide in Frank when he asked me if I was okay, but I couldn't. I was too ashamed.

I was also too humiliated to tell my sister or my Dad what had happened, so I reported that Jeff and I had a silly fight, but that we were okay. This drove an invisible wedge between my family and me — a wedge made from resentment and secrecy and silence. When Chloe tried to talk to me about it, I told her that everything was fine and we were moving on. I asked Sam not to tell anyone and convinced myself that it was no big deal that I was asking her to play pretend with me. I thought I understood the gravity of what Jeff had done — that he had aggressively pursued someone in a really creepy way, while I was asleep in our bed down the hall. That he lied through his teeth for days. I convinced myself that I understood all of it, but that I just didn't know how to handle it, and that's why I asked Sam and Chloe for their silence.

I had no idea then, all the pain that lie I was telling to myself would cause over the next year. But it felt safer if no one knew, so I didn't tell a *soul*. Time didn't stop just because I had a secret. I had less than 24 hours to figure out what I was going to do, and then the very next day I was back at The Restaurant, working shoulder to shoulder with Jeff and interacting with all our staff and friends as if nothing had ever happened. Life went on while I was drowning in oatmeal.

I felt the crushing pain of that self-inflicted solitude every single day for the next 15 months.

———

During the next few months I let Jeff beg for forgiveness. I let him fill my bedroom with yellow roses. I let him do the laundry and clean the tub. I let him take me to dinner and hold my hand, telling me how sorry he was and how he'd never stray again. I let him make love to me with all the passion in the world. A few months later, when we closed for the second week in August like we always promised we would, I let him take me far away so we could stay on a sailboat for a week. He brought me fresh coffee in the morning and we ate avocado toast on the dock while things went back to 'normal.' It was California all over again; it was what he did best.

Gravy fixes everything ... so I piled it on.

My heart repair took longer this time. Months went by and things were hard. I just kept applying meat glue to my wounds until the day came when I didn't hurt as badly. I walked through life as if conversations were landmines — tiptoeing around the questions people asked and doing everything I could to avoid confrontations with Jeff. I *wanted* to tell someone, more than anything. My coworkers were the people I spent the most time with, and they all might have suspected something was going on, but Jeff faithfully sent me love notes across the pass in the kitchen while they cooed over how romantic he was, vindicating him further. In the end, I was willing to exchange my silence for ease. I just wanted this mess to be over.

86

But the mess wasn't over, and a few weeks later, I got an email from Chloe, telling me so. It was hard for her to accept how quickly I had forgiven Jeff for such a deep betrayal. She also wanted to know why I hadn't reached out to Sam, even though I had promised her that I would. The truth was that I thought about Sam all the time. I wondered how she was coping, and if she hated me. But reaching out to her didn't fit my plan of staying silent.

I eventually caved, broke the spell of silence and tried to talk to Jeff about it. I told him that maybe Chloe was right when she suggested that we had moved on too quickly. "It doesn't really sound like Chloe is being a good friend," he urged. At first, I was angry but after a quick conversation and teary eyes, I began to believe him when he said that it didn't sound like Chloe actually *wanted* me to move on. He hugged me hard and asserted, "You don't need anyone else, baby. You've got me."

I felt full and empty all at once.

Chloe was angry with me for how I was refusing to deal with things. Jeff put the idea in my head that I should be angry at *her,* for not wanting me to move on. In the meantime, I made a peace offering by sending Sam a letter.

———

I crafted the letter carefully and concisely, with the intention of making amends. I wrote drafts and read it out loud to myself in the mirror, to make sure it sounded just right. I didn't want it to be harsh or judgemental.

In that letter, I told her that I was sorry for what happened to her. I told her what I had been telling myself since it happened — that good people can do bad things. I told her that I believed Jeff was a good man, but that because of *my* actions, he was incredibly lonely and during that solitary, sad time, he reached for something else. I told her that he was remorseful, and that we were working on our relationship. I wanted her to know that I wasn't angry at her and that I hoped we could all be in the same room again someday.

… I'm not exactly sure what I expected from that letter but I do remember everything about the moment I got Sam's response. I was sitting outside on an unseasonably hot autumn day and was drinking iced coffee. I can recall where my mug was on the table, and how my sunglasses rested on the side of that mug. I remember where my journal was and what pen I was using. I remember that my toenails were painted turquoise. I remember how I felt when I read her letter — it was more than just a punch-in-the-gut, lose-your-breath, heart-racing, cracked-wide-open moment. It was more like I'd been gutted like a sockeye salmon and was flapping around on the floor of a boat.

Sam told me that she was glad I was okay, and that she appreciated my loyalty and honesty. But she also told me that she did not, in fact, agree that Jeff was a good person who just did a bad thing. She told me that Jeff had *targeted* her. "*He sought me out and preyed on me,*" were her exact words.

Those words.

I blinked hard but I couldn't see straight. I didn't want her words. I didn't want any of it. All I wanted to do was destroy them. If I ripped that letter up or burned it or threw it in the river, it couldn't be true. I think, deep down, I *knew* it was true … but I had to do everything in my power now to avoid that truth and save the life I had built with this man.

Sam's words could have been a catalyst for great shifts in my life. *That letter could have changed everything.* It could have been my door to the Way Out. But at that time, it felt like there was no Way Out. So, instead, I sat on my porch in the sweet autumn sunbeam and read that letter over and over until it was creased and worn. And then I did the only thing that made sense to me at the time.

I folded that letter up and put it in a box in the back corner of my closet. I wouldn't go near it again for more than a year. Everything inside of me changed after I read that letter, but, at the same time, nothing changed at all.

I didn't want to be at The Restaurant any more than I had on day one, but I *needed* it now. My strategy became putting my head down and working. So I worked. Since the day I read Sam's letter, The Restaurant was the only thing I was willing to put my energy into and my work became all consuming. It wasn't the first time in my life that I'd used busy-ness as a numbing agent, and it wouldn't be the last.

———

My work week began on Wednesday and it always began the same. I woke up early with cramps in my calves and when my feet touched the floor I could feel where the new blisters began and the old ones were callusing. I dragged my hungover body to the bathroom where I would have a shower that was as hot as I could stand, massaging my upper arms, wrists, shoulders and neck. I'd stay there for as long as I could, half-asleep-half-awake. I'd get ready for the day with some mascara and my hair in a tight braid. While my coffee brewed, I put my chef pants and tank top on, pet my dog who didn't want me to go, grabbed an apple or banana and walked out the door.

On my way into work, I'd often stop to pick up groceries or fresh bread, and I would drive to The Restaurant with the same half-asleep-half-awake feeling I had in the shower. I'd either be the first one to arrive, or I'd be greeted by Jeff and get started on my day. I would unload the groceries if there were any, and would always hope that the painkillers I was taking for my shoulder pain had kicked in by then. If they hadn't, I would grab an ice pack from the freezer and sit in the dining room while I drank coffee number two and made my prep list for the day.

I liked the mornings I had to myself the most. Although I may have been good at faking it, I never really grew into enjoying my leadership role. I preferred any alone time I had at The Restaurant, the mornings being the only time I felt even mildly peaceful. It was quiet in the mornings, except for the hum of the fridge and the phone ringing for reservations. It brought me back to my previous life as a caterer, when I didn't live in such chaos. Occasionally I would listen to music or talk to myself, but most often, I would start prep for the day in the silence and solitude.

My vegetable farmer would arrive in the late morning, giving me more to do, but Frank would show up around the same time and get straight to work. By 11 a.m. we would have the prep list half finished, and the rest of the kitchen staff would arrive. By that time, I couldn't wait to go to the basement to seek more silence and solitude. Someone would offer to make me lunch every day, but I'd usually just grab the end of a piece of bread, dip it in a jar of peanut butter, pop a few more painkillers, drink some Diet Coke and head to the basement, or 'The Dungeon,' as we called it, to prep by myself. For the next few hours (assuming nothing went wrong at lunch) I would roll pizza dough, purée sauces, pick herbs or dice onions — no job was too big or too small, as long as I could keep my mind busy. My favourite task was to make fresh ravioli — if no one bothered me for an hour or more, I could get into a deep flow state and almost forget where I was completely. Some days it was peaceful, other times it was so turbulent, I wanted to crawl into the walls and never come out. The ravioli always tasted better if it was the former.

Around 3 p.m., Brandon would arrive and get started on setting up for dinner while Frank took a break or continued on the prep list, depending on the day. Every day, just after 3 p.m., I would have to crawl out from the blanket of solitude and join the world. I prepared myself with a deep breath each time, plastered a smile on my face and walked up the stairs as slowly as possible, hoping to prolong the inevitable. The service staff would arrive and ask how my day was going. I'd already been at The Restaurant for eight hours at that point, but I usually just responded with a generic, "Fine, thank you."

I would have a quick meeting with the servers before they got started on setting tables and cutting lemons. I would go through the menu with them, which I changed every single week, and write out the specials on the chalkboard. I'd answer their questions over a glass of wine or another Diet Coke and it was usually around this time that I'd realize how hungry I was. If there was time, I'd make a quick meal, usually pasta with butter, another peanut butter sandwich or something just as easy, and dole it out to anyone who was working. This was often the only time of day I would sit, and I'd sometimes be joined by Frank on the stoop outside the back door, but often ate in the dirty, cramped stairwell and hoped no one would bother me.

At 4:15, I would check in on everyone and make sure they were set for service. At 4:30, the doors would open and customers would begin filing in. It was always a combination of three of us on the line, but the kitchen was so small, if you had three arms, you could reach all of these stations at once. At 4:25 each day, just before the first order came, Frank would boom what eventually became our kitchen mantra: "Let's have a good service!" and away we went.

I was expeditor, plating every dish that wasn't a salad or dessert. For the next six hours I would be behind the pass, working as if my arms were tentacles as I quickly plated food, called out orders, organized chits, wiped rims and tasted *everything,* making sure it was perfect. I created on-the-spot tasting menus for customers who didn't want to order off the menu — another one of Jeff's ideas. I accommodated every allergy you can think of. I checked in with the front-of-house every half hour to make sure the dishwasher was available when they needed clean glassware. I reached. I stretched. I hammered out food. I had to be delicate and careful while I plated the handmade beet ravioli that took me all day to make. I had to check the sear of Brandon's burgers. I had to let all the servers know if we ran out of something and face Jeff's disappointment if we got any complaints on the food. I had to make sure the salad greens didn't wilt in the heat of the kitchen, and that the hot food was hot, even though we didn't have a working heat lamp. It was a mad rush for at least five of those hours.

91

In my former years, while I was a line cook, this is what I *lived* for. But now, I was falling apart at the seams and it was all I could do to turn off that darkness inside of me, for those five or six hours and put my energy into the food instead. A bittersweet saving grace that was quickly losing its sweetness.

At the end of the night, when it was just desserts left to be plated, and everyone had a quick break to shovel some food down or have a cigarette, I would make my way up the stairs to the staff room. I peeled off my pants and coat that were drenched in a combination of sweat and grime from the day. I would then head downstairs and sit at the bar for a final drink which was either a tea, a glass of wine, or a shot of straight tequila, depending on how service went. I would get started on the prep list for the following day, which was usually just as long as the day before.

I could see the kitchen from my spot at the bar and watched as my team cleaned up for the night, making sure everyone had a good day and being available to talk if they didn't. If it had been a tough night, I'd stay on the floor to help scrub the flattop or scour the sinks. I sometimes mingled with lingering guests during that last hour, or if I was feeling too anxious, hot or tired, I would sit outside and finish my prep list alone. Around 10:45 p.m. I would thank anyone who was left, consult with them on what needed to be done the following day, get in my car and drive home.

I did the same thing almost every single day.

On Sunday, business was a little slower, and we looked forward to a shorter prep list because by the following week when we re-opened, we would have a brand new menu and therefore an empty fridge to fill. On Sundays, we let loose in the kitchen. I let the guys listen to hip hop during prep time, and sometimes we would sit for 30 minutes instead of three, and have a proper meal together.

On Monday, Frank and I would usually meet to talk about the menu for the following week. We'd go to the bulk food store,

92

return empties and pick up cleaning supplies. We'd do inventory and place orders. It wasn't a full day, but it wasn't a day off either.

On Tuesday we would spend 8-10 hours prepping everything we needed for the next few days of service, and then it would start all over again.

I subscribed to my new way of living. I had a shoulder injury that would not heal, a sister who was sick, parents and pets who I didn't have time for, a man who slept beside me that I didn't trust and on top of all of it, I felt like I'd lost Chloe, my best friend. I walked around like a zombie while life at The Restaurant went on like clockwork. I tried to hold my head high even though it felt like I was wearing an industrial sized bag of flour around my neck.

————

I hadn't completely forgiven Jeff, but the romantic gestures and love bombing continued. When he came to work with fresh flowers, I let all the girls in the dining room go crazy over his gesture. While he was waltzing through the dining room with a wine glass in his hand, celebrating life and having everything he wanted, I was in the background, becoming so small that no one could even see me. I faded into the kitchen and let the food soothe me.

I forced myself to believe that if I lost everything, I would at least always have *food*. I could bury myself there in ravioli or mashed potatoes or lentil soup. I put what was left of my heart and soul into the food, because my heart was breaking, and cooking was the only thing that seemed to hold it together. It was the second time in my life that it felt like food had saved me, but now I feared if I lost my ability to cook, I would be swallowed up into the darkness that was creeping in and would never escape. All I had left was my trade. My skill. My talent. My craft. My hands. I pushed through my physical pain, as I let my profession consume me and did whatever it took to make it to work each day.

Even when things were their absolute worst, when I looked down at those perfect purées and my delicately minced herbs, I felt oddly at peace. Chopping hundreds of pounds of vegetables soothed me. Kneading dough for hours helped me forget. It was the one thing I could control now. I would stand over that bright, white plate in that tiny, ill-lit kitchen, shut off my brain, stop questioning myself and just *be there.* I'd be there by myself, while my whole world swirled around me like I was watching it on film.

Sometimes those moments felt sweet, and I was proud of myself. Other times, it felt like all I had was the food on that plate, and it absolutely destroyed me. I didn't belong to anyone anymore. That kitchen was all I had.

———

I really don't know how I made it through those next few months. My shoulder was completely ruined by that point and I was numbing the physical pain in whatever legal way I could. Eventually my doctor determined there was nothing *physically wrong* with my shoulder and stopped prescribing cortisol shots or any more T3s. For the first time in almost a decade, I actually considered buying a bag of blow just to get me through the pain.

Things went from bad to worse and I stopped caring. I didn't want to go outside. I didn't want to see my friends. I cancelled plans last minute, faking illness strategically so that no one would ask questions. I avoided public events. I stopped calling my parents. I stopped going on long walks with my dogs. I stopped recognizing how good the sunshine felt on my face. I stopped going to yoga. I stopped cooking for myself. I stopped caring what I looked like. I stopped being honest.

I gave up. On everything. On love and friendship. On faith and truth and magic.

Maybe if I would have told someone, or maybe if I had been writing at that time, everything would have turned out differently. But deep down, I *knew* what I'd done. I knew that instead of helping a woman in need, I pushed her under the rug, silenced her and ignored her pain. I was no longer the person I always thought I was; the girl I *wanted* to be was gone. I felt dirty, and although I wanted to scour the thought of her from my story, no matter how hard I scrubbed, I thought of Sam every day. Thinking about it made me so furious and so ashamed that I stopped writing for the third time since I was a child, because it hurt too much to admit what I'd done.

And with that, I was no longer a writer. I was no longer a happy, positive girl with a big, bright smile. I was no longer a good sister or daughter. I was no longer someone who told the truth. Everything I once was, everything that made me proud and everything that brought me joy was either blurry or shaky or gone.

And yet, my friends were all congratulating me. To everyone around me, it was completely normal to be so consumed with my work. I was a 'go-getter.' I was passionate. I was willing to *suffer* for my craft and for my budding business. When we won the highest honour a restaurant could have in our city that winter, and a shiny plaque arrived crowning us, "The Best Restaurant," I was completely indifferent. The newspaper came and took our photo. Flowers, handshakes and cards arrived in droves. I couldn't care less.

It made Jeff want even *more.*

He started planning a second location. He started talking about serving brunch. He started a plan to offer our products wholesale.

I was *So. Fucking. Tired.*

The more he demanded, the more depleted I grew. It didn't seem to matter how tired I was, or how much I was struggling with my shoulder pain, or how worried I was about my sister. It didn't seem to matter that I was circling the drain. He. Just. Wanted. More.

He wanted to sell t-shirts. He wanted to cater big festivals. He wanted an empire. He wanted his name on the side of that goddamn building.

He wanted me to rip off the end of an old loaf of bread and hastily dip it in an empty jar of peanut butter, scraping the sides for morsels. He wanted me to choke it down and move onto the next idea on his list. He wanted me and my peanut butter to be spread as thin as possible.

I wanted to take my time to toast the beautiful sourdough bread that took days to make and years to perfect. I wanted to toast it in a pan, evenly on both sides, butter it right to the edges and then slather on an obnoxiously thick layer of organic, chunky peanut butter. I wanted to eat it slowly, with intention, and lick my fingers until I was full.

I wanted lemon trees …

… He wanted more.

DUNGEON BEET RAVIOLI (V)

MAKES APPROXIMATELY 16 RAVIOLIS, OR 2-3 SERVINGS

Fresh pasta is a true labour of love. This recipe is probably the most complex one I've included in this book but it is well worth the time and effort. It requires a pasta roller and would benefit from an electric mixer. It is a wonderful activity for date night or to make with friends. You can also make it alone if you need to unwind and work some things out — in my experience, making fresh pasta is much cheaper (and as effective!) as therapy.

For The Beet Purée
6 medium beets
Up to ½ cup water

For The Pasta Dough
2 cups flour
¼ cup olive oil
1 tbsp salt
About 10 tbsp beet purée

For The "Ricotta"
200 grams (about ½ block) firm tofu
200 grams (about ½ package) soft tofu
¼ cup nutritional yeast
Juice and zest of half a lemon
1 tsp salt
¼ tsp black pepper
¼ cup chopped chives

For The Ravioli
1/4 cup flour + ½ cup cold water
Pasta dough
Tofu Ricotta
Beet greens (optional)

Method
The first step of this recipe is to make a beet purée. The simplest way to do this is to place raw beets in cold water, bring to a boil and simmer them until they are very soft, about 40-50 minutes. Drain and while warm, the skins should slide right off the beet. You can also roast peeled beets until they are very tender. Either way, once your beets are cooked, blend them until you have a smooth purée. You may need to add a few drops of water, but be careful not to thin it out too much.

If you're using a mixer to make your dough, combine everything listed except beet purée in your mixer and attach the dough hook. Mix on medium-low, adding beet purée, a tablespoon at a time, until the dough comes together. Continue to mix for 2-3 minutes on medium-low. If you are making this dough by hand, follow the same procedure, but make sure you knead well (10 minutes) to allow gluten to develop. When dough is finished (it should be smooth and elasticky) wrap in plastic and let the dough chill in your fridge for at least 30 minutes.

Meanwhile, make the tofu ricotta in your food processor. First, pulse the firm tofu a few times to break it up. Do not purée — it should be crumbly as this represents the "curds" in ricotta. Remove and place the granules of tofu in a mixing bowl. Next, purée soft tofu until smooth and add it to the firm crumbles. Season with remaining ricotta ingredients and set aside.

When you are ready to make ravioli, mix flour and water to make a "food glue" and set aside. Have extra flour nearby to dust dough if needed. Divide the dough into four equal pieces. Flatten one piece of dough as thin as you can by hand and then put it through your pasta roller. Continue until you reach level 4 or 5 (should be just a few millimeters thick) and then lay flat on your counter. Using a mason jar, cup or pasta cutter, cut rounds out of the pasta dough. You can gather any unused dough, ball it back up, and run it through the pasta roller again to make extra rounds. I recommend doing this only once.

Working with one at a time, use the "food glue" to draw a line around the circumference of the circle. Place a small amount of filling (no more than one tablespoon) in the centre of the ravioli and then place a second round piece of pasta on top. Seal the ravioli all the way around by using your fingers or a fork to press firmly. Set each finished ravioli aside, in a single layer, on a tray or surface that is heavily dusted with flour. Repeat until you've made all the raviolis.

When you're ready to serve, start by filling the biggest pot you have with water and lots of salt. Bring to a boil. While you're waiting, gently heat any remaining beet purée you have in a small pot or pan. You can also warm the tofu ricotta leftovers slightly, and if you really want to be fancy, you can sauté any beet greens you have with a bit of garlic and oil.

When your water is boiling, carefully drop a few ravioli at a time into the water, stirring often. Do not overcrowd the pot! Once the raviolis float to the top, sing a quick song (the alphabet works!) in your head. Remove with a slotted spoon onto a clean tray. Continue until each ravioli is cooked.

To serve, spoon some warmed beet purée onto a plate or bowl, with the sautéed beet greens if using. Top with ravioli and then spoon on any leftover tofu ricotta. Bonus points if you add fresh herbs to the top.

This dish will wow any guest and looks stunning on a bright white or wooden plate.

 We'd been open for more than half a year and we'd spent Christmas and New Years at The Restaurant. I knew I desperately needed to escape for a while, so when my friend invited me to her wedding in Bermuda, I leapt at the opportunity and bought a ticket right away. It was the first time I had travelled without Jeff in several years and although I was full of nerves leading up to my solo flight, I *knew* I needed this trip. I left Frank in charge of the kitchen for five days and away I went.

After a rough flight, I arrived at the resort feeling a little shaky on my feet and went straight to the bar and promptly ordered a double gin and soda. I ran into the bride who took my hand and dragged me to the dance floor. I reluctantly shook my hips, trying to remember how to dance and have fun, and before I knew it the gin hit me and we ended up dancing the night away in a techno bar with all her friends. I was a stranger to most of them — no one knew my struggles or baggage. The more gin I drank, the less I could feel the pain in my shoulder. For the next several hours, I lifted my arms into the sky and danced, caring about very little. I did shots of tequila and ate cheesy nachos at the late night restaurant and partied with my new friends until the wee hours of the morning.

All I really remember about that night though, was feeling *free.*

The following day I woke up on top of my bedsheets in the same dress I was wearing the night before. My mouth tasted like an ashtray, my contact lenses were glued to my eyes and there was an empty bag of potato chips on the floor. I reckoned I had a good night as I tried to pull myself together to make it downstairs in time for brunch.

I bumped into some of the people I'd met the night before who high fived me as I waited in line for waffles, all of them referring to me by my new nickname, 'The Dance Machine.' A man I barely recognized came up beside me, put his arm around my shoulder and chuckled, "Howdy, dance partner!" I shrugged, and headed for the omelette bar, wondering if I'd made a fool of myself the night before. It was unlike me to let loose like that since opening The Restaurant. I had become reclusive and was usually too tired after work to go out. It wasn't unheard of that I would pull an all-nighter in my past, but I certainly wasn't used to being the life of the party anymore.

While I was eating brunch with my new friends, my 'dance partner' from the night before pulled a chair up beside us. Nick, I found out, was a friend of the groom. He seemed friendly and full of joy. We sat at the table as a group, sharing stories of our lives at home while Nick told us all about his wife and kids. He even pulled out a photo from his wallet of his wife — he was so old school. A *classic*. And we became friends, instantly.

Nick and I spent the entire day together. We hunted for aloe vera to soothe our sunburns. We indulged with a second breakfast. We smoked cigars. We drank rum and banana and coconut drinks. We went down the kids slide. It was a perfect, silly, wonderful day. This vacation was working — my stress was melting away.

That whole week was a series of indulgent days and late nights, as resort life often is. All of the bride and grooms' friends from different circles were meeting and mingling and I sincerely liked everyone I met, but Nick and I connected more deeply than the others. Both of us were travelling solo, escaping the stress of our day to day lives, and we were both enjoying being a little rebellious — staying out late, smoking and drinking far too much. We spent our time lounging by the pool, swimming in the ocean, eating fried pineapple rice and nursing our hangovers. We spent evenings with our new group of friends in the lobby bar, rehashing our days and laughing until it felt like our sides were splitting open.

When my new friends told me they found me hilarious, it took me a while to even acknowledge it. *Yes, I am funny,* I thought to myself. *I am witty and quick and I just made a girl shoot bar-lime out her nose.* Perhaps it was just the alcohol, but I made people laugh on that trip, and I, too, laughed harder than I had in a long time. At The Restaurant, I often received compliments about my food, talent and the physical aspects of The Restaurant, but rarely about the human in me. People told me how inspiring it was that I changed the menu every single week, but they never told me that I was a good person or that I was generous or kind. I was always so busy at The Restaurant that I seldom had time to sit with friends, get drunk and be silly. When I was with Jeff, I found myself withdrawn, especially when we were out in public. It always felt like there wasn't room at the table for both of us.

Nick and I stayed up talking until the sun came up for days on end. We talked about his music career. We talked about his near suicide attempt. We talked about Louis. We talked about his favourite things about his wife. We talked about his father's death. We talked about The Restaurant. We talked about Jeff. We talked about my sister's tumour. Morning came, and when the whirlpools got turned on and we saw the bartenders shaving ice and juicing limes, I resented having to end our talk and go to bed. I never wanted it to end, but I of course knew it had to.

On our last night, we stayed up drinking gin straight from the bottle and playing a game which we called, 'The Desert Island' game. "If you were stranded on a desert island for the rest of your life … What five records would you bring? What three foods would you not want to live without?" We went back and forth until I asked him: "If you were on a desert island, who would you bring, if you could?" He couldn't answer the question in his drunken stupor, so we ended the game and went up to our rooms.

The next morning we lazily relaxed in the lobby waiting for our bus to take us to the airport. We shopped for souvenirs for him to take home to his kids. I bought the kitchen crew a dancing turtle. We took one last dip in the ocean.

I wasn't sure if we'd ever see each other again, but I knew our time was special and when I thought of him, I felt loved from the inside out.

———

When I got home from Bermuda, I told Jeff all about my trip. I told him about how beautiful the flowers at the wedding were, how smooth the sand had felt between my toes and I told him all about meeting Nick and the others.

What I didn't tell him was that I hadn't longed to come home.

Now that I was back to my old life, my anxiety had suddenly come back and the knot in my stomach returned. I missed the way I felt when I was with Nick, but no matter how platonic it had been, missing another man, made me feel guilty. I had nothing to be guilty for, but the feeling lingered and I didn't know what to make of it.

After I was home for a few days, Jeff and I were eating dinner one night and just for fun, I asked him, "Hey … if you were stranded on a desert island, and you could only bring one person with you, who would you bring?"

He was confused by the question, "Why am I on an island?"

"I don't know … the plane crashed. You're there for life," I explained.

"Won't I be rescued?" he asked, puzzled.

"No! You're there forever! … But you can pick one person to be there with you!"

"How does that make sense?" he laughed.

"Look … it's just a game … just *answer!* They can be dead or alive. Doesn't matter. Who would you bring?" I prodded.

Jeff furrowed his brow and thought about it for a few minutes. Finally he answered, "Probably Karl Marx. Or maybe Eddie Vedder." I laughed and started doing the dishes.

After dinner, Jeff went to the post office to deliver some mail and came back with a large, brown envelope in his hands. "Who is Nick?" he asked, sternly.

I answered honestly, "He's one of the guys from the wedding last week. I told you about him."

"Okay. But why is he mailing you *love letters*?"

I looked at the package Jeff was holding and noticed it was torn open at the side and that's when I realized it was a package from Nick. I barked at Jeff matter-of-factly that it wasn't a love letter — it was a copy of a record he'd made that he'd promised he would mail me, before we left Bermuda. I snatched the package from him and emptied the contents onto my desk. There was a CD and a letter, and I felt I had no choice but to read the letter while standing in front of Jeff. I tried not to let my face show any kind of reaction.

The letter read: *"Yoda. You asked me one night, if I could only bring one person to a desert island, who would I bring? I couldn't bring my wife, because my kids would miss her too much. I couldn't bring one of my kids because that wouldn't be fair to the other. I couldn't bring my Dad, because I know he belongs in heaven and I will see him there one day. My answer? I would bring you. You are a bright light in a dark world. Don't ever change. Nick."*

Those words.

My heart sank when I saw Jeff's face and I knew I had to do something. I breathed in deeply and tried to explain to him that Nick was just a friend and that we'd bonded on the trip. That it *was* a love letter, but not in a romantic way. I knew Jeff didn't understand and I was lost for words as to how to explain it to him. I could feel his jealousy seeping into me, like toast the way it soaks up butter. I knew I had done nothing wrong, but I spent the rest of the day, and the days following, trying to make up for it.

I wasn't perfect. Over the years we were together, there were times when I looked at other men, flirted a bit too long or thought

103

about other people. I wasn't perfect — modern romances rarely are. People get bored; people stray. But I dug my heels in when things got hard. I valued loyalty so much, it was always enough to steer me away from whatever impulses, hormones, loneliness, desire (or any other reason people give as an excuse for being unfaithful). The assertion that it would break his heart was *always* enough of a deterrence, despite the fact that he was never able to dig his heels in, the way I had. I never wanted Jeff to suffer. I never wanted him to know what it feels like when the person you love makes you think you're not enough.

Because he *was*.

He *was* enough for me. That's why I opened The Restaurant with him. It's why I funded it and worked myself to the bone. It's why I forgave him for something unforgivable. Twice. It's why I knew if I were ever asked who I would bring to a desert island, I would bring *him*. He was enough for me. I didn't even *need* the lemon trees — I just needed him to tell me that I was enough for him too.

I think that's why I was so drawn to everyone on that trip. Because when I was standing in front of them, being myself, I was enough for them. I was *enough* for Nick. I didn't have to be a famous chef or a doting girlfriend. In my core, my truest self, being me — silly and awkward —I was enough. And that's why I missed him when he was gone.

Jeff had never been betrayed before, but I hoped that he would recognize, in his own heartache, how much I hurt over Sam and Alisa and all the other girls. I hoped he would see how loyal I was and how much I wanted him to be happy. I didn't try to come up with an excuse and I didn't lie. I just apologized and told him how much I loved him.

I only told him one lie, which was that the letter meant nothing to me.

Eventually, after much convincing, Jeff seemed to get over it. Although I was relieved, there was something else nagging at me.

I *resented* not being allowed to feel the sweetness of my friendship with Nick. When I read his letter, it had meant the world to me. His kindness, his consideration, his love. It was a keepsake to remember our perfect week on the beach. To remember how free I felt.

Jeff *took* that from me, after he'd already taken so much. *And I let him.*

I decided, then and there, that there was no room in my life to be loved like that. So, with that realization, I wrapped up Nick's CD and note and put it in my closet next to the letter I'd gotten from Sam several months earlier. Something told me to hold onto it. Something deep inside of me told me that I would need to tell this story later. In the back corner of my closet, behind my diaries and my secret stash of cash, I was building a little nest of all the things that would help save me someday.

Someday soon.

ISLAND PINEAPPLE FRIED RICE (V) (GF)
SERVES 2 ENTREES
OR MAKES AN ATTRACTIVE SHARE PLATTER

This dish is a combination of all the best things I ate while travelling in Bermuda — fried rice, tropical fruit and some spice!

This dish is a great way to use leftover rice, and serving it in a pineapple has the extra wow factor. Feel free to substitute white rice for any grain — brown rice, quinoa or millet all work great. Also, feel free to swap the cubed, fresh pineapple for peaches; use peanuts instead of cashews; use any veggies you like; top with grilled shrimp, tofu, or avocado. Any way you make it, this recipe is delicious and beautiful!

To Make The Rice
1 cup brown rice
2 cups water
1 tsp salt

For The Wow Factor
1 fresh, ripe pineapple (see prep below)
½ cup whole, raw cashews
1 tbsp coconut oil
1 tbsp sesame oil
½ cup red bell pepper, small diced
½ cup carrot, peeled and grated
½ cup onion, fine diced
2 green onions, sliced
1 tbsp garlic, minced
1 tbsp ginger, peeled and minced
2 tbsp tamari
Juice and zest of 1 lime
1 tsp cumin
Hot sauce, to your taste
Cilantro, chopped (optional)

Method
This recipe works best with chilled rice, so it is a great way to use leftover rice. If you have the chance, cook the rice the day before. To cook brown rice, simply place rice, water and salt in a small pot and bring to a boil. Once boiling, turn down the heat to medium-low, stir once, put a lid on and set a timer for 22 minutes. The rice should have absorbed 90% of the water. Turn off the heat and leave the lid on until it cools and then refrigerate overnight for the best fried rice.

To prepare the pineapple, use a serrated knife and slice the pineapple lengthwise down the middle. Try to keep the top intact, but if it comes off, don't worry. Next, CAREFULLY use the tip of a small knife to carve out the inside of the pineapple. Get as close to the skin as possible without puncturing it. Set aside pineapple halves. Next, slice away the cores of the pineapple and finely dice everything you've got left. Set aside.

Heat a large frying pan on high for a few minutes. When it feels warm (hover your hand a few inches from the pan to test) empty cashews into the dry pan. Stir them aggressively in the pan on high for 1-2 minutes, until cashews are lightly browned and toasted. Set aside.

Next lower heat to medium-high and heat oils in pan for a few seconds. Add pepper, carrot, ginger, onion, garlic and green onion and sautee in oil for 2 minutes. They should be sizzling and browning slightly. (If not, turn up the heat a little. You need heat to properly fry the rice so it doesn't just absord the oil). Add cooked, cooled rice to the pan. Do not stir. Let it sit for 3 minutes and then stir vigorously for another 3 minutes total, until rice looks *dry*. Add chunked pineapple and cook for 1-2 minutes to warm through. Lastly, add tamari, lime juice and zest and cumin.

Empty contents of pan into the hollowed out pineapple halves. Top with toasted cashews and chopped cilantro. Drizzle with more hot sauce if you like it hot!

The rest of that winter is a blur. My shoulder pain got worse, my sister's health got worse and my stress level skyrocketed. There was nothing I could do about any of it so I continued to put my head down and worked. By the time spring rolled around, we were celebrating our first anniversary at The Restaurant. I couldn't believe I made it a whole year.

Jeff decided to celebrate by buying himself a ticket to a conference in Halifax. He would be away for one week, and even though it was a busy time at The Restaurant, I agreed that he deserved his own vacation. I had just gone to Bermuda and was still trying to make it up to him for Nick's letter.

Things went smoothly without Jeff around, and everyone let loose a little knowing 'the boss' was gone. Although I was technically also the boss, everyone agreed that he had a certain demeanour about him that overshadowed my authority. I was nervous to be the one in charge in his absence, but as the week passed, I felt more and more confident. We had zero complaints and everyone who came to The Restaurant that week was happy. My staff and I went out for drinks at the end of the weekend and I was overcome with the same feeling I had while I was in Bermuda. I felt connected. I felt worthy. I felt ... *light.* I felt different when he wasn't around, and that made me feel so much guilt I almost refused to acknowledge it.

Our staff had grown in the year we'd been open, but we had almost entirely the same staff since day one — a momentous accomplishment for any restaurant that survives a full year.

Frank had begun taking on more responsibility as my shoulder and mental state continued to decline. Brandon was as consistently calm as he'd always been, holding the team together. We added a girl named Sara to the team earlier that year. She was attentive to her work, albeit a bit antsy at times. She was ambitious, overwhelmingly thoughtful, sweet and fiercely loyal to me. Mackenzie was new to the team as well. I'd only hired her a few months earlier just after she graduated from culinary school. I actually hired her because she *pestered me* — she dropped off resume after resume, and after a while, I decided that I admired her determination. She reminded me a little of myself when I started in the industry — a little lost, but hungry to make it.

Marie, Scarlett and Rachel remained our main servers, whom I didn't interact with as frequently, but loved them all the same. We were a family who supported each other. We spent time together outside of work and were there for each other during divorces and death and celebrated milestones whenever we could.

My team worked hard for me and I tried to tell each and every one of them, every single day, how much I appreciated them. I tried my very hardest to be the best boss I could, even when things started taking a turn for the worse.

By June, my shoulder injury had gotten so bad that I was in physiotherapy every other day and wearing a sling. I was getting cortisol shots in my neck to manage the pain and was ordered bed rest by my doctor. The only thing harder than the physical pain in my shoulder was knowing I was going to *have to* take a step back from my kitchen. It really did feel like it was all I had left so I fought it for as long as I could. I came to work whenever I could physically bear it, and still clocked over 50 hours on the line each week. I would spend the morning icing my shoulder at home and then would come in for a few hours to help prep. When I was wearing my sling, it was impossible for me to even cut a sandwich in half or stir a big pot, so I would take my sling off and try to push through the pain. The pain was sometimes so intense, it hurt to stand up straight and fire shot up through my neck and into my ear, making me wince. I was forced to take a week off work, but if there was a silver lining, it was that it gave me time to be with my sister.

I still felt like I'd been a terrible sister because I was absent on the day of her brain surgery. I *wanted* to be by her side. I wanted to take the whole day off from work, but we were overbooked with reservations and short-staffed, so I had to be at The Restaurant that day to cook lunch service. *They* needed me; *she* needed me. I was like a piece of braised meat being pulled with a fork, tearing apart in every direction. I left The Restaurant after lunch that day and arrived at the hospital too late. I didn't get the chance to talk to her before she went into surgery, and I felt so guilty about that. The fact that it felt like there was no longer any room in my life or my heart, to love someone like that, made me resent The Restaurant and everything to do with it, more than I already did.

Thankfully, my sister's surgery went well, and I was able to be there for her while she recovered. Jeff was too busy to join me at the hospital. I *needed* him to be there. I begged him to come with me a few times, but he had orders to fill and floors to mop and he told me he just couldn't make the time. I was too exhausted to push harder, so I accepted it, and went each day for a week, alone.

After that, things became so strained that I decided to seek therapy, desperate for anything that might help. I told my new therapist, Di, that I was fine, and just needed someone to talk to, but the truth was, I wasn't fine. During my intake session when Di asked me if I was having suicidal thoughts, I paused and conceded, "I mean … I'm not making *plans* if that's what you're asking. But I suppose I do think it might be easier if I weren't *here* anymore …." Depression was something that affected almost all the women in my bloodline. It made me feel like I was somehow *rare* because I had dodged that bullet — I was strong. I was successful. I was independent. I didn't need help. "Self!"

So when Di asked me if I was depressed, I responded, "Being depressed is being so sad you can't move." I explained to her that I got out of bed every day; that I was able to get through each day and do what I had to do. I told her I was successfully running a busy, prosperous business. "Depression is when you feel like

111

tomorrow will be just like today. It's about being sad about your circumstances. Life hands you something so sad you can't move," I stated. "... And you can't go to family events or watch your kids graduate or pack their lunches or whatever else is important." My rambling left me to pause. My body sunk into the couch when I realized I was perhaps talking about my own mother. *Where was this coming from?* I wondered. Di interrupted my revelation and suggested that perhaps depression is about being sad *despite* your circumstances. It means feeling the darkness when your life is full. It means feeling like you are unable to move even though your life is everything you've ever imagined it would be ....

I cut Di off. "Depression is when you're sad *because* of your circumstances. My. Circumstances. Are. *Fine.*" I snapped, angry at my own comparison to my mother and to my sudden vulnerability.

———

I was walking around like a zombie. I had a short temper and seemed to have a permanent head cold. I had already started taking days off from The Restaurant so I could stay in bed all day. I used my shoulder pain as an excuse, but the truth was, it was my entire body that ached day in and day out. I ached and was numb all at once. *Depression is being so sad you can't move ...*

People were starting to notice. My parents were concerned but they never prodded deeper, I think because we were all so stressed and concerned about my sister. Ruby and Doug asked me if I was getting enough sleep and told me I seemed anxious. Friends reached out but their questions just annoyed me. It was no longer, *"Love me, but leave me alone."* I just wanted to be left alone, period.

I felt like I had abandoned my sister in her time of need. I was no longer a good boss, a good friend, a good person — I was short with people, cranky and downright rude more often than not. I was hanging onto any threads of my identity that were left, trying desperately to be a good chef and a good partner to Jeff. I broke apart more with each passing day, so one morning, late that

112

summer, I got dressed in my nicest skirt and walked down the street to the church at the end of our block. It reminded me of the church I grew up in. The exterior was a pale, yellow brick, worn down but taken care of. There were rose bushes out front and the inside smelt of Ruby's lavender perfume and moth balls.

I'd passed that church hundreds of times while walking my dogs and I sometimes wondered what it would be like if I ever went in. I was greeted by a few strangers who were incredibly friendly and curious, and settled into a quiet pew in the back so I could be alone. I listened to the opening hymns and quietly hummed. I hadn't forgotten the words to the songs or the prayers, but I was worried that maybe I had forgotten how to talk to God. I felt awkward at first; I fidgeted and considered leaving when no one would notice. But I felt compelled to stay, so I sat there alone on the pew in the back, quietly listening. Alone. In church. A little lost. *I've been here before.*

When it was time, I knelt and clasped my hands together and I started to pray. I wasn't sure what I was praying for, or if anyone was even listening, but I prayed and I kept praying until everything I felt was a puddle around me on the floor. I prayed for change. I prayed for something to budge; for something to give. I prayed for a sign to show me why I should stay here for another moment longer. Although I could barely acknowledge to my friends or myself how bad things had gotten, I felt it all in my heart, that day, in that pew.

I knew in that moment if things stayed the way they were, I wasn't going to make it out of this alive. And since I still couldn't see a Way Out, I began my Escape Plan.

———

When I walked home from that church, like soggy, overcooked pasta, I wondered if Jeff would be there for me, if I explained to him how bad things had gotten. I hoped in my heart that he would, but I wasn't sure if he was a source of light in my life anymore. I wasn't sure if he was going to be able to pull me out of the darkness. I mourned this realization and when I got home all I wanted to do was wash the feeling off of me. I got in the shower and turned the water on as hot as it could go. I scrubbed my skin as if I was scrubbing potatoes straight from the field. I felt like I'd done something wrong by questioning Jeff. I felt like I had betrayed him because just for a moment, *just a single moment*, I had lost faith in us. It was the first time I'd seriously considered leaving him in nearly six years.

When I got out of the shower, I wrapped myself in a towel and stood over the tub. I stared at all the hair that was in the bottom of the drain that I'd lost due to all the stress I was under. It'd been thinning for a few months, but now it was coming out in clumps. Quietly and earnestly, I admitted to myself, *"I don't think I can do this anymore."*

I again wondered if Jeff would be there for me, if I told him that I wanted to die; if I told him I had an Escape Plan in the works. But, in that moment in my bathroom, weeping over my hair in the tub and all the other things I'd lost, while I buried my face in my hands, instead of picturing Jeff comforting me, holding me, telling me things would be okay, I pictured him saying, *"Do you really think you'll be happier if you leave me? Do you really think you'll ever be able to trust someone else? How are you ever going to find someone who will love you with all this baggage?"*

He had trained me so well.

You are not enough.

As summer wore on, and my mental state got worse, Di recommended I take some serious time off from The Restaurant to get my health back on track. I looked online for some vacation ideas and found a retreat being held at an ashram in Montreal later that month, and I decided to give it a chance. I'd always loved yoga and saw my friends reap benefits from these types of retreats, coming back calm and enlightened. I needed a little calm in my life, so I decided to book the trip.

As always, we planned to shut down The Restaurant during the second week of August for our annual summer holidays. This year, when everyone returned to work around the 15th, I would head to Montreal for some additional time off. I would leave Frank in charge of the kitchen and when I came back, I would be as good as new. Everyone agreed that although it would be taxing, it was *necessary*, not only to heal my shoulder, but for my mental health as well. My kitchen team wanted what was best for me, and they were all waiting for me to return to myself after months of being distracted and withered.

Our week off from The Restaurant was fast approaching and everyone needed it nearly as much as I did. We were overwhelmed and overbooked with catering orders, a full dining room every day and had recently agreed to cater a big, summer festival just before our vacation started. We tread water for the entire week, and by Saturday night, we just had one more night of service and this festival to go, and then we would all have time to rest. And then I would be off to the ashram to meditate myself back into some state of normalcy. Or so I thought.

I was so numb at that point, I barely got upset when I found out Jeff was messaging with an ex-girlfriend on our shared work computer. I was searching through emails when I caught a glimpse of their messages but when I heard him coming up the stairs I quickly logged off and acted as if nothing had happened.

When I logged back on again, about half an hour later, the messages were gone. I tried not to let it bother me and went through service that night with questions lingering in the back of my brain. I didn't want to confront him — it felt like if I walked into an argument I was going to burst open — but he eventually got it out of me. When I told him about the message I'd seen on his computer, he laughed mockingly. He told me that she was just a friend of his who worked at a jewellery store. He told me that he had been chatting with her about getting a discount on an engagement ring for me, and boy did I feel stupid. It took him almost no effort to change my mind and I wish I could say that was the worst lie he ever told me, but it gets worse.

So much worse.

———

Saturday arrived and we left our staff in charge while Jeff and I went to cater the big, outdoor festival, which was looking like it might be rained out. We stood under a tent, soggy from having to set up in the rain, tired from a busy week at The Restaurant, stretched to our absolute limits. But to everyone else, we were *us*. The power couple. The ones with the adorable story.

Jeff knew how tired I was, and I think he noticed a few of my friends checking in on me, claiming they hadn't seen me in a while. As the music started up, and the doors of the festival opened, Jeff extended his hand towards me. "Dance with me," he urged, grabbing my hand and pulling me towards him. Without giving me a chance to respond, he guided me to the middle of that grass, and right then and there, where no one else was standing, and everyone was watching, he put my hand on his shoulder and started to slow dance with me.

A crowd began to form and everyone took notice. We held each other close and listened to the group of women standing nearby discuss how *sweet* we were. It was a moment of tranquility amid the mayhem of the day. My friends took photos of us dancing and posted them online using the hashtags *#SoInLove #DreamCrushing* and *#CoupleGoals*.

116

I wore his romance like a badge of honour.

———

The day wore on and the sun finally came out, shining on our booth as we barbequed and talked to customers. There was a folk band playing and incense burning all around us. Children were chasing bubbles nearby and there was an outdoor yoga class happening in the back corner of the yard. *Blissful* is how I would describe that afternoon.

Although we were tired and I was hanging on by a thread, Jeff made sure there were always threads to keep us going. Threads of romance woven together by him. And I hung onto those moments when he showed me love. It's why he slow danced with me that day, in the sun, where no one else was standing and everyone was watching. Not because he was romantic, and not because he loved me — but because he was *calculated*.

He crafted that moment, just like he had crafted all the others.

In a few days' time though, he would *miscalculate*. And less than two weeks after that day that we danced in the grass, we would close the doors of The Restaurant and he and I would be over, forever.

 I went to The Restaurant after the festival to help clean up and finish service and noticed that Frank seemed annoyed. I'd heard from the others that he was in a bad mood all night and when I asked him about it, he shrugged it off and claimed it was nothing. Everyone was exhausted, but the rest of us stayed in high spirits knowing we had a week of holidays to look forward to. We cleaned out the fridges and ate one last staff meal together, hurrying through a rustic pasta dish using everything that was left in the fridge, but Frank left on his own without saying goodbye. I didn't blame Frank for being cranky and tired — he had been working overtime since my shoulder injury had gotten really bad. All of us were stretched to our limits, so as each person went home, I thanked them profusely.

I would have said more if I would have known that was going to be the last night we'd *all* be together.

———

Our holidays started off relatively calm and I tried my best to relax and heal my shoulder. I spent the week attending to all the things I'd been neglecting for months — spending time with my dogs, my family and tidying the house.

Although I was relieved to be on holidays, I was distracted by Frank's distance towards me. It was unusual for us to go even a day without talking as we had become close friends since the day I hired him, becoming even closer in the last several months. He spent a lot of his time consoling me and was one of the only people I had opened up to about going to therapy. When he found me in the basement of The Restaurant crying, he would talk me through it and just give me a big bear hug to make me feel better. His apathy towards me that week was unusual, but I tried to tell myself that he just needed some time off to recharge. I had no idea it was because he was carrying the weight of my world on his shoulders.

———

On the third day of our staycation, Jeff told me he had found a cheap plane ticket to go to Halifax. He'd be gone just three days, and would be back in time for us to get everything set up for my week away. He'd just been to Halifax a few months ago, but told me that since he had been so busy with the demands of the conference he'd attended, he hadn't had much of a chance to see any of the sights or to fully relax. He confessed to me that he was running on fumes and really needed a weekend away by himself. I wanted him to be happy and it was only fair that he get some extra time off, since I was about to embark on my extended 'holiday.' I bought the ticket for him on my credit card and told him I *wanted* him to go.

He was due to fly out early on Friday morning, but we still had one full day of vacation together and wanted to make the most of it. We decided to drive three hours to the city, spend the day together and then I would drop him off at the hotel next to the airport for his early flight, and drive home by myself. Plans were made, the hotel was booked and we got up early that morning to pack the car and get an early start on our day of fun. As we were getting ready to pull out of the driveway he did something I'd never seen him do before — he *hesitated*. Usually steadfast and stubborn, he was having some sort of conflict about going on this trip. I didn't stop long enough to even wonder why … I just tried to calm his nerves and assure him everything would be fine.

"But there's just so much to do … and we really can't afford it … and I don't know … I just think maybe it's not a good time … like … *for us,*" he mumbled. I didn't typically put up a fight in situations like this, but this time I argued with him. We had both been working so hard since we opened The Restaurant, and as of recently since I needed more time off, he had been putting in even more hours. When he came back from his last trip, he seemed so rejuvenated and relaxed, which is part of the reason

120

why I didn't question his motives about taking such a last minute trip, and why I didn't ask him to stay. After a long conversation in the car, I finally convinced him to go. We started getting excited about our dinner plans at our favourite vegan restaurant, and to spend the day together wandering the city.

We arrived at his hotel in the afternoon and decided to go upstairs to drop his bags off before heading out to dinner. We were only in the elevator for a few floors before he started kissing my neck. By the time we made it to our room, I was half undressed. We had been together many times over the years and this time was no different.

Except, it was different. He was somewhere far away.

I tried to connect with him. I wanted to tell him that I knew I wasn't always easy to be with. That I knew it had been really hard since I found out my sister was sick, and since my shoulder started acting up. I knew working with me was a struggle sometimes, and this most recent conflict with Frank didn't help matters. I wanted to tell him that I knew that I wasn't always good enough for him, but that I was trying. If that meant letting him go on this mini vacation to figure some things out for himself, then that's what I was going to do. I wanted us to work. So, in the sweetness of that moment, while he was kissing my neck, I put my hands on his face and gently told him everything I wanted to say.

"Baby … we're going to be okay. I know it's been a really tough few months, and everything we've been through … but I want us to be okay. I'm going to take some time off and fix myself. I know it's been so hard for you and I'm so sorry …."

I started to tear up. "Shhhhh …" he said, as he kissed me softly, and then hard.

I would have said more if I would have known that was going to be the last night we were going to be together.

––––

We spent half the day in bed and the other half of the day roaming the city giggling about our sweaty hotel room session.

121

At dinner, we held hands and made eye contact and moaned simultaneously when we tried the first bite of vegan calamari. The 'calamari' were crunchy, slightly sweet and tasted like the sea — quite an accomplishment for some deep-fried palm heart rings and some powdered nori. The first time we had this dish, I had been so entranced by it, I asked our server if I could speak to the chef about it which resulted in receiving a tour of the kitchen and an autographed cookbook from the chef. I created my own version of the recipe to pay homage to the memory, and put it on our menu at The Restaurant. It was the only permanent dish on our menu and tasting it now, with Jeff across the table, sent shocks of nostalgia and joy through my body.

We were totally in our element that night — eating and drinking together. We clinked glasses and laughed with our heads thrown back. We gossiped about the couple beside us that was on a blind date that was clearly going badly. We met up with some friends for drinks after dinner and he was his usual charming self.

Wining and dining — it was when we were at our best. We met while he was bartending and I was cooking. We fell in love over conversations about our favourite foods and drinking fine wine in his living room. I fell more and more for him after every trip we'd been on, no matter how lavish or modest — food and wine was *our thing.* And now here we were, in the heart of one of my favourite cities, eating our favourite dish, playing footsies under the table and toasting to our success. I wanted that night to last forever but he had an early flight, so I went to drop him off at his hotel before heading home.

Before he got out of the car, he hesitated once more. This time, he *really* meant it. His eyes looked as if they were going to spill over as I struggled to understand his intensity. I touched the outside of his hands, which were cupping my face, and assured him, once more, "I'm okay, sweetheart. I love you … and we're okay. Everything will be better soon, you'll see."

During my drive home, I was not analyzing his strange reluctance to go. I wasn't thinking about the perfect palm hearts or the flavour of that delicious wine we had with dinner. My mind wasn't racing with what was possibly wrong with Frank or on my sister's brain tumour. I wasn't contemplating next week's menu or the next prep list. I wasn't concerned about Jeff's hesitation to go on that trip. (Perhaps if I would have been able to focus on that, everything would have turned out differently.)

But I wasn't focussed on any of that because I was fantasizing about our wedding day.

I was rehearsing the vows I would someday say to Jeff in our small, outdoor ceremony. I pictured myself in a white dress that my mother made and what his face would look like when I walked down the aisle. I closed my eyes and imagined Frank behind a barbeque, cooking our wedding meal for us. The Restaurant family would be at one table, our closest friends and family at the others. I was lost in a dream, picturing the kiss we would share with our dogs in the background and how perfect it would be.

It's all I wanted.

It's all I'd ever wanted since the night we fell in love.

CALAMARI... NOT! (V) (GF)

SERVES 6 APPETIZER PORTIONS

This recipe is adapted from Tal Ronnen's plant-based calamari served at Crossroads Kitchen in Los Angeles. You'll need to track down canned palm hearts for this recipe (which you can find at specialty stores or at the Asian supermarket). You'll also need some sheets of nori — the seaweed paper used to wrap maki rolls.

For The Cocktail Sauce
½ cup (1 small can) tomato paste
3 tbsp ketchup
3 tbsp horseradish
1 tbsp apple cider vinegar
1 tsp balsamic vinegar

1 tsp white sugar
1 tsp garlic power
Sprinkle of salt and pepper

For The Breading
1 cup coarse cornmeal
1 tsp chili powder
1 tsp salt
½ tsp pepper

For The Batter
¾ cup boiling water
½ cup raw, slivered, skinless almonds
½ tsp salt
Zest of 1 lemon
Pinch of white pepper (if you don't have white pepper, use black pepper)

To make the "Calamari"
2 cans of whole palm hearts (398ml cans)
4 sheets of nori
1 litre vegetable oil, for frying
2 lemons

Method
For this recipe, you'll need to set up a deep fryer (or pot of oil) and have everything ready to go before you start frying. First, mix all the ingredients for the cocktail sauce and set aside. Next, mix all ingredients for the breading and set aside in a large bowl.

To make the batter, pour boiling water over almonds. Add to a blender with other ingredients for batter and blend in a high-powered blender until very smooth. Set aside in another large bowl.

To prep the "calamari," lay out four sheets of nori on a flat surface (counter or butcher block works well). Open cans of palm hearts and drain. Using the handle of a wooden spoon or something similar, use the tip to poke the middle out of each palm heart. You want to hollow out each palm heart leaving you with empty cylinders. If your heart breaks, don't worry. *It will be okay.*

124

Once all palm hearts are hollowed out, slice these cylinders into palm heart coins, about 8mm-1cm thick. Place these palm heart coins onto your sheets of nori for about 20 minutes. This will allow the "from-the-sea" flavour of the seaweed to marinate the palm hearts, making them taste slightly "fishy," (in a good way!) Flip them once, around the 10 minute mark, for extra flavour.

Using a slotted spoon or your hands, dip each ring into the almond batter. Shake off excess batter and then dip into the breading. Repeat until all calamari has been breaded.

About 20 minutes before serving this dish, heat oil in a heavy bottom pot to 350°. You can use a candy thermometer, or just drop a small drop of batter or breading into the pot and once it bubbles rapidly and floats to the top, the oil is ready. **Remember never to leave the oil unattended!** You may need to adjust the heat throughout the frying process.

In batches, fry calamari rings until they are golden and floating (a few minutes). Stir and shake them often, again being careful with the hot oil. Drain on paper towels and squeeze fresh lemon over them while they are still warm.

Serve immediately with cocktail sauce or your favourite tartar. Laugh as people wonder if they're really vegan.

With Jeff gone, I had a quiet weekend by myself — self-care, long baths and packing for my trip to the ashram. On Monday, I had a meeting planned with Frank to discuss the menu for the following week. I hadn't talked to him all week but looked forward to seeing him and hoped whatever was bothering him had fizzled out during his week off. I always eagerly anticipated our Monday morning meetings — we would share tea and stories and sometimes our meetings would draw out into several hours. It was usually just him and I, discussing food and mulling over new menu ideas, or sometimes just talking like old friends do.

But this meeting was different … I knew it from the moment he walked in the door. He didn't make tea or playfully punch my arm and ask how my weekend was. He sat down solemnly, with dark eyes, and stared at me, coldly. I awkwardly tried to make light of the situation but his negativity wore on me. When I asked to see his menu ideas and he told me he hadn't even thought about it, I felt deflated. I could feel my temper bubbling up. "You're really letting me down here, Frank," I announced, trying to stay calm. He just stared at me, agitated. I wanted him to tell me what was troubling him but he wouldn't budge. It felt like hours passed when he finally blurted out, "I just … I don't understand why you're with him."

Those words.

I knew that Frank and Jeff had experienced some sort of altercation the week prior. I assumed it was the reason Frank seemed *off* on Saturday night. I assumed it was why he left without sharing our staff meal or saying goodbye. He wanted to distance himself because that's what Frank does when he's feeling uncomfortable or upset. But we were sitting in the hearth of discomfort now, and I wasn't sure if I had the emotional stamina for this. I was trying desperately to be calm but I felt like a pot of rice on full blast and the starch was bubbling over.

Finally, through clenched teeth I retorted, "Frank … you are my employee. You don't have to understand why I'm with him." His face was drenched in anguish and we were both at a loss for words. He sat across from me with his arms folded across his chest, staring at me — both of our shields up to maximum power. At a crossroads, I finally said the sentence that I was avoiding, "Jeff is your boss. If you can't get along with him, then you can't work here."

A line had been drawn in the sand and we both understood the gravity of what I said. The air between us remained heavy. I somehow got Frank to agree to go to a mediation session with Jeff when he returned from his trip first thing on Tuesday morning, to try to smooth things over. My train for the ashram left at noon on Tuesday, so as long as they could work it out, I could go on my trip as planned and then everything could go back to normal. Frank refused to tell me what he was so mad about, so I told myself that it was probably some small comment that was made, and it had been festering under all the stress and extra hours. *It's probably nothing,* I kept telling myself.

It wasn't *nothing* though. When we stood up to leave, Frank gave me a hug like he'd never hugged me before. He told me, quite seriously, that if I ever needed a place to go, he'd be there for me. He told me that if I ever wanted out, he'd help me. I pushed back; I *had* to make him understand. "Frank … I appreciate what you're trying to do here, but … I love Jeff. We are making it work. So please don't say stuff like that because you really don't know anything about my situation."

The statement stung us both, but at least we seemed to be leaving on better terms than when we arrived. I left the meeting with Frank feeling like there was a black cloud swirling around me. I yearned for Jeff's soothing embrace. I wanted to talk to him about how horribly the meeting went. I wanted his words of comfort. I needed him … but he wasn't answering his phone.

Jeff was on his way home and would arrive later that night, so I started mapping out 'worst case scenario' plans — the worst of which was Frank quitting after mediation meaning I would no longer be able to go to the ashram as planned. I spent a few hours working on menu stuff and eventually called my friend Monica to ask if she could help with some conflict resolution between Frank and Jeff. She was a long time restaurant veteran with some background in Human Resources. Plus, I trusted her. After she agreed, I knew that whatever was going to happen was now out of my hands.

———

Later that Monday, I went to therapy. I'd been seeing Di for a little over a month and I felt like we were making progress. The emotional heaviness of my conversation with Frank had caused a sudden surge of intense shoulder pain, so I was rubbing my shoulder when I sat down on her couch. Di was a psychotherapist, meaning she used a combination of talk therapy and energy work to heal people and help relieve pain. It sounded a little *supernatural* to me, and I was skeptical.

In fact, I was getting really sick of my friends telling me that my shoulder pain was due to some 'unresolved problem' within the masculine energy field of my body. I was at the point that if one more person told me that the "Universe had my back," I was probably going to slap them. *Fuck the Universe,* I thought.

Although I didn't really believe Di's energy work would magically heal my shoulder, I was willing to try anything at this point; any relief would be a godsend. I'm not sure if it was this moment that changed my life completely, or if this was just the first moment in a series of moments that would go on to be the worst, hardest week of my life. But what I do know is that something *happened* in that session with Di that day.

She started by asking me to sit with my legs and arms uncrossed — to be *open*. She explained to me that she wasn't going to put me into a trance or anything like that, she just wanted to work on my energy to hopefully remove some of the physical pain in my shoulder. She asked me to close my eyes, and told me that for the next few minutes, all I had to do was keep my eyes closed. It sounded easy, but as she got started, I began to feel dizzy. I started to sweat. My head started spinning and I felt like I'd been taken over by the flu or by several shots of tequila. All I wanted to do was open my eyes, but from the moment I met Di, something told me I could trust her, so when she told me not to open my eyes, I tried to obey.

She was calmly talking to me in a low voice. She started asking me questions and told me not to think about the answers, but to just say the first thing that came to mind. She started with simple questions and then swiftly moved to: "Why do you think you're depressed?"

I responded quickly and honestly, without opening my eyes, "Because of The Restaurant."

"Why does The Restaurant bring you so much pain?"

I responded, "Because I never wanted it."

"Why did you do it, then?"

I stated, matter-of-factly, "I did it for Jeff."

Di stopped asking me questions and told me that I could open my eyes. Over the course of the exercise, I thought she had moved chairs and was sitting right beside me. I could have sworn I felt her touch my shoulder at some point. But when I opened my eyes, she was sitting in front of me where she had been the whole time. My mind was playing tricks on me and I didn't like it. I felt violated and my tongue felt hot like it had been touched with pure cinnamon.

When I opened my eyes I was sobbing. This was big. I had admitted, out loud, the truth that had been following me around for the last 16 months. I opened The Restaurant *for him*. I gave up everything I had — my catering business, my happiness, my health, my sanity, my time, my family, my friends, and all of my money. I did it all, blindly, to make him happy.

Di and I talked until our time was up and I left her office in tears; my tongue still felt like it was on fire and I was utterly exhausted. By the time I got home, I had decided that I wasn't going to wait another minute. The moment Jeff walked through the door, I was going to tell him everything.

That I was miserable.

That The Restaurant wasn't what I wanted and that I couldn't do it anymore.

That I was afraid for my life; that I was making plans to escape.

That I needed him.

That I needed *out.*

I braced myself while I waited for him to get home. I had a few hours which felt like they went on forever, so I mindlessly got to work, tying up the loose ends on my to-do list. I quickly threw a menu together for the next week since Frank had been no help with that, and kept myself busy until Jeff got home. I drew up a plan of what I would say. I looked at it from all angles. I wasn't sure what that would mean for me, my reputation or my bank account, but I knew I simply couldn't go on like this anymore. I forced myself to accept the worst case scenario, which was that Jeff wouldn't love me if I told him I couldn't do this anymore.

When he walked in the door, he dropped his bag and gave me a warm hug. My stomach rattled with nerves about what I was about to tell him. We settled in and when I told him how upset Frank was, he scoffed and briefly complained about Frank's temper. He eventually agreed that mediation might be the best solution.

While we made small talk about his trip and my weekend, emotions started flooding forward. It had been an incredibly emotional day, and I just couldn't hold it in a moment longer. I knew that what I was about to say might change the course of our relationship forever, but I finally blurted it out. My words oozed out of me like brie from its rind, and I finally confessed what I'd been thinking for 16 months. I blurted out what we both already knew but were terrified to admit.

"Jeff ... I don't want The Restaurant. I never did. And I can't do it anymore."

I watched as he closed his eyes for a moment and collected himself. He was neither smiling nor frowning. There were no tears or scrunched brows. We were sitting close to one another on the patio chairs, with our knees almost touching. He opened his eyes and put his hands on my knees and said the one thing I didn't expect: "It's okay, baby. You don't have to do it anymore. Let's get you back to being happy."

I was thrown by his tenderness and sincerity. I was expecting him to be devastated.

We had a long talk and cried in each other's arms as we considered our options. We went to bed that night holding each other for the first time in months. I felt closer to him than I had in years, and he stroked my hair as I fell asleep. He whispered, "Tomorrow, you'll wake up, and we'll start a plan on how to make you happy again."

I almost couldn't recognize the feeling that blanketed me as I slept that night. I hadn't felt *hopeful* in so long. I thought back to the energy work I'd done that day with Di and thought that perhaps it had shifted something inside of me. I thought back to a week earlier when I had gone to church and prayed with everything in me that something would change. I begged for this. And the Universe, or God, or the cosmos had heard my prayers for change. The Universe, in all its glory, had brought back the man I fell in love with. He was tender, caring, thoughtful and kind that night — from the moment he walked in the door and gave me a hug, to bringing me dinner, to making me tea and brushing my hair as I fell asleep. No more crumbs. He was giving me the entire cake.

Maybe I really *was* enough for him, I thought to myself as I fell asleep that night, full to the brim, of *hope.* I thought about the moment when I could walk away from The Restaurant and how I could go back to living the life I'd always wanted for myself. Maybe Jeff could finally *see* how much this was destroying me. Maybe he wanted us to survive more than he wanted The Restaurant, and that's why he'd had this sudden change of heart.

It seemed too good to be true, and I was about to find out that it was.

PART TWO

"THE ONLY REASON FOR TIME, IS SO THAT
EVERYTHING DOESN'T HAPPEN AT ONCE."

– ALBERT EINSTEIN

 I was done grasping for unrequited love. Jeff *loved* me, and this is how he was going to prove it. He was going to help me *get out.*

Relief washed over me and I felt my jaw unclench for the first time in over a year. I felt my shoulder blades soften and my brow uncurl. I felt myself fully surrender to the softness that space created. I didn't know if it meant a farm full of dogs in Costa Rica, but I believed it meant the start of something wonderful. I left the house feeling *full* of hope. Excitement, even.

We drove to work separately so that Jeff could meet Frank at mediation and I could make sure everything was in order before departing for the ashram in a few hours. I checked my phone out of habit shortly after I arrived, as I was counting our inventory of milk and lemons. There was a message from Frank saying that he had thought about it, and decided he wasn't going to go through with the mediation session. He said he didn't care if it meant he lost his job, he just never wanted to see *"that motherfucking asshole"* again.

This was more than a punch-in-the-gut moment. My rage broke through the vessel I had created for it and by the time I was dialing Frank's number, I was explosive. My jaw re-clenched. My chest tightened. I didn't want to hurt Frank, but this was where I drew the line. I wasn't going to let him quit a job like this, or the little family we'd built, over what I perceived as *nothing.* I thought about all the things I was going to say to him while the phone rang, and braced myself to tell him off.

The next moment *really* mattered.

In the next moment, Frank saw my name pop up on his caller ID and, because he was in the middle of a conversation with a friend, he hovered his finger over the 'Ignore Call' button. In that moment, his finger was millimetres away from doing *nothing*; from changing *nothing*. That moment was a fragment, a flash, a flicker. A sliver, a shred, a scrap. The teeniest, tiniest moment. In that moment, Frank's finger missed and pressed the 'Answer Call' button instead. As a result of that miniscule moment, I heard everything he said to his friend because he had bluetooth headphones in. What I heard was, "I have every nerve to get a lawyer! Jeff is fucking some girl in Halifax, and he tried to fuck a server. He's a scumbag and Yoda has no fucking clue."

Those words.

It was *those words*, or some version of those words, that caused time itself to come to a complete stop. That moment seemed to go on forever — the little things sometimes last the longest. It was like I was in a movie scene where things are moving around the main character in slow motion and there is no sound, except for maybe a ringing — like a loud, high pitched ringing in your ears. I dropped my phone to the floor and clasped onto the counter for support. Hope so violently ripped out from under me and all the optimism I felt that morning was suffocated out as quickly as it had arrived. It was a crushing, devastating, sobering blow, amplified only by the realization that I had been here before.

My mouth. My heart. My chest. My head. My skin. My jaw.

Every part of my body felt amplified. I couldn't see straight. All I kept thinking was, *I've been here before.*

I wanted to give that moment back. I wanted to go back in time and pretend it wasn't real. I wanted to go back to the night before, when I was lying in Jeff's arms and he was telling me that everything would be okay. I didn't want *this* life.

But you don't always get to choose how things turn out when you beg and plead and pray; you don't always get to choose how the Universe acts on those prayers. You don't always get to choose the trajectory of how the Universe steps up for you.

I wasn't thinking of that now, though. I was pacing my tiny kitchen, not knowing what to do. The mercury level regulating my body was rising to what felt like the point of no return. I realized that if what Frank was saying was true, it would explain why Jeff had wanted to spend so much time in Halifax the previous week. How could I have missed that? While I was at home worrying about him, thinking about him, missing him, he was having an affair with someone he'd met two months ago, on his first trip to Halifax. While I was in bed crying after my sister's surgery, he was in his office, forming a plan to go visit her again. I didn't want to admit that he had 'tried to fuck' one of the servers — I simply couldn't believe he would do something like that. I couldn't even begin to believe that Frank could be right, and that I had missed all the signs.

While I was stood there, motionless, in total shock, sifting through the destruction of my life as if it was flour for a delicate cake, Jeff walked through the back door. He saw me, panicked and shaking, unable to move or speak, and immediately asked what was wrong. He stood beside me and when he tried to hug me, I slapped him, pushing him hard against the door and demanding he tell me the truth. I asked him to tell me exactly why he went to Halifax. He told me that he did go to see friends, and then confessed that he *did* visit with a girl that he'd met on his last trip. After I adamantly demanded details, he told me they'd gone for dinner and on a walk. "So, you went on a *date* with her?!?!" "I swear," he pleaded, "Nothing happened."

The excuses started. He told me he had gone to Halifax to say goodbye to her. That he'd been *tempted* but that he actually went there to do some 'soul searching' and upon realizing how important I was to him, he ended things with her. That's why he hugged me so tightly when he walked through the door last night. That's why he was so kind and sweet to me — not because he loved me, but because he had a dirty conscience he was trying to make clean.

139

I couldn't even look at him so I stormed out the back door, got in my car and sped off. I wasn't sure where I was going but I knew I had to get out of there. I needed to hear Frank's side of the story from his own mouth, so I pulled over and tried calling him again. This time, he answered. He had no idea that I'd heard his conversation earlier, and that just like that, he had changed my entire life.

I calmed down long enough to tell him that I'd heard everything he had said to his friend and that I needed to know the truth. I could hear Frank's stiffness through the phone. I could hear his uncertainty of how to handle what came next. He told me he was sorry I found out the way that I did and that he wanted to tell me, but didn't know how. He told me that someone from The Restaurant had come forward to say that Jeff was being *'really inappropriate'* at work. I demanded to know who, and he replied with, "Why? So you can fire her? … So you can *hate* her? … And just … *forgive* Jeff? That's what you did with Sam, isn't it?"

I was stunned. I thought all this time I'd hid my secret well.

Frank confessed that earlier in the year, he'd bumped into Sam while he was running an errand with Jeff. He noticed she seemed really anxious so he questioned Jeff about it. Jeff told him that she was 'just some crazy girl spreading lies.' Frank realized something was up and eventually asked Sam about it personally. When he did, she told him what had happened last year in June. I had no idea that Frank had known everything this whole time, but it made sense now, that he was always trying to protect me. It made sense now that he was always pushing me to tell him the truth about what was really going on behind the scenes.

"Look, Boss," Frank began. "I'm sorry you found out this way. Really. I am. But … you're better than this, you know? You can leave … you can stay with me … I'll help y——" I cut him off. I simply could not handle what he was trying to tell me, so I did what I'd been doing for 16 months — I lied through my teeth. I told Frank to stop pretending like he knew my situation. I told him, matter-of-factly, that he didn't know anything about my life

140

outside of work. I explained that although Jeff had been unfaithful to me in the past, we were *working* on it … a lie.

I told him that we were in couples counselling … a lie.

I told him that I believed whatever may have been said to the server in question was probably blown out of proportion … *a lie.*

"He's not a bad guy, Frank. And I know you think you know everything about this, but you don't. So you need to back off and let me handle it!" I hung up the phone and started my car. A few minutes later, I got a call from Monica wondering where everyone was — I'd completely forgotten to call her to cancel the mediation! She heard me crying and asked me to meet her at the park so we could talk.

I drove there in an epic fog. My eyes stung. My face hurt. I was nauseous beyond anything I'd felt before. I was burning up. I didn't want to talk to anyone. I just wanted to figure out the truth. (Or maybe I didn't even want to do that.)

Monica met me in the park and told me that she had talked to Frank, and gotten a bit of the back story. She asked me what my *gut* was saying about the situation. I told her that although Jeff had been unfaithful before, I couldn't let myself believe that he would do something like this *again*, given everything we'd been through, everything I'd done for him, everything that was at stake. " … But?" she speculated.

"… But Frank has never lied to me." I replied.

Monica was a dear friend, and I trusted her discretion. She'd worked in restaurants for a long time, so she was no stranger to the drama that restaurant life sometimes entailed. She had a close friend who worked in Human Resources that she was going to call, to consult on the best way to handle this situation. Monica advised me to go home and rest, and that no matter what we decided to do, we should keep The Restaurant closed until the weekend. She agreed to talk to Frank again, and try to find out more information.

When I left the park, I think I went home. I think I crawled into bed. I think I cried. I might have slept. I know I hastily cancelled my trip to the ashram. I know I cleared my schedule for the week. I know I turned off all the lights and hugged my dog and wondered what was going to happen. I couldn't write. I couldn't think. I couldn't pray. The only thing I wanted was for the day to be over. I wanted my life to be over. I feared what would happen if I moved, so I just stayed there.

———

I must have fallen asleep because when I woke up, it was dark. Monica called and explained that she had spoken to Jeff. He was on his way home, she told me. She advised that I should hear him out. Jeff came home looking wrecked and relieved all at once. He climbed in the bed next to me and hugged me from behind. I was so weak from the day that I didn't push him away. He squeezed me and insisted, "Baby ... it's going to be okay."

He told me that he had done some investigating and discovered that it was Rachel who had felt *a little* uncomfortable with a few of the comments he had made at work. She had confessed to Mackenzie, after a night of drinking, that she found Jeff to be a little *creepy*. Mackenzie took the confession very seriously and when she realized she couldn't tell me (because of my relationship with Jeff), she went to the next manager in line, which was Frank. When she told Frank, he already had this big secret about Sam, so *he* took it seriously, too. I sympathized with Frank, because I had been in the same business of keeping secrets for 15 months.

The whole thing, according to Jeff, was a giant misunderstanding and everyone wanted to put it behind them. Rachel told Monica how embarrassed she was that Frank made such a big deal out of everything and reiterated that she just wanted to come to work like nothing happened. She wanted to sweep it under the rug. I wasn't sure how Frank or Mackenzie were feeling about the situation, but Monica and Jeff seemed to think that everything would be fine tomorrow.

Finally, a break in the day. It felt like the hard shell of a chocolate had broken, allowing the caramel to ooze out. I gave way to the softness and wanted to lap up the sweetness.

In those final moments of that day, I let Jeff hug me close and tell me that it would be okay. He whispered that we would make it through this, together. I wasn't sure if I believed him, but I was so exhausted, I let myself fall asleep in his arms for what would be the very last time.

WEDNESDAY

On Wednesday morning I woke up with the normal chest pain and uneasiness I'd felt for 16 months, but amplified. *Everything* weighed on me that day.

Monica asked us to meet her at The Restaurant first thing in the morning and when we arrived, she was sitting with three papers in a row, on the table in front of her. She hugged us both but was a little more solemn than the day before. I've always known Monica to be a straight-shooter, and today was no different — she started our meeting by telling us that We. Were. Completely. Fucked.

She reported that after discussing things with her friend in Human Resources, Jeff and I were *both* liable if Rachel or Mackenzie wanted to take legal action. We did not have the proper procedures in place, so it was determined that it was not in our best interest to keep Rachel employed. I looked at the piece of paper in front of me and quickly deduced that it was some kind of contract for Rachel to sign. "Monica … what are you saying? We have to fire Rachel? She didn't do anything wrong …"

"You're right," Monica said, firing a look at Jeff. "And we're not firing her. We're letting her leave and giving her severance, in exchange for her discretion. If we don't do this, there's no telling what she could do or say."

Monica slid the next set of papers across the table and urged, "I think Mackenzie has to go as well."

"Mackenzie definitely didn't do anything wrong!" I protested. "She saw something that wasn't right and reported it. If anything, we should be rewarding her!" Monica explained that when she spoke with Mackenzie, she confirmed that she didn't feel *safe*

145

around Jeff. Unless we wanted the labour board knocking on our door, Monica concluded it might be best to ask her to move on. "Mackenzie will be getting severance too," Monica explained.

My whole body flooded with rage. I looked at Jeff and demanded, "What have you done? What have you done?!?!?!?!?!" He claimed, once more, that he did nothing serious and that it was all blown out of proportion. My ears where ringing again and I barely heard the words coming out of his mouth. He had tears in his eyes and reached out for my hand. I recoiled.

I snapped back to reality when Monica said, "And Frank …."

My fists were clenched so tightly that my fingernails were digging into my palms. "I. Am. Not. Firing. Frank. Frank is my friend. He didn't do anything wrong …." I vowed. Monica took my other hand and said, "Babe … you *know* Frank can't work here now. You *know* it's true."

It felt like Monica had taken a boning knife to my entire life. I wasn't angry with her — she was speaking on behalf of the HR representative she'd consulted for us. She was suggesting what she thought was best for us.

I needed more time. I wanted to sit with it and investigate. I wanted to have tea with Frank and talk it over. I wanted to hug Rachel and Mackenzie and tell them I was sorry. I wanted to call my Dad and ask for advice. There was no time though, because we had to act quickly if all of this was going to blow over. We were supposed to reopen in just a few days ….

Monica explained the contracts to us in detail. They stated that each one would accept their severance and in doing so, they would not speak about their reasons for termination. It was a fancy word for *muzzle.*

When we calculated what the severance packages were going to cost, I realized that we were, in fact, *fucked.* Just one week ago, I had been on the verge of breaking. I couldn't imagine being there for even another day, let alone months or years. I didn't

146

know how we were going to run a restaurant when half of our staff was *gone.*

Monica hugged us and left Jeff and I, so we could start exploring our options. We opened the books for The Restaurant and for the first time since we opened, I saw all our debt, laid out for me, clear as day. I saw the huge loan he'd convinced me to get. I saw the expenses that I didn't agree to. I saw all the payments made in only my name. I saw the credit cards that had been maxed out. And now I saw the taxes we owed, that I was unaware of. I couldn't believe how stupid I'd been for putting someone who was terrible at dealing with money in charge of all the finances.

After calculating everything we owed to current staff, suppliers, vacation pay, as well as what we now owed for severance, we realized we would have to wait until our lease was up (in about two months) before we could afford to close our doors without running the risk of claiming bankruptcy. Since everything was in *my* name, this meant personal bankruptcy for me, so we came up with a plan for the next two months. The plan meant I would likely never see any of the cash I had invested into The Restaurant back. It essentially meant that I would be paying for his mistake to save myself from bankruptcy. It wasn't a perfect plan — but it was *the only plan.*

We were going to try as hard as we could to pay off some of our debt, and make sure all our employees and suppliers were paid up to date. We would scrimp every penny we could, and start selling off any remaining inventory. We called a professional accountant to help sort out the mess Jeff had gotten us into with our taxes. He explained, "Whatever salaried employees are left will have to put in extra hours to keep costs down." That meant Jeff and me.

I had no idea how I was going to make it. I had no idea how I was supposed to heal in the environment that had made me so sick.

I had no idea how I would make it through without Frank, Rachel, and Mackenzie, or how I was going to work beside Jeff each day knowing what he did.

I had no idea this is what survival would feel like.

————

As we packed up the books and receipts, we sent an email to our staff asking them all to meet us at The Restaurant for a staff meeting the following day, before we reopened for the weekend. We lied to them (and the rest of the world) and claimed we had 'plumbing problems,' to explain the few extra days to sort things out.

At home, I lay still and quiet, for the first time that day. My thoughts started swirling and paranoia set in. One thought in particular swirled above me, weighing on me heavily since that morning — something about Rachel's story didn't add up. It seemed strange that Rachel would tell Mackenzie about Jeff being a creep, but then later say it was no big deal. It obviously bothered her, so I wondered why she had been so quick to backtrack. I asked Jeff what he thought. "We can't think of that now, baby. We've got to look out for ourselves. For our future. For our family. *For us.*"

We hadn't discussed 'us' or what we were going to do about his escapade to Halifax. We hadn't discussed how *we* were going to make it through. But I was too exhausted to think of any of that now. I needed sleep.

As I started to doze off though, I couldn't stop thinking of Rachel.

THURSDAY

Reality set in upon waking on Thursday morning. I knew I was going to have to rally in a way that I never had before. I tried to stomach some toast and tea, got into my car and drove to The Restaurant. Jeff was already there and greeted me with tender eyes. Perhaps he realized the gravity of the situation, finally. Perhaps he realized what I was about to give up for him. I ignored his need for affection, put my head down and got right to work.

I spent the entire morning in my kitchen, alone, with a gargantuan prep list. My mind wandered everywhere, so I tried to focus on the food to steady myself. Everything felt like a challenge. My arms felt sticky and heavy; my hands refused to work with the speed and accuracy they usually did. It was a thick fog I was in, made thicker by the fact that every time I looked up, I saw Jeff in the dining room. Bitter doesn't begin to describe how I felt in those moments.

At 1 p.m., it was time to meet Monica. She had taken charge as our unofficial HR rep, and was going to help facilitate the exchange of the paperwork and severance cheques. She was going to meet with Rachel and Mackenzie later that afternoon, but given Frank's sometimes unpredictable temper, she thought it would be best if I was there when she gave him the contract to sign. She was right — out of all of them, Frank was the wild card. He was so angry at Jeff it was uncertain how he would react. I gathered my things and told Jeff I had to go meet Frank, feeling full of shame and tension. Jeff rubbed my shoulder and told me it would be okay. "How? How will it be okay, Jeff? I'm going to fire one of my best friends and he didn't do anything wrong."

Jeff turned my body so it was facing him. The alchemist spoke softly this time, declaring almost verbatim the same words he'd said to me about Chloe last June. "Frank is not your friend, Yoda." I shook my head but he continued, "He's the guy who you work beside. This isn't friendship. It's … proximity! You and Frank fight all the time. And to be honest, it kind of sounds like he wants to fuck up your life. Does that *sound* like a good friend to you?"

His voice was soothing like chamomile tea; it went down smooth and I drank it up. By the time I got to the coffee shop, I had let it sink in. I had made up my mind that Frank was not, in fact, my *friend*. He was upheaving my whole life, as if it was some kind of game to him. I'd made up my mind — he was going to sign this piece of paper, keep his mouth shut and move on.

———

I drove to the coffee shop to meet Monica and Frank. I sat down at the table as calmly as I could. Monica had the paperwork in front of her and began explaining things. I could feel Frank's eyes on me, but I couldn't bear to return his gaze. My eyes stayed planted on my hands, clasped under the table, my body poised to bolt. When Monica asked if he would sign the paperwork, Frank interjected, "So basically you want to pay me to sign a piece of paper that says Jeff did nothing wrong?!?!"

I snapped. "No, Frank. You are going to sign this piece of paper that says *I* did nothing wrong. Don't you understand? If Jeff goes down for this, I'm going down with him. If he harassed someone, under my watch, and I did nothing … that comes back to me. I didn't have the right procedures in place to make sure something like that didn't happen. So if Jeff goes down for this, I'm done." I paused, barely realizing what I was saying but understanding that it was the truth. It felt as if someone had thrown jalapeno juice in my face — I was burning in all directions. "If you really care about me, and don't want to see me get dragged through the mud, you'll sign this fucking piece of paper. Right. Now."

150

Frank looked back at me with the saddest eyes I'd ever seen. And I'd seen him through a lot. He picked up the pen and begrudgingly signed the paper. I slid him the cheque and before he picked it up, he grabbed my hand and pleaded, "You deserve so much better than this, Boss. He doesn't love you. I know you think he does. But this is so fucked up ..." Before he could finish his sentence, I got up from the table and fled from the café. The only thing I was grateful for was that I had time to get out of sight before the tears came.

Monica caught up with me before I got in my car. "Well ... *he signed*. That's good," she noted optimistically. She was going to see Rachel and Mackenzie next and told me she'd update me as soon as she had news.

"They *have* to sign, Monica. *You have to make them sign,*" I begged, bursting with desperation.

"I'll do my best, sweetie," she replied as she kissed my cheek. "This could all be over in a couple of hours ..." she whispered.

———

I knew what I'd just asked of Frank was wrong. I felt it in every pore of my body; in every gram of my being. I had to believe that Frank would follow through with the contract, and not do anything to hurt me. All the power was in his hands — all he had to do was renege his contract and tell someone, and I would be *done*.

It turns out, I would find out months later, that when Frank left that coffee shop he considered it. He considered it while he sat down at his computer wanting to tell the world about the fucked up thing that had just happened to him. That he had just been told by two strong, female leaders in our industry, that we basically supported muzzling sexual harassment victims. He deliberated on it — I don't know for how long, or what really went through his head that day or the days after. I know that his wife (who was my good friend) intervened in some way, but I don't know what

151

exactly changed his mind. All I knew was that I would never forgive myself for what just happened.

———

After leaving the café, I went back to The Restaurant for the staff meeting we had scheduled and forced myself to put on the happiest face I could manage. We'd been closed for more than a week and although we greeted our staff with wine and smiles, it was obvious to everyone that something heavy was about to happen.

I let Jeff speak while I sunk into my shame. I was overflowing with sorrow after days of extreme stress. I wished Rachel was there — Monica was probably giving her the contract right now. I longed for the composure Mackenzie brought to our meetings. I missed Frank already.

Jeff explained to everyone that we'd had a difficult few months. Morale was down, tensions were high. He explained that we'd made the decision to close for lunch service, thus eliminating the need for some of our staff, which justified why Frank, Mackenzie and Rachel weren't there. We were going to be cutting our hours so that we could have more time for each other, more work-life balance, and hopefully that would make it a happier place to work. He told them that they were the ones we'd *chosen* to join us on our new journey.

It would have been a sweet moment if it hadn't been total bullshit.

My face was stiff from trying to stop the tears. Scarlett, as sweet as maple syrup, told us how happy she was that we were finally doing something for *us*. She'd been in the business for a long time and knew what it looked like when people were burnt out. My heart cracked a little more with each word she said.

We had a group hug at the end of the meeting as we thanked them for their patience and understanding. We told them that things were going to be better from that moment on. It would have been another sweet moment if we weren't lying through our teeth.

Sara approached me in the kitchen while everyone was leaving. "Chef...?" Her voice shook. "Where's Frank?" We hadn't fooled her — it didn't make sense to her that Frank all of a sudden wasn't there. I wanted to run from her innocence. I set my knife down calmly and turned to face her. Brandon was standing beside her now and they both had tears in their eyes. They knew something had happened, but I couldn't tell them anything. I gave Sara a hug and told her that we were going to have to go on without Frank.

Every move I made from that point on, was about making it out of this alive.

———

Once everyone was gone and it was finally quiet in the kitchen, I stood in disbelief knowing that I would be forced to come into work for the next two months and pretend like everything was fine. I still had work to do, to prepare for the next day, so I focussed my attention to slicing onions and searing eggplants. I actually wanted that prep list to last forever because when it was over, I'd have to go home and the thought of being near Jeff made me feel like I'd put my face into a carton of sour milk and inhaled deeply.

As my mind drifted to thoughts of food, my phone rang and I hurried to answer it. I knew it was Monica, and I wanted desperately to hear the words that we were in the clear. I needed to know that everyone had signed the paperwork and we could start moving on from this wreckage. She told me that both girls decided that they wanted to read over the contracts and think about it over the weekend. I sighed heavily. Monica reassured me by saying, "I think they're both going to sign. I really do. So don't worry about it. It's done."

Then she said, "You and I really need to talk."

I was more drained than I had ever been in my life so I declined her offer stating, "Not tonight." In her way that I both respected and avoided over the years of knowing her, Monica argued, "Listen, babe. I know you've had a tough day. But I've done a lot for you in the last 48 hours. You can make time to come have a beer with me." She was right, so I agreed to meet her in 20 minutes at a pub near my house.

———

When Monica arrived at the pub, she gave me a long hug. She took a deep, deep breath as we sat down and ordered a drink but before it arrived, she grabbed my hands from across the table. Next, she told me that she was sitting there, not as my mediator and HR rep, but as my *friend*. She took another deep, deep breath and started, "I talked to Rachel. It's *bad*."

" … What the hell does that mean?!?" I scoffed, my back already stiff.

"It means that I talked to Rachel and what Jeff did to her was the *textbook definition* of sexual harassment. It's *bad*, sweetie."

Those words.

Monica was one of my own. We were both women working in a male dominated industry and we both had an understanding that all women in our industry seemed to be equipped with. We both understood that sometimes inappropriate things were said in the kitchen. We had been taught that there was a fine line between friendly comradery and inappropriate behaviour, but sometimes that fine line was a little blurry and it was hard to tell what side of the line you were on. If you couldn't decide, you were better off to stick to the former and not make a fuss. When Monica listened to Rachel's testimony, she knew, definitively, that what Jeff did to Rachel was *wrong*. There was no grey area. This wasn't just one of those things that *happens* in restaurants. It wasn't a cavalier comment here and there, as Rachel had originally led us to believe. It wasn't just a joke or two friends being silly, like we sometimes were in the kitchen. Rachel had been sexually harassed *for months.* Black and white. Textbook definition. It was clear as consommé.

Rachel described a moment at The Restaurant when Jeff detailed a 'sex dream' he had about her. He made physical advances at work on many occasions and when she didn't reciprocate, he started cutting her shifts and giving her the cold shoulder. He made comments about her appearance that were distasteful and forward. He was aggressive and threatening. It was all there, in black and white. *Textbook definition.*

As Monica continued, my mind felt like it was comprised of mushy peas. I was able to recall how a few months earlier, Jeff wanted to cut Rachel's Sunday shift and when I asked him why, he told me it was because she was lazy and mouthing off. I'd never observed anything like this from her, but I trusted him so I let him make the call. I *should* have pried. I *should* have looked into it more. I *should* have hired an HR rep a long time ago. I *should* have been in that meeting when he told her he was cutting her shifts. I *should* have stuck up for her when my gut told me to.

My list of 'should haves' was growing longer and I had to physically give my head a shake to be able to come back to the conversation with Monica.

Monica told me that when she showed up at Rachel's door with the contract, Rachel broke down. She confessed everything to Monica and showed her the proof. She had texts, emails and photos dating back for months. She didn't want to leave The Restaurant, or sign the paperwork, but she said she would do it, because she didn't want me getting dragged down for what Jeff had done.

Monica paused her story and asked me if I had inquired about the girl from Halifax, yet. That's when I started with the excuses. *Sweep harder. Scrub. Pile on the lies.*

Next, she asked me about Sam. It turns out Frank had told her everything he knew, hoping that she could use it to talk some sense into me. I lied and told Monica I had *handled it.*

155

She asked if there were other women I knew about. I told her it was none of her business.

She pushed. She asked about all the times he'd betrayed my trust. *Sweep harder,* I told myself.

She pushed a little more, asking me to look her in the eyes and say that I trusted him. I begged her to stop.

She didn't.

Instead Monica mused, "You told me that you prayed recently."

"Yeah? So?!?" My voice raised, defensively.

"Well, maybe God heard you." She inched forward a bit. "Maybe *this* is it. Maybe *this* is what you prayed for. Maybe this is your *Way Out.*"

The truth I'd been ignoring was finally here for me. It wasn't gently knocking. It wasn't tapping me lightly on the shoulder. It was standing straight in front of me, staring me in the face and wringing my neck. It was waiting for me to make what might be the most important move of my life. This moment mattered … possibly more than any single moment in my life so far.

There had been many moments over the last several days that *could have* changed my life. On Monday, when I had that therapy session with Di and she cracked a hole in my shield. The light had poked through the darkness, just enough for me to speak the truth for the first time in years. It could have been on Tuesday when the Universe finally answered my pleas for change and I heard Frank's phone conversation and everything flipped upside down. It could have been on Wednesday when I was lying in bed and every fibre of my being was telling me that I was not going to be on this earth for much longer and I wasn't even sad about it. Or the moment that came earlier that day, when Frank tried one last time, with everything he had, to look me in the eyes and get me to see the truth.

156

None of those moments had penetrated the surface of my shield enough.

This moment though … was *different.*

I felt my consciousness leave my body for a moment and I could feel it floating above me. My consciousness, my "Self!" was whispering to me that it was safe for me to speak. She told me I didn't need all the excuses I had conjured up for him that I was storing in my shoulder, my ribs, my jaw and my belly. She was on a mission to find and speak the truth. Real, raw, undeniable, honest, ugly, total *truth.*

What happened next was like nothing that had ever happened to me before. Instead of staying silent and lying, I told Monica *everything.* I said all the things I had never said out loud. I said all the things he had made me promise not to say. I told Monica about every time I snooped on his laptop and found him talking to someone from his past. I told her about all of his exes and stories of him being unfaithful. All of the broken hearts. All of the boys' nights. All of the trips he went on for work. All of the shady excuses. All of the vacations he took me on and romantic gestures he used to make up for his deceit. I told Monica about Charlotte and Alisa and Sam and all the women I *knew* he had hurt. I told her about every woman he *might* have hurt.

I started questioning that if he could do what he did to Rachel, someone we considered family, and hide it so well, what else was he hiding?

I finally began to consider the secret girl from Halifax and how thick that betrayal had actually been.

Every single lie came to the forefront of my mind, like I'd cracked some kind of code. Every single lie he'd ever told me, and every single lie I'd ever told for him, came crashing down on me, in a single moment. It was as if I was a glass ketchup bottle being held upside down, and each lie was a tap-tap-tap on the bottom — all the truths wrapped up inside of me came gushing out of me and I couldn't stop it. Suddenly, I didn't care about him

157

and his lies. I didn't care if it killed me. I didn't care if it burned. I didn't care if it tasted salty and sour. All I cared about in that moment was the truth.

It was as if an actual light switch went on in my head. The more truths I told, the more my cells opened up. It was invigorating and terrifying all at once.

I didn't *choose* to go through this moment. This moment *took* me.

It was like I was in the eye of a hurricane; I was swirling around in a vortex of the destruction he had caused. I was in the centre of it all, and a strange sense of calmness was contained in me. It gave me a sense of safety. A sense of strength. A sense of *self*. "Self!" Where was she? I'd nearly forgotten about her completely.

In that hurricane moment, my consciousness returned to my body. My nausea diminished; my fists unclenched. It was an eerie feeling all over my body, but now that it was there, it wouldn't leave. And, I didn't want it to. I wanted to hold onto this sense of self, and I wanted her to tell me what to do next.

In the short time that I left my body, it had shed its former state of fear and anxiety. It was different now — *I* was different now. A different, *calmer* version of myself had taken over. She was brave, independent, powerful and confident. She wouldn't be silenced this time. I was listening now, to that Little Girl who resided inside my chest as she told me what I needed to do.

Instead of running, I lifted her up.

I told her we were going to be okay.

I asked for her help, and she joined me.

We do not change until we must, she whispered in my ear.

I knew in that moment that the only way I would make it through this darkness, would be without Jeff. If I stayed with him, it would mean giving up absolutely everything that was left of my

158

life, including my friends, my sanity and whatever integrity I had left.

That Little Girl inside me knew it was true. She had been there for me the whole time, waiting for me to see the truth. She'd never left my side and she never, ever will. She'd loved me from the beginning of time. She was powered by equal parts self-love and desperation. She was powered by the notion that there is no right way to do the wrong thing. She was fed by love and forgiveness and strength and girl power. And she was going to take her Fucking. Power. Back.

I barely recognized the Little Girl, but I clutched onto her tightly. She was ready to brawl. She was completely unafraid of the truth. And the truth, was here.

The truth was that he wasn't who I thought he was. I could no longer hold onto the fact that if I gave him everything he ever wanted, that he would finally be good. He. Simply. Wasn't. Good.

I had hoped for a long time that if we closed The Restaurant or moved away, or went to therapy, that we would *make it.* I always in my heart of hearts, believed that we would end up together. The fairy tale would be kept alive if I just kept pushing ….

But it wasn't time for that now. Now it was time to face the truth, and I *knew* what I had to do.

I collected myself, calmly got up from the table, and told Monica I had to go.

———

By the time I pulled into our driveway, my calmness had morphed into some sort of super human strength. Everything felt so simple now.

I turned off my car, got out, glided up the steps and through my front door. Jeff was in the kitchen at our table, looking like he'd been crying. I insisted that we needed to talk, sat down and kept my distance. I swear, I didn't even flinch.

In our six years together, I'd never been the one to speak first. I'd never been able to stay calm. I'd never chosen to fight instead of flee. I'd never had a voice that was loud enough to not be interrupted or talked over or hushed. I'd always been the one who needed comfort. It has always been my move to end an argument by any means necessary — it was part of what had gotten us into this mess. I'd never loved myself enough to *fight* for what I wanted.

But that girl was *gone*. She'd been replaced with this Little Girl who spoke the fuck up. She was determined and steady and strong. Her convictions were about to pour out of her mouth.

She began: "Jeff ... I need you to admit that you *sexually harassed* Rachel. I need to hear you say Those. Words.*"

I was a brick wall.

"I need you to go to therapy." He opened his mouth to argue with me, but I continued, "I don't want to book your appointment or find a therapist for you. I just need you to go. It starts by admitting, out loud, that you need help."

My list of demands got longer and as the strength rose up in my body like the kitchen thermometer on a night in July, I finally said all the things I wanted to say. By the end of it, I commanded, "You can't stay here anymore. You can stay on the couch tonight, but tomorrow you need to pack a bag and I need you to leave."

We'd crossed some sort of threshold and as I finished speaking, I knew my strength was wavering.

Jeff knelt on the floor in front of me, begging. Snot spilt from his face and tears rolled down his cheeks and he held onto my waist with both arms. He told me that if I wanted to, we could leave tonight. We would go straight to the airport and get tickets to some far away land and start from scratch. He told me we could grow lemons or tomatoes or coconuts ... he didn't care, as long as I didn't leave him. He wrapped his arms around my stomach tighter and kissed my sides.

160

Tomorrow we would reopen The Restaurant, after being closed for almost two weeks. We needed rest, I told him, and we went to bed in separate rooms. I lay down, the colour of grey, flat on my back on top of the sheets and stared at the ceiling. My strength was now decimated.

That night was the longest night of my life. Alone and afraid — I didn't sleep a wink. If there were ever a night that Jeff was going to do something desperate or dangerous, tonight would be the night. I wasn't scared of him and I didn't believe he'd ever physically hurt me, but I wasn't brave enough to sleep either.

So, I lay awake, my mind racing, and my strength finally spent, I curled up into a ball and wept. It was different than any of the other times I'd cried; like every horrible thing I'd ever done was coming to the surface. During the course of the last several days, weeks, months and years, my heart had been poked, prodded, punctured and squeezed. All the little cracks that had been developing were finally shattering into dust. This is what *rock bottom* was.

I deserve this, I thought to myself.

This is my penance.

On Friday morning, Jeff packed a bag and left early to prepare us to open that evening for dinner. Our reservation book was overflowing after almost two weeks of being away. I had a significant amount of prep to do and was going to have to do it without Frank and Mackenzie. Sara and Brandon were up to the task, but they arrived to work looking grave and concerned.

As Sara, Brandon and I got to work, I gave myself a silent pep talk. *"You can do this. You have to do this. 75 more days and you're out."* I tried to act normal and made small talk with them, and when that stopped working, I blasted hip-hop to break the heavy silences. When Scarlett and Marie arrived, everyone hugged. This was everyone who was left.

Just before service, there was a sharp pain in my stomach that took me a while to recognize as hunger. I hadn't slept more than a few hours in the last several days, and the only thing I'd been able to stomach was a few bites of toast. It wasn't uncommon for restaurant chefs to neglect their health, but this was extreme and I felt *very* ill. I didn't dare take a break from cooking, though. It was the only thing keeping me from dissolving into a puddle on the floor.

I somehow plugged through service, which was a total blur, with a menu I'd haphazardly pieced together. As the night wore on, I watched as Jeff interacted with Scarlett and Marie. I watched and watched and couldn't take my eyes off of him, my paranoia becoming debilitating. I watched closely as he looked at Sara when she went out to the bar for a drink of water. I watched for signs of inappropriate behaviour. I watched to see if he was standing too close to Scarlett when he spoke to her. I watched for signs of flirtation. I watched to see if any of the girls looked afraid or uncomfortable. I looked into every move he made. I studied him. I didn't take my mind or my eyes off of him for the whole evening. This was more than just anxiety or uneasiness. I felt physically ill in every corner of my body.

There was no way I could withstand this for 75 more days.

———

When the orders finally slowed, and it was just a few desserts left to be plated, I asked Sara and Brandon to take over while I went upstairs. They were tired too, I could tell, but they responded in unison, "We got you, Chef!" I knew it was true. I knew that they had my back, and I had to have faith that if I chose to close The Restaurant they would still have my back. I had to believe that was true as I walked up those stairs otherwise I might not have made it. Once at the top, I collapsed. I didn't faint ... it was just that one moment I was standing, and the very next moment I was not. I wasn't sure if I could get up, so I stayed there a while.

I was lying on the floor of our staff room at the top of the stairs, above the kitchen. I lay there and looked around at everything in the room. The first thing I noticed was the corner where I held job interviews with Sara and Mackenzie. I saw the wall that Frank and I had torn down and then drywalled, mudded, taped and sanded. I saw the table where we held our weekly menu meetings. I saw the stack of bowls from our lunch that day and the recycling bin overflowing with energy drinks and coffee cups to keep us awake. I saw the First Aid kit that I had clumsily ripped off the wall when Brandon had cut his fingertip off last month and I had to mend him. I saw the ironing board and the washing machine where we cleaned our coats each week. I saw the mat in front of the fireplace where I had taken a nap last year on New Year's Eve in between seatings after coming down with a horrible stomach flu.

I saw all the memories, self-doubt, fear, lies and fights. Through everything, I'd *pushed.* Always.

Something clicked in that moment, as I was lying on the floor, that I had pushed for long enough.

I wasn't going to let this be my fate. I wasn't going to lose everything for a man who didn't love me like I needed to be loved. Or who didn't love me at all — I had yet to figure that out.

I had already lost so much … but I knew that if I was going to make it through this alive, I was going to have to pull the plug. Not only that, but I was going to have to come clean. I knew that I would never be able to live with myself if I silenced another woman who Jeff had hurt. I knew I wasn't going to be able to look at myself ever again if I went through with this lie. It had gone on for long enough.

I had to do *something*. Something other than what I had always done. For Rachel. For Mackenzie. For Sam. For Scarlett and Marie and Sara and all the girls who were left. For all the girls I didn't know about. For Frank and the men who tried to stand up for us. I had to do something, so I gathered my energy and crawled to the desk. The first thing I did surprised me. I called my mother.

It was late and we didn't typically call each other unless it was on a Sunday. I'm not entirely sure why I called her, other than the fact that I needed to tell *someone* in my family what I was about to do and I needed to hear it was going to be okay. "Baby, are you okay?" I told her that I hadn't been okay for a long time but that I would be. I told her that I was leaving Jeff and that I was going to close The Restaurant tomorrow. With urgency, I asked her to tell my family, so that they wouldn't be surprised if they heard the news online. My mother asked me if I was sure — she wondered if perhaps this was just a bad fight. I told her that I was *sure*. I told her that Jeff was a bad man and that I couldn't stay here a minute longer. "Oh, baby …" my mother blubbered, her voice breaking under the weight of my news.

The next thing I did was call Monica. I told her about the paranoia and anxiety. I told her I knew I couldn't do this anymore and I couldn't go through with our plan to stay open until the end

165

of our lease. She asked too, if I was sure. "I'm actually calling you because if I change my mind, I need you to come get me." I knew in my fragile state, I might be talked out of this. "Bring rope," I added. I wasn't kidding. Then I pleaded, "Monica … I know you've done a lot for me. But I need you to do one more thing, okay?"

"Anything, sweetie."

"I need you to call Rachel and Mackenzie and tell them that they don't need to sign those contracts," I said. It was as if I could *feel* Monica's relief through the phone.

"Are you … are you sure?" She wasn't doubting me, she was checking to make sure I understood the consequences of what I was saying.

"Yes. I'm sure. Tell them to burn them. And tell Frank I'm going to destroy the one he signed. Please, Monica," I pleaded. "Tell them. Tell them that I said so, okay? They can keep their severance money, too. If Jeff cancels the cheques, I'll write new ones … From my own account …" I was sobbing and rambling now. "They don't have to sign anything. Can you tell them that from me?"

She agreed and told me how proud she was of me. "It's going to be hell before its light again, sweetie."

I knew she was right. And I knew, as Jeff made his way to the top of the stairs, that it was *time.*

———

"Jeff … I thought I could do this. But I can't." He opened his mouth but I stopped him before he could speak. "I've been through enough. And I am not willing to put myself through this anymore. You can't ask me to do this, Jeff." I stiffened my back, trying my best to appear strong and steadfast, finally declaring, "The Restaurant closes tomorrow. I've. Been. Through. Enough."

He stared me down. "We just have to hold on a little while longer, Yoda. And then we can pay off all the loans and you and

I can figure this out." His desperation started seeping out, "Let's go out with a bang! We can't go out like this … don't make me do it like this …" He was whimpering now, proposing every solution he could think of, landing on the original plan of me finally going to the ashram and letting him sort everything out.

For just a moment, I considered what he was proposing. But there was one major problem: I couldn't trust him alone with women I cared about. "I'm not a *predator*, Yoda. Come on … you *know* me." But I didn't *know* him, not like I thought I did, but I knew in that moment I didn't trust him. The more he pleaded, the more I held my ground. I was done being obedient.

He frantically suggested that if that wasn't an option, that perhaps he could be the one to take a step back from The Restaurant. If I really didn't trust him, he volunteered to work from the sidelines but still be involved. He would create the wine lists and do the bar inventory, taking over all the scheduling and menial office tasks. He'd never even show his face at The Restaurant but instead, we would promote Marie and make it work until our lease was up.

There was a problem with that scenario too. It meant that I would have to stay there, cleaning up his mess, further destroying myself for something *I never wanted in the first place*.

I chose my next words carefully, like pulling taffy from my teeth. "Listen. In 10 minutes, I'm going to go downstairs and I'm going to tell the staff that *it's over*. You can either come with me, or you can stay up here and be a coward. I don't really care, but I'm doing it. I'm out …" He hung his head but I remained steady. "You can't do this without me, so we're done here."

I'll never know what was going through Jeff's head at that moment. He'd not only been defeated, but he was about to lose his dream. I walked away from the desk and started down the steps — actively telling my legs to move one foot in front of the other. My body was buzzing and shaking, wanting to rest but being forced to not only stay awake, but to go through more trauma. I took a seat in the dining room and quietly pretended to work on the prep list for the next day. Scarlett was wiping tables and Marie was polishing glasses. Sara was scrubbing the sink and Brandon was mopping the floor. Those details, although insignificant, are branded on my heart as some of the longest, saddest moments of my life. As the moments passed and his time was up, Jeff came down the stairs and joined me in the dining room.

I had held in tears for long enough. I was tired and starved and worn and broken. By the time everyone gathered in the dining room and we choked out the news, tears were streaming down my face. It seemed as if they all knew what was coming.

I stood still with my arms crossing my chest and my jaw clenched as tightly as it could go, bawling my eyes out, while Jeff explained to all of them that it was over. We had made the decision to close The Restaurant, and had one final day of service tomorrow. I didn't have it in me to say a single word — I just grabbed Sara, who was standing closest to me, and hugged her harder than I've ever hugged anyone before. Brandon came to join us and we stood in the dining room weeping together.

It was intensely emotional for obvious reasons, but what I wasn't prepared for was the resentment I felt towards Jeff in that moment. It was irrelevant to me that we were possibly going to close The Restaurant *eventually*. It didn't matter that I had one foot out the door already. This was too damn sad to do on my own, so I let Jeff stand with us in the dining room as we hugged and cried. He shouldn't have been there though. And in those final moments, I both resented him for being there, and myself for allowing it.

After everyone left, and I was getting ready to go home, Jeff gently grabbed my arm, turning me towards him. He was desperate for a hug, or some kind of affection, and I, too, needed something to soothe me. I almost caved and let him scoop up my body and hug me, but ended up turning away and walking out the door to go home.

I knew then that any microgram of energy or love I had left, had to be saved for *myself* so that I could go back to the home we once shared and make it through the night, alone.

I woke up and felt my bones crack with every move I made. I tried to swing my legs over the edge of the bed, but they wouldn't budge. I imagined myself as a chicken carcass lying butterflied on my butcher's block, all of my joints broken apart. My body ached so much from the stress of the last few days. I almost didn't recognize my shoulder pain as *pain*. It was something that was a part of me now; integrated like an elbow or a tooth.

I stayed in bed for as long as I physically could, and then finally forced myself to get up. More cracking. Popping. Searing pain. I had a shower that was hotter than hot, pulled my hair into a quick braid, and made my way to The Restaurant for what was going to be the very last time. The last service. The last time I would walk into what now felt like a prison.

I pulled into my parking space and my heart sunk, competing with every other organ and body part over which was heaviest. A lump formed in my throat and my body buzzed with anxiety. It took absolutely everything I had to walk into The Restaurant that day.

Surreal and unfair was a fucking understatement.

———

Jeff was in the dining room when I arrived. This wasn't unusual, as he typically arrived first thing in the morning to get the dining room cleaned and set up for lunch service. His shoulders were slumped and his eyes were bloodshot. I had one job to do — make it through this day intact. He asked me for a hug, which I coldly obliged, keeping my distance and not looking

171

him in the eyes. Next, we found seats side by side on the bar stools in the dining room, and set up our laptop so we could start crafting the Facebook post that we had both been dreading.

This wasn't a dream … it really was *over.* I put one knee up on the bar stool and hugged myself closely. Tears were forming but there was no time.

We somehow found a way to work together to write a letter to our customers and friends, explaining our sudden closure. In that letter, we announced that the timing was 'right' for us to 'move on,' and that we had decided to 'choose' our happiness and health over our business. We spoke about a 'big opportunity' that had come our way that we simply couldn't pass up.

We made ourselves look brave, when we weren't.

I helped Jeff appear virtuous, when he wasn't.

I didn't have time or energy to think about how important our final words really were, so I just did the best I could with the energy I had left. When we finished curating the perfect, fake story, we clicked 'post,' and it was done.

There were a few hours until we opened and as Jeff swept and mopped the dining room one last time, I wrote the prep list for the day, as I usually did around this time. We both kept busy doing all of the pre-service tasks we were used to doing. I cut root vegetables as thin as I could on the mandolin for our signature root vegetable chips with chili salt. I prepared mayonnaise and meringues. I seared mushrooms on the flat top and grilled lemons for vinaigrette.

As I worked away, the staff began filing in. Instead of everyone getting straight to work as they usually did, we each paused to hug. Everyone was visibly emotional, myself included, and knowing I would have to say goodbye to everyone at the end of the night left a bitter taste in my mouth. My kitchen crew had gone from five to three, in what felt like the blink of an eye. Brandon and Sara both looked crippled by our swift decision to close … and there was something else plaguing them both — they wanted assurance that I was okay. I was so broken, I didn't have the energy to be empathetic to their needs or questions. I just wanted the night to be over. I could see that they needed me to be their fearless leader in that moment. And they deserved that much, so I did the only thing I could think of. I tore up the prep list I had written out earlier that morning, and told them both that they could come up with any single dish they wanted, and we would serve it that night. I told them this was their chance to put anything they'd been dreaming of, on the menu. They could use anything and everything in our fridges or in dry storage; nothing was off limits. It was up to them, I told them, and I was cheering them on with the only strength I had left.

I watched as Sara created a beautiful, refined mixed melon gazpacho. She added mint from our patio, then she strained it over and over until it was finally as smooth as cream. She used the techniques I had taught her, she asked all the right questions, and she waited anxiously for approval when I tasted it. Brandon made a rustic green curry with zucchini and potatoes — he always did best when we cooked without rules or recipes. His curry was mild and sweet and tasted like love and mourning. As they both buzzed around the kitchen checking in on me and cooking away, I felt a brief sense of peace wash over me. I knew, deep in my heart, that they would both be okay. There was *ease* in that moment, and for a minute, I allowed myself to feel proud of them.

Sara and Brandon continued prepping and we had our regular pre-service pep talk as Scarlett and Marie finished setting the dining room. It wasn't long until our loyal customers and friends started to arrive. People brought cards, gifts and well wishes. People brought questions. People were confused and concerned. But overall, people came to celebrate one last night at The Restaurant they loved so dearly. People came in droves and it was the busiest night we'd had since our opening night, 16 months earlier.

As orders started flooding in, all I wanted to do for the next few hours was focus on the food. I wanted a reprieve from what was happening all around me. I wanted that rush from the line —

173

when things were really busy, and everyone found their groove during a busy night. That rare feeling of pride in my work had kept me going, despite feeling like I was in a prison. Getting that rush, that I think only a chef can truly understand, made me believe, even if just for a minute, that things would be *okay*. Like I was making some kind of truce with my pain to just *let me be* for a few hours while I cooked my heart out.

I *deserved* to feel that rush one more time. I deserved to enjoy these final moments; to bathe in what I had built; to feel proud of the business I had created with my bare hands. Even if restaurant life made me miserable, I still deserved one final moment with my team, in my kitchen, with my craft.

But when I looked out and saw Jeff's face — his smiling face, hugging one of our regular customers, pouring champagne — I felt a rage bubbling up. His presence there that night felt like a dirty deal.

In that moment of chaos and rage, when the chit board was overflowing and orders were coming in faster than I could call them out, I *could have* given up. I could have thrown my arms up in the air and stormed out. I could have taken every single chit off the board and thrown them in the trash, linked arms with everyone who was left, walked passed Jeff and out the back door. I don't think anyone would have blamed me.

I kept going though. And I realized when I was staring at him in the dining room with all the rage in the world, that *this* moment wasn't my darkest hour. My darkest hour was in that church a few weeks before, when I was down on my knees praying for a reason to live. My darkest hour was when I sat across from Frank and told him that the truth didn't matter to me. My darkest hour was when I silenced a woman who was targeted by the man standing across the pass from me. My darkest hours were behind me, which gave me the strength I needed to make it through this one last night.

"Are you okay, Chef?" Sara asked. I'd been staring at the chit machine and not moving, for the last several minutes. Her voice snapped me back to reality but I felt unable to respond to her very loaded question. She held a spoon of melon soup up for me to eat and I let it coat my throat. It was cool and smooth, seeming to soothe every ache in my body for a millisecond. I can still taste it. I'll always remember it.

I gave my head a shake. "Ready? Ready!" I tightened my apron and, as Frank had faithfully boomed every night at 4:30 p.m., I filled in, my voice cracking under the pressure. I took one more sip of that minty melon nectar. "Let's have a great service!" I shouted.

Brandon and Sara moved swiftly and with intention; they did everything I had taught them. When we started running low on the food we'd prepped for the night, we offered tasting menus and we all feverishly cooked until we eventually ran out of literally everything. The fridges were empty and we had given it our all. Like most services, by the end of it, we were exhausted and hungry. I told Sara and Brandon to grab a beer and sent them to the back stoop for a quick break.

Finally alone, I stood in my kitchen and took a deep breath in. I smelled mushrooms, organic lettuce, bleach, coriander seeds and mint. It smelt of familiarity. It smelt of blood, sweat and tears. Of memories and family. Of shame and secrets. Jeff saw me standing alone and I got the sense that he wanted me to flash him a fake smile, from across the line, like I always did. He wanted me to pat him on the back and tell him that he'd done a good job that night. He wanted me to reassure him that he was a good man. But it was impossible for me to give him that.

So I did nothing, but he continued to look at me with hopeful eyes, and walked towards me. He put his arm around my waist. I shuddered; my reaction startling me. He put his head next to mine, touching my shoulder with his chin and whispered into my neck, "Yoda ... if we make it through this, I will make you the happiest woman on the planet. I will give you everything you've ever wanted."

For a moment, I was paralyzed; completely unable to move or respond. I felt like my emotions were going to bubble over like sugar turning into caramel. I made it through that rage by assuring myself that this would be the *very last time*. The last time I would help him clean up his mess. This would be the last time I would help him look benevolent.

Brandon and Sara came back in the kitchen and Jeff left. We didn't bother cleaning the kitchen that night, neglecting the end-of-shift cleaning list for the very first time. When it was time to say goodbye to everyone, I filled everyone's arms full of canned goods and unopened bottles of booze. Brandon scooped me up in a big hug before he left and told me he couldn't wait for my next big project — his innocence so welcome in that moment.

I found Sara in the stairwell, sobbing. Embarrassed, she hastily wiped her tears and told me she was being stupid and asked me to leave her alone. I wiped her eyes and she confessed that she knew there was something I wasn't telling her. "I can't tell you anything else right now," I explained, "But I'm going to need a friend over the next while, so don't go far, okay?" She nodded and we hugged once more before she left.

There were still a few customers in the dining room paying their bills and saying their goodbyes. Some wanted a photo or for me to autograph the final menu as a keepsake. I was too drained and broken to give them their memories. I mustered a quick goodbye to anyone who was left, gathered a few of my things, and left out the back door without looking back. I couldn't. I only made it a few blocks away when everything I'd been holding in for the last week was about to leave my body in a swift purge of words and rage. It started with a few tears, and then my whole body shook. I pulled my car over and started wailing and hitting my steering wheel with all my might, until my hands felt bruised and I was exhausted. It was like a cork popping from a bottle of champagne, the way my shame spilled out of me that night.

I called Frank and started to mourn my mistakes of the last six days over a voicemail. I told him how sorry I was and begged for his forgiveness, even though I wasn't sure if he'd even bother listening to a voicemail from me, after what I'd done to him. I told Frank that I wished he would have been there that night. If I would have decided to go on without Jeff, and kicked him out before that weekend began, I knew Frank would have supported me. That's what I *should* have done.

I also could have refused to show up to The Restaurant at all. Jeff would have been unable to do it without me, so it could have been as simple as that.

Or perhaps I could have barred the doors, threw away the key and never looked back.

There were a lot of things I *should have* done, but there was a part of me that thought I needed *one last night*. I thought we needed to give our customers an explanation, even if that explanation wasn't the truth. I thought we needed to give them one last 'hoorah.' I thought I needed to put out one more menu so I let my ego — and Jeff — talk me into staying open for one last weekend.

If I could go back in time, I would have chosen to close the doors of The Restaurant before that weekend began. I thought I was doing the right thing for everyone, but by the time the night was over, I felt like such a sellout. *There is no right way to do the wrong thing.*

It would take me a long time to wring the shame of that out from my story.

It would take a sincere apology to Frank. When I told him that it should have been him there with me that night, instead of Jeff, I meant it. But it would take truly acknowledging what I had done to him, face to face, to start repairing our friendship.

It would take checking in on Sara and Brandon and making sure they found work and were doing okay. It would take time and effort to nurture my friendships with them back to health.

It would take trying to make amends with everyone I hurt or let down.

It would take an apology to Mackenzie, if she would hear me.

It would take helping Rachel pay for a lawyer if that's what she decided, and telling her I would stand up in court next to her, and really meaning it.

It would take me walking away from my restaurant and eventually filing for bankruptcy. It would take losing *everything*.

It would take letting go of people and friends who no longer fit into my complicated life. It would take realizing that not everyone was going to accept my apologies.

It would take moving back in with my Dad when I was 29 years old.

It would take saying goodbye to one of my favourite dogs.

It would take me accepting all the consequences of everything I'd done.

It would take working on this book for 35 months until I was brave enough to release my shame.

———

I'd been building a shield of lies around myself for nearly two years now. My shield was thick and heavy; it had become impenetrable. When Frank had tried to break through it, I resented him for it. It's why I couldn't open up to him. It's why I believed Jeff's lies about him. It's why I stopped going out with my friends; why I stopped calling my parents. I was afraid if someone broke through my armour, they would know all my secrets and they would see the darkness building inside of me. So I built my shield up and plastered it with lies. My shield had made me blind and ignorant to what was really going on around me. It made me abrasive and short with people, and most of all, it kept the lies in and kept the love out.

Sitting in my car that night, I felt like an overstuffed ravioli that was going to rupture. I called my sister and asked if she would stay with me that night. I picked her up and drove home. We stayed up for a while as I confessed my fear of what was to come.

178

As I started worrying and wondering about who would get our dogs, our friends, our money and our stuff, there was something else lingering in my heart.

It was a feeling I *barely* even recognized. It was soft and quiet — just a glimmer. Like a dot of cream in a giant pot. It clawed at me as I finally closed my eyes and tried to sleep.

I thought it was maybe a sense of *relief* that the weekend and that chapter of my life were *finally* over. As my eyes got heavy, and my sister's breath slowed as she fell asleep, I finally realized what that feeling was. It took me by such a surprise, if I'd had an ounce of energy left, it would have brought me to my knees.

... It was *hope*.

Sometimes a moment can look and feel like salt on our fingertips, but when we look closer and bring it to our lips, we find out that it is actually sugar.

SARA'S MELON GAZPACHO (V) (GF)

MAKES 2 LARGE BOWLS, 4 SMALL BOWLS OR 6 TEACUPS

This soup is best made in the middle of melon season (which, where I'm from, lies somewhere between early August and mid-September) but if you're craving something super refreshing, you can make this any time of the year. You can swap out the melons in this recipe for your favourite. Just make sure you find the best, sweetest melons you can.

For The Gazpacho
250 grams (about 1 cup) cantaloupe, peeled, seeded and chunked
250 grams (about 1 cup) honeydew, peeled, seeded and chunked
200 grams (about ¾ cup) cucumber, peeled and roughly chopped
¼ cup white onion, peeled and roughly chopped
1 thumb sized piece of ginger, peeled

½ cup coconut milk
15 leaves of fresh basil, plus extra for garnish
15 leaves of fresh mint, plus extra for garnish
1 tbsp sugar
½ tsp salt

Zest and juice of 1 lime

Sara's Method
Blend melon, cucumber, onion and ginger in a high powered blender until smooth. There is no need to add water — the melons should be juicy enough on their own. Strain this mixture through the finest strainer you have (or cheesecloth) using a spatula or spoon to push everything through.

Return to the blender and add coconut milk, mint, basil, salt and sugar. Blend for one minute and strain again. Lastly, add lime juice and zest, stir well and adjust seasoning if necessary.

This soup should be served very cold. It will taste better a few hours after you make it. For bonus points, garnish with extra fresh herbs or slices of melon or cucumber.

PART THREE

"WHERE THERE IS RUIN,
THERE IS HOPE FOR A TREASURE."

- RUMI

My sister was lying beside me when I woke. I decided not to wake her and quietly moved to the living room by myself. I pet my dogs a little longer than I usually did and then curled up on the couch with a blanket as my anxiety and coffee both percolated. The idea of not rushing to The Restaurant like any other morning haunted me more than it comforted me.

I scanned my living room walls and the memories of Jeff poured in. I pulled the blanket tighter around me so it partially covered my eyes as if I was a child watching a scary movie. I sat with my eyes closed for a while and when I opened them, they gravitated towards my journal sitting on the edge of my desk under a pile of receipts and half written menus. I opened it to the most recent entry and it hit me how long it'd been since I'd written. I remembered that moment, because my diary entry had frightened me so much that I decided to seek therapy that very day.

I used to have marathon writing sessions when I was young. Even as a child, I would write endlessly about my little life, often becoming a play by play of my day, sometimes sinking deeper into my aspiration for fitting in. When I got older, I would get high and write about bigger things — confusion about my sexuality, stories of addiction. When I found my love of food, I would obsessively scribble new recipes and stories about my successes and failures in the kitchen. It'd been a long time since I wrote like that — I'd lost my words over the last few years and when I did remember them, I was terrified of what I might say. I picked up the pen resting in the spine of the book and started to swirl the pen on the paper. My mind raced, and as I swirled, words began to form.

Exactly one week ago I was sitting on Di's couch, speaking the truth for the first time in a long time, and I wrote about that, and how everything was different now. Once I started, the words rushed out of me like cutting into a perfectly baked molten lava cake. My words raced towards the edges of my paper, just like chocolate to the corners of the plate. My writing turned to fury as I feared not being able to get the words out fast enough. If I didn't put them down, right now, they would disappear, so I wrote and wrote until my hand cramped so badly that I couldn't write anymore.

I closed my eyes for a moment and took a deep breath. It'd been a long time since I'd done that too.

As I began to massage a cramp from my hand, I looked down at my fingers. I had a callus on the inside of my right middle finger that had developed after those marathon writing sessions and it never fully healed. I rubbed it gently with my thumb — it was faint now, almost entirely gone, but this sudden burst of writing had caused it to flare up and I wanted *more*. I wanted *clarity*. I wanted to analyze how I got here.

My sister was awake and looking for me. She sleepily poked her head into the living room and asked if I was okay, which triggered a vivid memory that knocked the wind out of me. Jeff used to stand in the doorframe of the living room. Some mornings, when I got up early for work, he'd peek around the door, in his boxers, lean his head on the wooden frame, and sweetly beg me to come back to bed. I looked forward to it. I'd be sitting there at my desk, writing emails or planning menus, and I'd hear his footsteps coming gently down the hallway. I knew that in just a moment, his messy hair would poke around the doorframe, followed by sleepy eyes and a mischievous grin. "Come back to beddd," he'd say. Then a flash of that charm, "I'll make it worth your whiiiile ..." I would mutter something coy and keep sipping my coffee but moments later, I'd scurry down the hall, jump in the bed and cuddle up next to him.

I was reminded of this, and when I saw my sister standing there, it stung like raw garlic, fresh from the field, on the tip of your tongue.

184

My sister sluggishly walked over and curled up next to me on the couch. We held hands as I quivered with exhaustion and remorse. "I'm sorry I didn't know how bad things had gotten ..." In that moment of realness and rawness on my couch, I clutched her hand and made a confession. I told her that, for a long time, I felt like I couldn't talk to her because she was sick. I didn't want to burden her and add to her stress. It felt impossible to complain about *anything*, when she had a brain tumour. "I could have helped you," she pointed out.

Another confession crossed my lips, "You *did* help me." I told my sister that when my thoughts were getting really dark, I knew I had to stay here until she was fully recovered. I told her that I knew if she woke up in the hospital after surgery and her little sister wasn't there, that she might not make it through, and that I couldn't do that to her, so I stayed. There was a time in the thick of that darkness when she was the *only* reason I stayed.

My sister went on to tell me that sometimes she got so tired of being sick that she didn't want to go on living with her tumour. But that she couldn't leave me either, so *she* stayed.

————

I spent the next several days and weeks leaning on my sister, often crying or having a meltdown. She was my rock — strong and sturdy — despite being sick. She helped me mend my wounds and took care of me. She would eventually help to lead me back into the light and give me hope to start my life over. In the darkest moments when I felt hopeless, she would braid my hair like when we were kids and tell me things would be okay.

We spent nearly every single day together for the next several months and depended on each other in a way that only sisters or best friends can. I took her to dozens of appointments each month, and sat and waited with her when she needed scans or tests. She cooked me dinner and made me tea. I helped her pay for an expensive experimental treatment with some of the cash I had stashed away in my sock drawer. She let me sleep in her bed for days on end when I couldn't face the world.

Some days, I would cry and she would comfort me. Some days, she would cry and I would try to comfort her. Some days, we both cried. A day would come when neither of us would cry. But for now, she was my person and I never hid anything from her again.

My sister was there when my life fell apart.

And she was there as I put it back together.

I retreated inward by turning off my phone and checking out of all my social media accounts. Aside from spending time with my sister, I didn't do much of anything or see anyone for four days.

I felt like I'd been run through the meat grinder; like my nervous system was being pulverized. I was anxious and paranoid and didn't want to see the outside world. I didn't want to explain myself. I didn't feel like being vulnerable or honest anymore. I didn't want to make amends. I didn't want to talk about it but on the fourth day, I had an appointment with my therapist so I reluctantly got out of bed and put myself together enough to leave the house.

I hadn't seen Di since our session 10 days earlier and didn't feel ready to talk to anyone, even her, about what had happened. When I entered her office, she told me that I looked different.

It was true, I told her, I *was* different. There was now a 'Before' and an 'After.'

Before and After — The Restaurant.

Before and After — Jeff.

Before — I was innocent; After — I was a terrible person. I had turned my back on my best friend. I had silenced a woman who had done nothing wrong. I had fired my friends for trying to look out for me. I had lied to the whole world about what happened. I had wished I was dead.

It was as if I was being strangled by my guilt. It was difficult to even look at myself in the mirror, I told Di. "I knew he was dangerous," I kept repeating. "I *knew*. I had evidence. Years of evidence. And I just … let it happen." My voice was weak and feeble. My throat feeling stretched, trying to get the words out, trying to move past the shame I felt consumed by. Di let me finish venting and when she finally spoke, she assured me that even if I couldn't feel hopeful right now, that in time, I would. She promised me that time would heal my wounds and that there was something simple I could do, every day, until then.

Ho'oponopono she explained, was a Hawaiian prayer used to help families with conflict resolution. Modern day therapists use the ancient prayer as a technique for releasing shame, helping with forgiveness and for meditation. The prayer, in itself, is simple. 10 little (big) words:

I'm sorry.

Please forgive me.

Thank you.

I love you.

I felt awkward when she asked me to say it out loud. "Bow your head, clear your mind, say those 10 words and repeat," Di instructed.

"For how long?" I muttered.

"Until you believe them," she replied.

———

If I went straight home after therapy, I'd be going home to an empty house. I wasn't ready to be by myself yet, so I decided to drive to Monica's house instead. "Come on in, I'm baking cookies," she beamed. We hugged and I told her about therapy. "I'm so tired," I blurted out. She offered coffee, and went to the kitchen, but by the time she returned, I had fallen asleep on her couch. She let me rest there and when I woke up, she more or less forced me to eat some cookies and have a tea. It was the first real rest or food I'd had in days.

I ate and we talked, and she told me I looked different too. I was about to launch into the speech I'd given Di about 'Before and After,' but Monica interrupted by stating, "No, it's not that. You look *lighter.*"

I started to cry and she hugged me, hard. "The last time I saw you, you were planning your escape," she observed. "It wasn't your time, babe," she added quietly with tears in her eyes, *"It wasn't your time."*

"I know," I echoed, wiping snot from my face and crying harder now. "And I'm so grateful," I whimpered, barely able to get the words out.

"Me too," Monica said and she held me close.

For the first time in a long time, I meant it — I didn't want to go. I didn't want to leave this world. I had my sister to think about. Sick or not, she needed me to be here for her. I had parents who loved me, people who believed in me and friends who wanted me to live a long, full life. I wanted to watch my dogs grow up.

I felt a little better after leaving Monica's, but I still wasn't ready to go home. It was a beautiful, sunny, bright day, so I decided to take a walk by the river. I watched as a nearby dog lapped water and played on the shore — a tranquil sight as the sun was beginning to set. I found a seat on a damp rock that was nearby and stared into the water.

For the second time in two weeks, I prayed, having gone nearly a decade without talking to God.

I sat there on that rock and thanked God for Monica — she had saved my life that night at the pub, and this was the first time I'd sat and truly acknowledged how grateful I was for her. I knew not everyone got this kind of a chance and I promised God, and myself, that I wouldn't squander it. I asked for guidance. I asked for the strength to make it through whatever was coming next. I looked into my own eyes in the reflection of the river and told myself that I didn't want to go, and I was sorry for wishing that I was dead. I thanked God for this beautiful life; for my second chance, and for my blank slate. I prayed for the strength to start from scratch.

With tears in my eyes that felt as thick as mayonnaise on the end of a spoon, I said, "Thank you for this gift." I recited it over

189

and over. "I'm sorry. Please forgive me. I love you. Thank you. Thank you. Thank you."

———

When I finally went home, I was exhausted from my outing. I instinctively turned the kettle on and started pacing my hallway. I felt uneasy about being alone with my thoughts, so I paced. I shook. I wanted to flee my own body. I paused for a moment to examine one of the pictures hanging on the wall. Memories flooded my mind as if I'd broken a poached egg and the yolk was flowing toward me. Every room of our home was lined with photographs of trips we'd taken and memories we'd made, and now they were all just staring at me.

The photograph I was staring at was from our trip to Panama together. Jeff had invited me to join him at a friend's wedding, just a few weeks after we'd started dating. I leapt at the opportunity to stay with him at a fancy hotel on the beach for a week. We spent that week drunk-in-love, rolling around in our king size bed. I met all his friends including Charlotte, and it was on that trip where I learned about what he'd done to her when they were teenagers. It was on that trip that he wrote our names in the sand and got down on his knees and told me how even though we'd just met, he knew he wanted to spend the rest of his life with me.

I walked further down the hall to look at the other photos — the time we drove to Montreal to visit a friend who was studying there, and stayed in a funky hostel. We ate cheap Chinese food and played board games late into the night. One night, we climbed to the roof of our friend's apartment and shouted like wolves into the city below. As I looked at the photo of us smiling on the roof, I recalled a fight we'd had just a few hours before that photo was taken, because I felt insecure about how friendly he was acting toward one of the girls on the roof. He told me I was acting crazy, which resulted in me feeling silly, for being jealous.

Next, there were several photos from our favourite destination — California. He took me to Napa Valley and surprised me with dinner at the French Laundry once. I ate Oysters and Pearls, which was one of the dishes that made me want to become a chef in the first place, and it was *perfection*. I was as swollen with joy as the oysters were with salt water. We giggled at how many different types of butter they served and stuffed my $8 purse with the complimentary $40 chocolate truffles they gave at the end of the meal. I was invited into the kitchen after dinner where the chefs autographed my menu and I thought I might die from happiness.

Later that week, we rented a car and drove down the coast where we stopped to take photos with the rocky cliffs on one side and the sea in the background, on the other. We each put one arm out the window of our shitty, little rental car and flapped our arms like birds as we drove. We walked along Venice Beach, went to comedy shows, got day drunk on wine tours, walked foggy cobblestone streets, bargained our way through farmers' markets and ate dinner in the park with our legs intertwined.

I looked through every photo I could find from that trip to California. I looked so fucking happy. Was I happy? I wondered. I know I was hurting. I hurt so much every time I thought about him and Alisa together in his truck. But as that week wore on in California, I started to forget.

I was beginning to see a pattern and I didn't like it.

I completely forgot about making tea as I stood in the hallway, holding each memory up to the light. I had to look closely at the photos from the middle years — 'The Happy Years' — 'Before' The Restaurant and 'After' his first betrayal was far behind us. There was a photo of him slurping spaghetti in Italy. We stayed in a vineyard deep in Chianti. There were winding hills and narrow roads — my fear of heights and driving had become unbearable, so I closed my eyes as we whipped around sharp corners. He soothed me, and I let him. It was all part of the *pattern*.

We stayed in a stone farmhouse and slept naked, with our windows wide open, overlooking the grape vines. We ate pasta

191

until we couldn't eat anymore, we drank wine and played ping pong on the terrace. We ate bread drunk with olive oil and a broken ball of mozzarella with the moon and a candle as our only light. We danced in the moonlight on a bridge in Venice. We stayed at the Waldorf Astoria and I wondered to myself, as I fell asleep under the hot, Italian sky, if I would *ever* be this happy again?

I wondered that now as I paced our apartment, alone, and I wanted to smash that stupid photograph of him slurping spaghetti to bits.

———

Jeff understood that when in a foreign country, I would rather visit grocery stores than museums. He let me wander the isles of markets for hours and never complained. He also didn't seem to mind that I always requested a seat at the bar, even at fancy restaurants where we could have sat at a private table. I wanted to eat in silence as I watched the chefs in the background work, always in awe. It was *our thing*. Jeff was my match when it came to eating and drinking — the ideal travel mate. He was silly and adventurous, and he was also the calm, sensible one in moments of high stress. He was the spontaneous one who took my hand and ran into the ocean in his suit in the middle of the night. He was the one who could make me forget all the hardships going on in the back of our relationship, and each trip we took, I fell more and more in love with him.

Travelling together became part of our identity — we were the power couple with thousands of happy selfies from all over the world. Now I was staring at our walls, alone, with one of the most recent photos of us staring back at me. It was a photo of us on the patio of a swanky restaurant in Toronto. He was there taking a course and called me in the morning to say he passed his final exam. He informed me that he was going to be staying an extra night to celebrate. I was over the moon for him and decided to surprise him that afternoon. I got dressed up, took the train to the city and showed up in the lobby of the hotel. We hugged and kissed and then decided to go for a quiet dinner, just us two. We ordered the tasting menu and a bottle of wine that was older than me. We posted a picture — the picture I was now staring at — being sure to use the hashtags *#DateNight #DreamCrushing #CoupleGoals*. We stayed at that restaurant until it closed and stumbled back to our hotel room and had drunk, ravenous hotel sex.

At first glance, it *was* a happy photo. But then, like the others, I held it up to the light. I recalled why I had decided to surprise him, in person, that day. It was because I felt threatened by one of the girls in his class. I knew he would be having dinner with her, if I didn't go steal him away. I couldn't stand the thought of them having dinner together because I worried it might lead to more, so I impulsively bought a train ticket, as a desperate attempt to make a memory with him, instead. And although we *look* happy in that photo, and perhaps we were in that moment, the deeper I looked at that photo and all the others, I realized that we weren't going to be okay when that photo was taken. I realized in that moment standing in my hallway, that we *never were.*

I continued scanning every photo that my hallway bore until my heart was black and blue. I picked apart each memory until I understood each and every one, for what they truly were. Hours had passed, as I held each one up to the light. There were red flags in every smile, in every glass of wine, in every family outing, in every memory. My grief was now a bottomless cup.

———

Later that evening, when I was ready for bed, I called Chloe. I wanted to calmly tell her everything, but as I started to speak, my shame began to spill over, like a carelessly poured pint glass. I was so remorseful, for everything I'd done, but especially for being willing to walk away from a two decade long friendship with her because Jeff *told me to.* I told her how sorry I was for letting him convince me that she wasn't a good friend, even if it was just for a moment. I told her how sorry I was for not reaching

193

out to Sam when she asked me to, and I cried and cried into the phone.

"It took me two whole days, Chloe," I stammered, choking back tears. "It took me two whole days to see that giving those girls those contracts was *wrong*. What kind of person does that?! If I were a *good* person, I would have seen it right away. If I were a good person I would never have asked you and Sam to——"

Chloe interjected, "You were a *tired* person, Yoda. You were a beaten down person. You were a manipulated person." She repeated the word 'manipulated' again, slowly and broken into its syllables for emphasis. "When that happened with Sam, that wasn't your fault. Okay? Yes, you could have done things differently … but you were being manipulated by someone who is really dangerous, so you can't blame yourself. You are a victim in all of this too. We all are. You. Me. Sam. Those girls. It's not your fault, and I need you to know that."

Chloe had known all along that Jeff wasn't good for me, but she also knew that if she pushed, she might lose me forever. So she tried to grin and bear it, for over a year. I think she hoped I would see it someday, and was just waiting for me to come back to reality.

She stayed on the phone with me that night until I could assure her that I would be okay for the night. When we ended the conversation she told me that she was proud of me. "Sam is proud of you too, you know that right?"

Those words.

When I hung up the phone, I sunk deep into my pillows and I thanked Chloe over and over for not leaving me despite everything I'd done. *I'm so sorry. Please forgive me.* She was the one person in my life who understood my entire story from beginning to end. She'd been there, through everything, even when I tried to push her away. *I love you. Thank you.*

Chloe continued to check in and would continue telling me that what happened wasn't my fault until I believed it was true. It would take time, like everything else, and we had many lessons yet to learn, as friends. The next time we spoke on the phone she told me I sounded *relieved.*

I was relieved, I suppose. Relieved to be free from The Restaurant and all the responsibilities it entailed. Relieved to have time to rest and heal. Relieved to finally be able to tell the truth. Relieved to be doing the right thing.

But mostly, I was relieved because I felt like Chloe and I could maybe go back to being the type of friends we were, 'Before' all of this happened. Maybe the 'After' was something to look forward to.

MONICA'S CHOCOLATE CHIP COOKIES

MAKES 12 LARGE OR 25-30 SMALL COOKIES

Monica made me these cookies during one of my lowest lows and I don't know if it was the cookies or her love that cheered me up, but either way, I knew this book would not be complete without this recipe.

Dry Mix
2 cups + 1 tbsp flour
½ tsp baking soda

Wet Mix
225 grams (2 sticks/1 cup) butter, softened
¾ cup brown sugar, packed
¾ cup white sugar
1 tsp vanilla (use the good stuff!)
2 eggs

2 generous cups semi-sweet chocolate chips

Monica's Method
Preheat oven to 315°. Line 2 cookie sheets with parchment paper.

Mix dry ingredients together in a bowl. Set aside.

In a mixing bowl, use the paddle attachment to cream butter and sugars together until light and fluffy. If you're doing this by hand, really use your muscles to incorporate some air. Add vanilla. Next, on low speed, add eggs, one at a time, letting them combine fully (scrape down the sides) before adding the next. Next, on low speed, add your dry mix in three stages, scraping down the bowl each time. On your last addition, add the chocolate chips as well.

Using a large spoon or scoop, place balls of dough on cookie sheets, making sure to leave 2-3 finger widths in between to allow them to spread. This recipe will make 12 large cookies, which you should bake for 15 minutes. (If making smaller cookies, bake for 12 minutes.)

Either way, check cookies at the 10 minute mark — you want to see the edges slightly browned. Bake for additional time if necessary but remember — your cookies will continue baking for a minute or two when they come out of the oven (from the residual heat of the tray,) so it's best to take your cookies out of the oven just *before* they are done, so they remain chewy.

Jeff was on his way to the house to pick up some clean clothes. I hadn't seen him since the day The Restaurant closed, and although we'd talked on the phone a few times, I was so nervous about seeing him, I chewed my fingernails like I was gnawing on an olive pit.

I spent the morning lying in bed, mentally preparing myself. Spending time alone in our apartment felt like I was torturing myself, and I knew I couldn't stay there much longer. If we were going to give notice that we were moving out, we'd have to do it by the end of the month, which was fast approaching.

What I really wanted was to stay in bed forever and not have to go through with the day ahead, so I stared at the ceiling for a while. My eyes were pulled to the heart on our wall, just above our bed. Jeff had drawn it with chalk on the day we'd moved in, and put our initials in the middle. I reached up and closed my eyes as I traced the edges of that heart with my fingertips.

I let the truth sink in.

The truth was that all I wanted was for Jeff to be a man that I could be proud of.

But he *wasn't*.

Resentment bubbled up as reality set in. Memories came up from all angles and all sides as I considered the fact that we would soon have to move out of the home we'd shared together for years. The day we adopted our dog. Morning sex. Family Christmas. Eating pizza at our table while we played cards late into the night. Watching movies in a fort. Slow dancing in our underwear. Even silly things like folding laundry and eating breakfast together. The times he opened a bottle of expensive champagne *just because*. We'd drink it straight from the bottle and when I asked the occasion, he would say, "You." I yearned for that version of that man, even though I knew it was all an act.

I got out of bed and sat on the front steps of our home while I waited for Jeff. When he arrived, I noticed he was thin and dishevelled, and had bags under his eyes, showing obvious signs of not eating or sleeping well. I'm sure I looked just as rough.

He took a seat next to me on the steps and we started discussing the logistics of our dogs and car payments. After a few minutes, he went inside to gather his things, and I stayed on the steps to give him some privacy. I stared out onto the yard while I waited, actively gathering all the bravery that it was going to take to bring up the topic of moving out of our home for good. I didn't want to rock the boat or hurt him, but now was not the time to spare his feelings. I took a few deep breaths and joined him inside. I found him standing in the doorway of our bedroom, looking at that heart drawn on the wall, with big, hearty tears in his eyes. He leaned in for a hug and before I could think twice about it, I was hugging him back. I *needed* him in that moment as much as he needed me. Maybe more. As I held him, he began to say all the things he should have said.

He told me that if he could take it all back, he would.

He told me that he was an idiot and begged me to forgive him.

He cried into my t-shirt until it was soaked. "If I could take it all back and buy you flowers every single day, and come to bed with you every single night, I would. I never would have opened The Restaurant. I would have listened to you and we could have just gone to Costa Rica like you wanted …."

He lifted his head and looked me square in the eyes. I knew with every piece of my being that I *had* to leave.

Right then, in that moment, I had to go, or I never would.

Moments matter.

As I began to push away, he pleaded with me. I recoiled and as he saw me slipping away, he took one last stab at convincing

198

me to stay when he uttered, "You would make such a good mother ……." His voice cracked while he wept like a child, holding back nothing. I stiffened my back, let go of his hand and gently pushed him away from me.

Like a skilled butcher scraping every last piece of meat from the bone, I summoned the last bit of my strength and told him I had to go. I had finally chosen to leave the table because there was nothing left there, to serve me.

As I walked away, I turned and told him that I was giving notice on our apartment and moving back home with my Dad. He let out a gasp and melted onto the floor. There was a piece of me that wanted to stay and comfort him, but I shut her up and summoned more strength. Scraping together every morsel I had, I squeezed his hand one last time, and walked out our front door.

I was not strong then.

But I am strong now.

I had been wrapped around a man's finger for more than six years. It wasn't going to just be unwound because I said so.

For the next month I stewed in my anger, eventually adopting the mantra that Men. Are. Scum. Every single one of them.

This new belief I had adopted in an effort to protect myself and soothe some of my resentment towards Jeff arrived just in time for the #MeToo movement. Each story I heard for the next several weeks reaffirmed my belief — *Men. Are. Scum.* The evidence was clear.

The heaviness of this deep, dark, core belief weighed on me as much as my grief did. It would cause me to run from anyone who tried to love me, and it ensured that I would never have to care about another man again.

Men are scum — simple as that.

And then …

… I remembered my father.

I called my Dad on the morning of August 20th and declared, "Dad... I need to move back home for a bit ... And I need you to not ask why, okay?" Within a week, my old bedroom (which had been converted into a pseudo storage unit), was cleared out and I was back to sleeping on the small twin bed I slept on when I was a child.

My Dad's house had not only been the place where I'd grown up, but it was also the place I ran to whenever life got hard as an adult. The truth is that I loved it there, but I certainly didn't see myself ever moving back, especially when I was almost 30-years-old. I knew how lucky I was to be able to go back to the home where I was raised, and how lucky I was to be there, in my safe space, with such a wonderful human. On my first night, he barbequed a pizza, poured me a glass of wine and asked what happened.

Before that night with my Dad, I thought I might save some of the poignant details, to spare my Dad from any discomfort. But as I sat across from my father in our living room that night, the words just poured out of me, like hot butter over popcorn. I told him the story from beginning to end like it was the first time I told it. We talked in his living room that night, for hours. When I was done, he looked as heartbroken as I felt.

———

My Dad has never been one to say, "*I love you.*" Not because he's cold — in fact he's actually incredibly kind, warm and light-hearted — but because he's always been a bit emotionally withdrawn. He has a social awkwardness to him that causes him to keep his distance in difficult situations. Strong emotions had always been challenging for him, but as an adult, I grew to know him as a man who was sensitive and thoughtful. He just didn't think he knew the way into peoples' hearts, so he often stood on the sidelines.

When I moved back home with him, I don't think he fully knew how to handle it, but he found his way. We had a deep-rooted, close relationship, and I think we both considered each other a friend more than the traditional father-daughter dynamic. My Dad didn't cry with me like my sister had, but he brought me tea when I couldn't get out of bed. He didn't threaten to beat Jeff up like some of my male friends had, but he told me I did the right thing and he was proud of me.

Over the next few months, he found ways to be my friend and father. He set up a fridge for me in his garage so I could get my catering company back up and running again, if and when I was ready. He hung a single string of Christmas lights on our houseplant when I told him how much I was going to miss Christmas with Jeff's family. He drove me to the airport when I went travelling. He welcomed my friends into his home and made them feel warm. He took care of my dog when I couldn't.

My Dad might not be the type of father who openly says *"I love you,"* but every single time I left the house that winter, he'd caution me to, "Watch out for deer." Every. Single. Time.

That year, my Dad stepped up to be *my parent*. Not my friend, not my buddy, not my roommate who just happened to be blood related. That year, he was *my father.*

———

Eventually, my Dad's home became my home, again. Each morning when I woke, I listened for the familiar creek of the front door being opened to let the morning sun in. I listened for the sound of the broken burner on our ancient gas stove taking a few times to light, when my Dad would get coffee started in the morning. I listened to what sounded like laughter through the windows, but was actually the alpacas at the farm down the road. I spent the afternoons in the hammock he hung for me on a tree limb. On the days I felt able to get up and be productive, I helped

204

him in the garden. We harvested chamomile flowers and dried them for tea. We shingled his roof. We made pizza and cooked it on the barbeque and had dinner together almost every night. We played cards until we were too sleepy to keep our eyes open. We listened to old records and talked about the world. We shared wine and stories of travel and every time I'd leave the house he'd remind me, "Watch out for deer," and I'd say, "You too, Dad."

What a relief it was to be spending the rest of that summer in the hammock, sitting next to a soy field, reading a book by the light of the sun, listening to laughing alpacas, feeling safe and wanted.

———

After a few healing weeks at my Dad's house, I knew it was time to visit my mother as well. I knew she would take care of me and not ask too many questions. The trip to her house was the farthest I'd been outside for weeks, and by the time I made it to her apartment door, the act of just leaving the house had made me feel drunk with grief. My mother helped me over to her couch and as I began telling her what happened, she motioned, "Shhh, baby. You sleep now."

When I woke up I was covered in a blanket and my mother was in the kitchen. I knew without asking that she was making chicken soup. I could hear the broth bubbling on the stove and the blade of her knife sliced through what sounded like carrots or onion. I could hear her humming while she tasted the base of her soup, and without being able to see her, I could tell she was adding a pinch of salt. Later she would strain the broth, add some fresh vegetables and herbs and serve me a big bowl of hot, steaming soup.

After my mother left, I waited nearly a year to go see her new apartment. I'm sure she needed me then, but she also knew I needed space to work through her departure in my own way. My mother understood me in a way that I'm not sure I ever truly appreciated. She didn't push me when I was young and screamed, "Self!" She didn't question my motives over the years, no matter how unusual my decisions. And she didn't demand anything from me now. She was just *my mother*. My mother who made me soup, loved me endlessly, bought me books and wanted nothing but the best for me.

"Things will be okay," my mother insisted.

"How do you know? ... And don't say, *'Because I'm your mother.'*" I replied, snidely.

"I know you'll be okay because I lost the love of my life and I'm okay ... And because I'm your mother." She winked.

My mother knew what it felt like to *stay* — to try your hardest to make something work that wasn't meant to. She empathized with what it felt like to lose everything and feel broken. I think I understood my mother more in that moment than I had ever even tried to, and I didn't feel confused or angry anymore, for the first time in a long time. We'd both been through hell and back. We'd both lost love. We both knew what it felt like to be alone.

In that moment, while I was eating the soup she'd made, I felt like a warm blanket had been draped over me. I realized that no matter what, my mother would *always* love me. She didn't care about my shame or my guilt or what I had done. She loved me, unconditionally, in a way that maybe only a mother can, and she'd been showing me that in one way or another since the day I was born. She showed me with books and memories and chicken soup and love.

As I began to let go of everything I had been holding onto since the day she left, my belly full and my heart a little lighter, I started to feel tired. As I began to fall asleep, I could hear her whispering how much she loved me, as my eyes got heavier and heavier.

DAD'S PIZZA
MAKES ONE 13" MEDIUM THICK CRUST NY STYLE PIZZA OR TWO 8" THIN CRUSTS

My father has been making this pizza every Friday night for years. It's a ritual in his home, and if I ever visit him on a weekend, I know there will be cold pizza waiting for me. He goes all-out sometimes and makes his own cheese and sauce, but you can keep this simple by putting your efforts into the dough itself. This recipe is very easy — you just need a hot oven, some pantry staples and your favourite pizza toppings. It's a fun recipe to make with kids or for your next summer barbeque.

For The Dough
½ cup warm water
Pinch of sugar
½ tsp active dry yeast
220 grams (1 ⅓ cup) flour
½ tsp salt
½ tsp olive oil
Semolina flour, for dusting

A Note About Pizza Toppings
According to my Dad, "Anything goes."
A traditional pizza is just tomato sauce with mozzarella cheese on top. My Dad's favourite pizza goes like this: 2 cups of mixed grated cheese, sliced yellow onion, mushroom, peppers (fresh or pickled pepperoncini and pimento), olives and homemade pepperoni slices. Whatever you do, make sure you sprinkle on a good dose of dried oregano and some garlic powder. Then a good overall drizzle of olive oil just before shoving it into a hot oven or barbeque. This is the secret to really good pizza.

A Note About Pizza Sauce
A good sauce is important. Use a good ready-made or make your own. You only need about ½ cup for a medium size pizza. Use crushed or whole canned tomatoes, blend them up with a fork (you don't need to purée it), add 1-2 tsp of tomato paste to thicken it. Add a hearty pinch of dried oregano, black pepper, and garlic or onion powder to spice it up. Spread it on the pizza evenly.

207

A Note About Barbequing Pizza

Pizza on the barbeque is easy and a lot cooler on a hot summer night! The crust tends to get done quicker than the top though. Placing it on an overturned pizza pan will help shield the crust. Bake on barbeque, with the lid closed, same as above — 450° for about eight minutes. Because all barbeques tend to heat differently, you must check the pizza regularly.

My Father's Method

Measure water (make sure it's warm, like the temperature of a bath) in small dish. Add pinch of sugar and stir to dissolve. Sprinkle yeast on surface and let it sit to dissolve and activate (about 15 minutes).

Measure flour and salt into mixing bowl. Add the oil to the yeast mix when it's ready and pour into flour mix. If using stand mixer, use the dough hook attachment for about 2 minutes. Scrape sides down and continue to knead for 2-3 more minutes. If kneading by hand, stir flour and yeast mix with spoon until it forms rough dough. Empty onto floured surface and knead for about 5 minutes until dough is smooth looking. Dough is at right stage when it is soft, silky, not wet and has a give when pressed — like the inside of your forearm. Coat the inside of a large bowl lightly with olive oil. Place dough ball in the bowl and cover with plastic wrap. Place bowl in a warm place (at the back of your oven, on a table close to a vent or near a sunny window) to rise to 2-3 times its original size (about 2 hours).

When dough has risen, sprinkle your work surface with some semolina flour — this will give it a crunchy crust. Scoop dough out of the bowl onto surface, and sprinkle a little flour on the dough. Press and flatten into a disk with palm of your hand. Rotate and flip dough while doing this until formed into about a 9" diameter with the centre a bit thinner than the outside edge. Begin stretching by grabbing an edge and pulling slowly while holding the centre with your other hand. Spin dough a bit and repeat until dough is about 14" diameter. Dough can also be stretched by lifting it up, draping over fists and pulling out. Toss and spin it in the air if you feel lucky!

Drop stretched dough onto a lightly oiled pizza pan and pull lightly into position to edge. Cover with a towel in warm spot to let rise again a bit while you get the toppings prepared. Also, now is a good time to preheat your oven or barbeque to 450°.

When oven is up to temp, and your pizza is topped with a great sauce and lots of toppings, slide pizza onto the middle rack of your oven, or into a hot barbeque. Set timer for 8 minutes.

Check for doneness by lifting edge of crust. It should be slightly stiff and lightly toasted underneath. Let it bake a minute or two longer if it's not done, but check it every minute. It'll burn very quick once the underside starts to brown. Once ready, remove pizza from oven/barbeque. Toss on some rough chopped basil or your favourite herbs.

Now for the tricky part ... it's best to let your pizza cool 10 minutes before slicing! The last step is to crack a beer, play some CBC radio and eat at least half of your beautiful creation! This pizza is also delicious the next day, reheated, or eaten cold.

 I'd been avoiding visiting Ruby and Doug for over a month despite them constantly calling and checking in. I didn't feel ready to face them and their perfect marriage.

Although I was not related to Doug and Ruby by blood, I always wished I had been because that would mean inheriting some of their seemingly flawless genetics. Doug was tall and thick, a full head of just slightly grey hair despite being in his late 70s. He had been my pseudo grandfather, or maybe great uncle, since I was a child. Ruby was his stunning counterpart — always dressed up, full face of makeup and she always smelt of cinnamon and lavender. She treated me like a grandma would treat her only granddaughter.

I loved Ruby and Doug as much as I loved anyone in my actual family. I'd grown up thinking of them as even more than family — they were a part of me. But, when I finally went to visit them that day, my guard was up. I felt anxious and uncomfortable and told myself the visit would be quick, and then I could retreat back to bed, back to grief.

When I walked into their apartment that day, Ruby was sitting at the kitchen table eating a grapefruit and told me Doug was napping. Ruby motioned for me to sit down. We'd shared hundreds of hours at this table, sharing food and stories. Ruby was an incredible storyteller, having moved to Canada with just $20 and the clothes on her back, escaping from a war zone when she was just a teenager. She told a few short stories that afternoon as I contorted in my chair, until I finally caved and told her what had happened between Jeff and me.

Despite being determined not to, I started to cry. Ruby got up from her chair and hugged my whole body with her frail arms. I took a deep breath in, cinnamon filling my nostrils. "Life is hard, sweet girl. Isn't it? I know exactly how you feel darling. It will be

211

okay. It will work itself out." She patted my back and moved back to her chair, handing me some tissues.

I wasn't sure what she meant when she said she knew how I felt — she had been happily married to Doug for over 50 years. Their marriage was part of the reason I desired their genetics — I had hoped to inherit some of the qualities that were responsible for one of the most happy, healthy relationships I'd ever seen. Ruby and Doug loved each other wildly. They stared at each other from across the room and smiled back at one another, brimming with deep love. They hugged and kissed like they were teenagers and expressed their love for each other constantly.

I didn't know it when I sat down that day, but today was the day that Ruby was going to tell me her own truth.

———

For the next half hour or so, Ruby shared the story of Doug's affair with me — a story I had never heard even a whisper of and almost didn't believe. She told me that when they were young, Doug had an affair with one of his colleagues at work. It was the 1960s at the time and with no job and two young kids, she felt trapped. So, she did everything she could think of to save the marriage. This included calling Doug's mistress on the phone one day to threaten her life, if she didn't leave town.

For years after the infidelity, their marriage struggled. They both felt empty and hopeless, but wanted to honour the vows they made in front of God when they got married, so they were willing to *try*. They wanted to try to save the family for their young children and to save themselves from what they viewed as public humiliation. There were many reasons to stay, Ruby explained, but in the end, Ruby stayed for *love*.

"Sometimes people get lost," Ruby stated. "And if we love them, and believe in them, we stick around to see if they find themselves." She put her hand on my knee and looked me straight in the eyes and smiled genuinely until I looked away. I didn't know what to make of the story but her deep-rooted grief mingled

212

with my fresh grief in a dance of silence, meaningful glances and tears.

Shortly after my tears had dried, Doug wandered sleepily into the dining room. He hobbled over to give me a hug and kissed Ruby's head, asking if she wanted a grapefruit. After making coffee, he sat down at the table and I explained to him too, what had happened with Jeff. We sat at their kitchen table for a long time, holding hands on their antique, linen tablecloth. Doug leaned in and lifted my chin to wipe the tears from my face. As I looked into his eyes, him gently smiling back, I decided, almost involuntarily, that I wasn't going to be angry with Doug.

He was flawed, like all of us, but I *knew* he was a good man. I knew it because I had witnessed it my whole life. He had loved me like a granddaughter and had been nothing but good to me — I didn't even need to look for the evidence. I was witnessing it right now as he wiped my tears and held my hand. Doug was a good man who had made amends for what he had done.

———

Sometimes people get lost, and if we love them, we stick around to see if they find themselves. It was a powerful revelation and although I wasn't sure if I fully believed it yet, I was choosing to believe in that moment of forgiving Doug, that good people are capable of doing bad things.

The problem with Ruby's theory was that it didn't explain what to do when *bad* people do bad things.

When I asked myself that question, I wasn't asking about Jeff. I was asking about *myself.* I had made up my mind that I was just as bad of a person as he was. It was time for me to start making amends.

I started my pursuit of amends with Frank. He, along with Rachel and Mackenzie were the ones who I felt I had wronged the most. I contacted each of them with the intention of apologizing, and making sure that they were all okay.

On Frank's birthday, I drove over to his house with a wrapped gift under my arm and knocked on his door. I was nervous but to my surprise, he gave me a warm hug and told me he was happy to see me. I fidgeted nervously while we stood in his hallway making small talk, feeling like I wanted to throw my gift in the air and flee. Instead, we went for a walk and sat in a quiet sunbeam with some tea. The warmth of the sun and the chamomile tea made me feel safe enough to open up to him. We talked for *hours* that day, sharing every single detail of the days and weeks leading up to The Restaurant closing. He told me what it had been like for him, what he observed and how he felt, and I did the same. We weren't two friends just casually catching up — we were reliving some of the most painful days of our lives. Out loud. Face to face. This was a situation I would normally have sprinted from, as fast as I could, but here we were, being brutally honest with each other and it meant everything to me, to stay.

Frank showed me his anger that day, and I countered with understanding. I showed him my remorse, and he responded with compassion. We found a way to meet in the middle of anger and remorse, and told each other the truth. It wasn't an easy conversation, but by the end of it, I think we both felt at peace.

Frank told me that it was easy to forgive me because he knew that the decisions I made weren't my own. He had seen Jeff's hold on me since the day we met, before we opened The Restaurant, when we were renovating and making simple design decisions. He watched me struggle for 16 months, and didn't know how to

215

tell me how bad it was getting until it was too late, so he just tried to be there for me and be a good friend.

That day, I told Frank that he *was* a good friend, and that I was sorry for allowing Jeff to ever question that.

When it got dark, we retired from our sunbeam that had slipped away and went back to his apartment to talk a while longer. I was glad I got the chance to look him in the eyes and apologize for everything, and to tell him how grateful I was for his friendship. "I'm just glad you're okay, Boss." I knew he was being sincere when he playfully nudged my shoulder like he used to do every day at The Restaurant. I didn't *feel* like I was okay though. I confessed to him how scared I was about my financial situation and how life as I knew it was a total mess. "I know it's hard because you have all this shit to deal with and he's just out there walking the world ... but *you got out.* You can live your life without someone like that dragging you down."

"It just took me *so* long——" I trailed off, my shame seeping out of every pore.

"You know what I think?" Frank asked, interrupting my thoughts. "I think if you hadn't gotten out exactly when you did, we would have found you at the end of a rope."

It had been an incredibly narrow escape ... but I had *escaped.* I got out. Like Frank said, I had to find a way to be grateful for my chance to start over.

———

A few weeks after that day, Frank came to The Restaurant to help me pack up the last of the glassware and kitchen equipment. When we finished packing, he asked what I wanted to do with the box of expensive glassware that was sitting on the bar. I opened the lid and examined all the fancy crystal wine glasses and decanters I'd bought for Jeff over the years. I looked up at Frank and it was unanimously decided: Smash It! It was the last day either of us would ever step foot into that place, and our violent whipping of glasses across the ceramic floor felt more like a celebration than a funeral. It felt like we were celebrating my narrow escape and that someday, he and I would be okay.

As Frank swept the floor that day for one final time, I picked up a piece of glass and decided to keep it. To this day, it still reminds me that life is fragile and friendships take work.

———

The conversation I had with Frank that day gave me courage, so I decided not to waste any time, and went to visit Rachel. After The Restaurant closed, she followed her dreams of opening a boutique store, so I decided to visit her there on the day of her Grand Opening hoping we could talk. She might turn me away or throw me out, but I had to try.

When I arrived, Rachel saw me through the big glass windows of the front of the building, burst through the door, ran across the parking lot and hugged me *hard*. I thought I knew Rachel's side of the story because it had been told to me by people I trusted. But hearing her account of what happened in her own words shook me to my core. I wanted to flee … but I came here for the truth and I wasn't leaving now. This was my chance to expand and listen and give her the love that she deserved. So, I sat and listened. I listened as she told me how aggressive Jeff had been with her. How much she dreaded coming to work every day; about how she was scared that if she told him to back off, she would lose her job. She didn't know how to tell me, she said.

"I *really* didn't do anything to encourage his behaviour. I swear."

Those words.

When I heard those words come from her mouth, I realized how much *damage* had been done. Jeff may be innocent until proven guilty, and Jeff may have his *own* version of what took place at The Restaurant. But there is only one truth. And everyone who was there in those final days and weeks knows what that truth is.

It was easy for me to believe Rachel because I'd lived through similar moments of feeling unsafe and uncomfortable in my workplace. I knew it was something that happened frequently in the hospitality industry. But I needed her to know that sexual harassment is *not* okay. It shouldn't be a thing that we excuse just *because* it happens. I needed her to know that just because our industry had all kinds of ways to justify it, it doesn't make it *her* fault. I needed her to know that I was sorry for creating a work environment that failed to protect her from that kind of thing. I needed her to know that if she needed anything, I would help her. So, I told her that if she needed to talk to a therapist, I would help her pay for one. I made it crystal clear to her that if she ever wanted to press charges, I would help her financially, physically, emotionally... whatever she needed, and I meant it.

Before I left the store that night, Rachel and I embraced and I felt a weight lifted from my shoulders that had been there for so long, it actually made me dizzy now that it was lifted. I left feeling hopeful not only that Rachel would be okay, but that she and I could be friends.

———

The final person I desperately wanted to make amends with was Mackenzie. She was so young and innocent in all of this. I had heard from Frank and a few others who were keeping in touch with her that she was so traumatized by what happened that she moved away. I texted her several times to tell her that I was there for her if she needed anything, but I never heard back. I eventually asked Frank to pass along a message for me. He told me he would try, but added, "I think she just wants to move on ..."

Eventually I decided to respect the space she was obviously creating between us. All I could do now was hope she was happy, and hold faith that someday I would have the chance to tell her I was sorry, in person.

———

I checked in on the rest of The Restaurant family often, to make sure they were coping with the aftermath. Forgiveness came in waves and then tapered off. There were ebbs and flows and a nuanced grief that hung around for a while when I spent time with Rachel or Frank. The moving on and letting go that had to take place in our little family was full of heart and earnestly complex.

When I finally felt strong enough to tell my closest girlfriends bits and pieces of what Jeff had done, they all immediately reassured me by saying that if they ever saw him do *anything,* they would have told me. "I know you would have," I assured them back. I knew that if they had told me they'd witnessed him doing something shady, I probably wouldn't have believed them at the time. It was hard to accept, as the truth often is.

Over the next several months, I sat with a lot of my friends and told them how sorry I was for being absent for so long. *I'm sorry.*

I asked for forgiveness for allowing him sway my trust in them or create a rift between us. *Please forgive me.*

I told them how grateful I was that they were here for me now. *I love you. Thank you.*

I started compiling a list of all the people I could trust with my story. I watched as some people in my life turned away when I got to the hard part. I watched as some people retracted when I told the truth. I watched as people pushed away or slipped through the cracks, unable to face the reality of my situation.

It didn't take me long to realize I had a lot more letting go to do.

October arrived, and we could no longer avoid the mountain of tasks that required our attention at The Restaurant. There were accounts to be closed, invoices to be paid, reservations to be cancelled, phone calls to be returned. There were gift certificates to be reimbursed and meetings with our landlord. It seemed like we had to answer questions at every corner. The stress was unbelievable so my priority became getting *out*.

Getting out wasn't as easy as I thought it'd be — there was so much stuff to sort through, sell and divide up. I tried to make the best of it, filling my sister's cupboards with restaurant quality dishes and glassware. I invited Rachel to bring boxes and fill them with things she needed at the store. I boxed up all the small wares and donated them to the Men's Mission. The only things I took with me were the antique tools we had hung on the wall, and my knives. The gas range and fridges were returned to the rental company, and just like that, the kitchen was transformed into an empty shell. It was heartbreaking. And it was a relief.

The day I stood in that shell wasn't the first time I'd stood in a space that was once my own and felt the crushing blow of vacancy. When I had moved from my first tiny catering kitchen to a bigger facility, I remember sitting on the floor of my now vacant space and not knowing how to feel. I wanted to cry, but I just sat there in silence and looked at the hollowness of that now empty, hopeful room. However, on that occasion, I was moving into a bigger, brighter kitchen. Even when catering felt overwhelming, I absolutely loved going there to cook and clean and work and sweat. I'd never felt more of a sense of "Self!" as I did when I was in that kitchen. It was my own, and I loved it there. After we opened The Restaurant, I went to that very kitchen that I loved so much and packed everything into boxes and it went from being a place that I loved more than anything to being an empty shell in almost the blink of an eye. Although it devastated me, I still had somewhere else to go. I wasn't certain that The Restaurant was 'bigger and better' at that point, but it was *something*.

This time around, while I was standing in that vacuum of emptiness, I had nothing. Just an empty restaurant and nowhere to go. Just a few weeks ago I was rolling pasta downstairs, calling chits, and rearranging lettuce on plates. And now … I just … *wasn't*.

I stood in the shrill nothingness, with absolutely no plan, except to get out of there as fast as I could. I walked the perimeter of the dining room which now felt too grand and too little all at once. I caught a glimpse of the letter we'd hastily taped inside the front window the day we closed. It was a copy of the Facebook post we had crafted so carefully. *What a crock of shit,* I thought to myself now.

When we published that letter, there were all kinds of reactions. Some people congratulated us and told us how proud we should be for making such a 'brave' decision. Others formed their own opinions that we were bankrupt or that we weren't busy enough. Customers came in and saw my arm in a sling and they must have seen the bags under my eyes, and those people made their own assumptions that we were just *tired*.

We *were* tired.

But the truth is — The Restaurant did not close because we were *tired*. We did not close because we had another opportunity. We did not close for our family, dogs, or for our future. We did not close The Restaurant so we could launch another dream, as we'd said in that letter hanging from the window, now slightly yellowed from the sun.

We didn't close our doors so we could move to Costa Rica and grow lemons.

We didn't do it for *us* — there was no *us*.

222

We closed The Restaurant because we had to. Because of what *he* did. Because we didn't have another choice.

If I thought for a minute that we could have, I *would have* soldiered on. I would have done it for as long as it took, if I had a single gram of fight left in me ... but I didn't. I had been through so much in those 16 months. For over a year, I *did* soldier on. I *pushed* myself. For 16 months, I stretched myself to my absolute limits and all I was trying to do in those last few weeks and months was stay *strong.*

Even in The Restaurant's final moments, I fought to keep going. I did it for my family and friends who supported me for all those years. I did it for my staff. I did it for the strangers and customers who donated to our crowdfunding campaign because they *believed* in us. I did it for my own ego, too. I did it for the Facebook status. For the happy selfie. For the glory. For the recognition. I soldiered on through whatever physical pain and deprivation I experienced for so long because I knew if I left, I would be financially ruined. I did it because my shoulder was so fucked up that I sincerely believed that any chances of me cooking professionally somewhere else again were slim. I did it because I was *stuck.*

As I stood in my now empty dining room, staring at that letter, I thought about how stuck I felt for so long, and how *free* I was now. And even though that freedom had cost me plenty, I was not willing to go back. Not ever.

As I contemplated this, I started wrapping up the last of the items that mattered in the dining room and I caught a glimpse of my hands in the light. They were worn and scarred from chopping and slicing, hot oil marks and wounds from a decade in the industry. There were blisters and burn marks, calluses and cuts. I stood there, looking at my hands, frozen, thinking long and hard, once more, about *everything* that had transpired here. I took one more walk around, just to be sure I wasn't missing anything. I peeked outside and saw the patio pots that I planted and tended to for two summers. I peered into the bathroom and ran my finger along the chip in the 300 pound sink that I polished by hand until it was shiny. I looked at the baseboards that I scrubbed and stained and the floor that I made white. I looked up at the ceiling that I primed and painted, painted and primed. It was here that I found out I was good at drywalling. It was here that I learned how to properly hang art on the walls, use a drill, cut boards and strip paint. It was here that I lifted, stretched, organized, scraped and chipped away for months until this place sparkled.

I walked into the kitchen and thought of Brandon working the sauté station and smiling even as the long, sweltering summer nights wore on. I touched the contours and curves of the pots and pans hanging on the walls. I thought about Sara's trial shift, and how we all knew immediately that she belonged with us. I thought about Mackenzie and wondered if I'd ever see her again. I thought about Frank consoling me while I curled up into a ball in our dry storage area when the stress got to be too much. As I thought about it, my shoulder ached with muscle memory.

Goosebumps covered my body. It was eerily quiet since all the fridges had been unplugged and the phone ringer turned off. I tried to tell myself that I could be *proud* of what we'd done there. I literally held a stack of comment cards in my hands, praising my food, and under my arm there was a plaque that said we were the city's Best Restaurant. But the proof I held in my hands meant nothing to me in that moment — all I felt was regret and remorse and rage and ruin.

I knew once I left, I could never come back, so I left my keys on the bar and walked out the back door. My shame finally spilling over; my eyes overflowed; as I turned one last time to face all the magic we'd made here, and all the mistakes.

Except, there was no '*we.*'

———

A few days later I would leave another set of keys on another counter and have the same thought. This time, it would be the keys to the home Jeff and I shared and it was almost more than I

224

could bear. I packed up our things, room by room, and ached all over. More muscle memory.

As I tied up all the loose ends of our life together, washed off the heart written in chalk above our bed, and took the pictures in our hallway down, I was angry. I was *so* angry at him for doing something so careless that we could no longer be together. Even when we were at our absolute worst, I always thought that we would make it through it *together.* Even when things were the darkest they'd ever been, I always thought it would be him there, lifting me back into the light. I believed we would handle any storm that came our way.

But not this. We couldn't make it through this, and that's what caused my rage that day.

I'd known it for a while, but it didn't fully sink in until I set our house keys on the counter that day. When I closed my eyes I could still feel his arms around me, slow dancing in that kitchen. I could still feel him waking up next to me in our bed.

I missed him so much in that moment, it quite literally took my breath away. I slid down the wall until I landed on the floor.

We were over. It seeped into every pore like dunking bread into olive oil.

There was no 'divorce' because we'd never actually gotten married. There was no ring or document. But in those moments, it was a divorce. A severance. A complete dismemberment of me from him. We. Were. Over.

There was no 'we.'

When things are messy and it's obvious, people naturally want to comfort you by using all kinds of clichés like, *"This too shall pass,"* and *"Time heals all wounds…"*

We all learn these clichés to be true at one point or another — that everything, even immense pain is temporary. But when you're in the thick of that suffering, and someone wistfully tells you that *"This too shall pass,"* it kind of makes you want to scream in their face. At least, that was my experience.

People offered all kinds of words because they didn't know what else to say. *"Well at least you didn't have kids involved …"* was a popular one.

… As if I was somehow supposed to be celebrating the fact that I was not yet a mother.

I had made the decision to stay at my Dad's until I got my life back on track. I had no idea how I was going to make money because for the first time since I was 19 years old, I didn't want to cook. I'd never even considered doing anything else, but every time I stepped behind the stove or picked up a knife, I got that punch-in-the-gut, lose-your-breath, heart-racing feeling and it was *just too damn hard.*

I had been largely ignoring job offers and avoiding clients, but every once in a while, I found myself at an event with food in hand and coolers in tow. But, each time, no matter how well the event went, or the positive reception I got, something about it didn't feel *right.*

People kept telling me how glad they were that I was back, but I didn't feel like I was *back.*

———

In November, I went to a catering consult for some long-time clients of mine, Martha and Dan. My nerves melted away as they warmly invited me into their home. Martha made coffee and we sat at their kitchen island discussing their upcoming event. While we were finalizing the menu, Dan asked me how Jeff was doing. I froze. My stomach dropped. Perhaps he could come with me to the event to offer some wine pairings, they suggested.

"You guys make the sweetest couple," Martha cooed. I was choking back puke. *What the fuck lady?* I thought to myself. *Can't you read between the lines??*

I collected myself and made an excuse to leave before they had a chance to give me their deposit. I left with a fake smile on my face but as soon as I got to the safety of my car and out of sight, my emotions poured out.

It was *too hard.* I wasn't ready for this. I wasn't ready to be professional, let alone honest or graceful.

I messaged Martha a few days later, giving her a fake excuse about being double-booked for the day of her party, and cancelled. She emailed me back but I couldn't look. I knew she was innocent in all of this, and I couldn't blame her for her ignorance, but the incident rocked my world enough to see that I couldn't handle another experience like the one I'd had in Martha and Dan's kitchen. Every time I thought about cooking, anxiety burst through the seams that I had been trying to sew up since the day The Restaurant closed. I was lucky I was strong enough to flee from Martha and Dan's kitchen before those fresh stitches ruptured open … *this time.* But, I knew next time I might not be so lucky and if I had any chance of salvaging whatever reputation I had left, I knew I had to take a step back from catering, maybe permanently.

It was one of the most difficult decisions of my entire life and I felt like I was not only letting people down, but I had lost a piece of me that meant so much. Cooking had always been such a massive part of my identity, I wasn't sure what I was supposed to *be,* if I wasn't a chef. But no matter what I did, I couldn't seem to get that joy for cooking back. I had based all of my worth on being a chef, and being Jeff's partner. Now I was neither and I couldn't decide which broke my heart more.

I missed cooking so much that it cracked me wide open. I was deeply ashamed of my own exhaustion. I knew I couldn't go back though, not yet, so I temporarily disabled my website, packed up my knives and turned down any job offers that came my way for kitchen work.

I tried to find the silver lining — perhaps this change would allow me to be more empathetic to the people out there who didn't have everything all figured out. Perhaps it would give me a chance to connect more deeply with people who were going through loss, a breakup or a career change. I thought about going back to school. I thought about travelling. I thought about getting an office job somewhere until I figured it out. I thought about what it would look like if I published this book.

This was new to me. I'd been obsessed with my work for the last decade; I'd been self-employed for seven years, and all of a sudden, *I wasn't*. For a moment, I felt myself returning to that young woman who had returned from Australia feeling so lost. I felt myself return to the girl in high school, confused and alone, frantic to fit in. I felt myself return to a childish version of myself, desperate for love.

Over the years, I had tried to *belong* any way that I could, because I believed belonging equaled love. I dabbled in over-achieving and lying, but then I discovered that becoming a party girl and drug user was the quickest route to belonging. I lived in that belief for a while, but then traded it in for success and perfectionism — and that became my key to belonging. Cooking had been the perfect industry for all of these things to take place. My addiction to being busy was celebrated among my peers and family, disguised as 'ambition' and 'drive.' And now that I decided I wasn't going to cook anymore, I was lost, once again, needing to find a place to belong.

The obvious way to find love and belonging, would have been to find a new partner, so I tried. I shared a second kiss with the boy who was my first kiss, who was now all grown up and in a band. When we were 15 and neither of us knew how to kiss, we shared a sweet peck under the streetlights in my hometown, after the county fair. I had a crush on him that felt like it would go on forever. One night that November, after watching his band play, I ended up in his car, with his tongue in my mouth. I wanted him to take me home that night but this soft spoken, soft lipped, soft-hearted boy whose hands I couldn't take my eyes off of, was trying to save me from something he knew I wasn't ready for. (I thanked him for it later.)

When I realized that 'the boy who got away' wasn't going to save me, I tried harder with others. I stayed up late once with a quirky girl who kissed me on the walk home. She was beautiful and forward and I could taste her lip chap on my lips long after we said goodnight.

I went on picture-perfect dates with men who pulled out my chair, paid the bill and opened doors. I usually ended things quickly and swiftly at the first hint of actual intimacy. Once when a man gave me a card with a black and white bouquet of flowers drawn in it, once when a man baked me a chocolate cake for our third date and one time, all it took was him telling me I was beautiful, for me to flee. The thing they all wanted from me was the one thing I couldn't give — vulnerability. I could be sweet and flirtatious; I could put on an act. I could let myself be happily distracted for a while by men with strong arms and long fingers, or women with beautiful lips. But my heart was still totally off limits.

I eventually got bored and tired of exposing my skin but never my soul, so I started to explore the other areas of my life. I started to ask myself, "Who am I?" That December, instead of my usual roster of catering holiday parties, I learned how to make all natural soap and lotion at my friend's boutique store. I made soy candles, sold used records and worked at an olive oil tasting bar. I did pretty much everything that winter, except *cook*. I was lucky to have a few entrepreneur friends who took me in to help them through the busy Christmas season. I wasn't sure at that point, if I was doing odd jobs for friends who needed help, or if my friends were giving me odd jobs because I needed help, but either way, I was doing *something*. I worked a few hours here and a few hours there, and somehow found a way to make ends meet.

I wasn't worried about money at the time, since I was living at my Dad's house and still had enough cash stashed away from the sale of some restaurant equipment to survive a few more months of unemployment. It was the first time I'd been unemployed in over a decade; it was the first time I'd been *bored* in as long as I could remember. The hardest thing was giving myself what I knew I needed most: *time*. Time to mourn; time to heal. Time to answer the question, who am I, when everything else fades away?

232

So that's what I tried to do.

I spent long, leisurely days being with my sister. We went for walks, picked apples and sat eating them in the shade. Sometimes we'd curl up in her bed and watch classic movies and laugh like we were kids. We went on day trips when she was feeling well enough. We had picnics, went to galleries, fed ducks and made memories.

I went back to my roots and embraced being a country girl. I helped my Dad outside, harvesting the garden. I started every day for the next several months with a quiet walk in the forest behind my Dad's house. We made pickles and preserved the peaches that were making the tree in our front yard sag to the ground. He showed me how to use the tractor and how to change a tire. We had card tournaments and he taught me about space and science and all the cool things about my Dad that I'd forgotten were there. I never once let myself forget how grateful I was to have a safe place to live, and to be surrounded by nature and memories of my childhood.

I walked my dog and reconnected with her after being absent for 16 months. I gave her too many treats and hour-long belly rubs and my undivided attention. Sometimes I would lie in the hammock with her underneath, and I'd read my book with one hand and pet her with the other. I made sure she knew she was loved.

I visited my mother often and watched her cook the foods that I loved. I let her take care of me in a way that she hadn't done since I was a child. And I took care of myself too.

I watched movies in bed. I got massages. I went to bed early. I slept in. I listened to my body. I ate what I wanted. I moisturized my chipped, cracked, wounded hands. I worshipped my calluses. I appreciated every inch. I detoxed. I skin brushed and tongue scraped and salt bathed until my body felt better.

I explored my body and told myself it was okay if I craved another person's touch. I touched myself and learned about self-pleasure. I let my mind wander late at night and fantasized. I explored my identity as a bisexual and tried to make sense of my sexuality.

I continued making my list of whom I could trust and whom I had to let go of. Both lists grew. I acknowledged the various shades of support and curiosity within my friend group. I surrounded myself with people who are kind to themselves. I sat and told stories with Ruby and Doug. I went to parties every once in a while and I was social when I could be; I was alone when I needed to be. I listened to my heart.

I watched as my girlfriends made tiny humans and my closest friends became fathers. I witnessed loss and death and extended my time, space and love because I *could.* I offered to pet sit for friends who needed it. I baked casseroles and dropped them off for people who needed them. I walked my neighbour's dog just because. I spent time petting the alpacas and horses who lived down the road. I connected with the animals and babies in my life.

I went to therapy. I talked. I released shame. I made a list of everything bad I'd ever done, read it to myself in the mirror, lit it on fire and watched it burn. I cried it all out. I read the books Di recommended. I wrote down what I was anxious about on one side of a paper, and wrote down what I couldn't control on the other. I burned that one too. I talked about forgiveness. I practised Ho'oponopono every single morning, and every single night. I put the prayer on a post-it and stuck it to my mirror, beside my bed and on the dashboard in my car so I would see it as often as I could and try to remember those 10 little (big) words: *I'm sorry. I forgive you. I love you. Thank you.*

I went to healers and had my chakras aligned and sat in front of the singing bowl while I talked to God. My new church became a rock beside the lake and I sat there with Spirit as I made lists of everything I loved in my life. I found ways to be grateful even when it was hard. I had faith. I held space for everything good. I asked for what I needed.

I counted my blessings. (Literally.) I wrote them down and I counted them. Daily. I oozed gratitude. I chose to live my life in a way that I knew was good.

I went back to yoga. I got up with the sun and stretched in the yard. I sat in my hammock with my books. I tried to stay present and recognize how beautiful the sunshine felt on my face. I recognized my privilege. I hiked. I went canoeing. I meditated. I sat in the quiet with just my thoughts. I relearned everything I had forgotten about the power of breath and started intentionally breathing again. With that, I got healthier and started jogging. I joined a boot camp class and punched and kicked while the instructor shouted at us to *let it go*. I started loving myself again … or perhaps for the first time.

By the time fall started morphing into winter, I noticed that my shoulder *didn't hurt* anymore. I nearly cried when I realized that the mind-numbing pain I'd felt for 16 months had subsided. I knew it was thanks to all the rest I'd given myself, so I continued to rest and let long naps, deep sleeps, hot baths and meditation fill the cracks that had been created in my joints and bones, and in my spirit. I lay in the grass and let it ground me. I stargazed. I daydreamed. I danced in the rain. I watched clouds. I picked blackberries. I harvested wild leeks. I painted pictures; I added glitter. I helped my friends. I baked bread. I talked a lot. I listened a lot. I smoked pot and drew pictures. I rode ferris wheels by myself.

The most important thing I did that fall was being willing to sit with the loneliness. I sat in the only-ness.

I did everything I ever wanted to do while I was learning about all the other things I could be instead of a chef. I was a *person* first — a good person. A kind person. I was a good daughter — one who checked in on her parents and genuinely cared for them. I was a good sister and friend. I was a dog sitter, a yogi, a long distance runner, a poet and a painter.

And *I was a writer*. My journal had barely left my side for a moment that year. I wrote in my car, on trains, on the grass, in trees, by the water and in my bed. I wrote and wrote and wrote. I went to writers' workshops and would have huge purging sessions where I would sit and write 5,000 words at a time. I filled journals upon journals and sat at my desktop and started working on this very book. I wrote, constantly and feverishly, about everything that happened. I analyzed Jeff's every action from the last few months, from the time we spent at The Restaurant and for the six years we spent together. I poked and prodded and inspected and interpreted. I wrote about it until my hand and heart were numb.

I also learned that writing was like anything else I wanted to do. When I started, I would write for 8-10 hours a day without stopping. I was purging — getting it all out. But when I got to the good stuff — when I arrived *here* — I realized that if I was going to finish this book I needed to be kind to myself. So I took breaks to stretch. I drank lots of water and sometimes whiskey. I wrote letters to myself with lots of self-compassion.

I often wrote about the girl I *wanted* to be. When I closed my eyes and thought of her, she was twirling, carefree, on the grass, in a sundress. I was ready to be her — the girl that always chose love over fear. The girl that hugs strangers, who will never let someone cry alone. The girl who touches your arm when you're sad, rubs your back when you're hurt. She's compassionate and gentle. She's a good listener and she's graceful. She's healthy and she loves herself. She's strong and resilient. She looks in the mirror each day and thanks God for her body and everything it does for her. She wakes up and tells herself, "You're a fucking warrior."

Instead of trying to figure out where I belonged in the world, I spent the next several months trying to recognize myself in that girl I wrote about — the girl I wanted to be. She was so close I could almost touch her; I could almost feel her breath when I inhaled. There was no rush and no reward, but I yearned for her.

Each time I worked on this book, I felt closer to her. I felt closer to the truth. So I continued writing and purging and I even

236

convinced myself to start sharing my writing online and doing public readings. During one reading, it came to me that if I wasn't going to be a chef anymore it'd be okay. I was more than that now — I was a *storyteller.*

———

That time I spent with myself taught me something more important that anything I'd learned in school, as a business owner or as a chef. The time I spent with myself uncovered a lesson that would lead me to my life's work — the deep knowing that I did not belong to someone. I did not belong to my parents — I'd been striving to disprove this since I was old enough to crawl by screaming "Self!" every chance I got. I did not belong to my friends — I was carving out space in my life for a community of like-minded people whom I loved, but I did not *belong* to them. I no longer belonged to Jeff and did not want my next partnership to feel similar to ours. I did not belong to my identity as an addict, a bisexual, a victim, a restaurant owner or to anything external.

At first, when I realized this, a loneliness inside of me took over that I honestly thought would kill me.

But then, the silver lining came, when I realized the lesson in its fullness.

Love does not come from belonging.

Love comes from within. (It has to.)

When friends and family asked me about Jeff, I would repeat the same thing, over and over: *It does not serve me if you hate him. It does not help me to know that he is suffering.* There were nights that I cried myself to sleep missing him, and there were moments when I swallowed my screams, but one thing I knew for certain was that when I didn't speak to him for a while, I felt *calmer.* When I was without him, I felt like I was sitting on a chair with four thick, sturdy legs that were supporting me. I felt balanced. When I let him in, even for a moment, I all of a sudden felt *unsteady* … like a leg had broken off the chair I was sitting on, and I was forced to try to balance and find steadiness all over again.

There was one thing still tying us together though — we shared two dogs. We had an arrangement that we would meet every few weeks so the two could play together. Gnowee, the gorgeous mutt we adopted together four years earlier, stayed with me at my Dad's. Gracie, the 14-year-old, goofy, golden lab, would live with Jeff. We had taken Gracie in as a 'foster dog' from his sister a few years earlier, but fell in love and ended up keeping her. She technically didn't belong to me, but I ached from not seeing her every day. At Christmastime, I asked Jeff if I could have her for a few days. He agreed, and I was glad our relationship was civil enough for now. Thoughts of, *Maybe he's changed,* no doubt entered my mind that day.

———

Before going to pick up Gracie that day, I met my friend Nancy for a coffee. It had grown increasingly important for me to spend time with the strong, inspiring women in my life, of which Nancy was a perfect example. I had been cheering her on as she grew her small café over the last few years. Although we had always been friendly towards each other, I always felt like there was a strange distance between us. Nancy was a bit shy and reserved, slightly cynical and incredibly smart.

When I arrived at the café, we made small talk for a while, listing business accomplishments and exchanging travel stories. The conversation flowed freely and seemed to welcome intimacy so when she asked how I was doing since The Restaurant closed, I opened up to her. At some point during that conversation, she admitted, "I have to tell you something." *I've been here before.*

She started by telling me about the time she spent sitting beside Jeff at the business school they both attended right before we opened The Restaurant. Both of our businesses had received a big grant from the city, to which attending the six week intensive coaching was a requirement. She told me that when she met him, she liked him immediately, finding him funny and charming.

Then, he changed. He started by giving her compliments about how she dressed or looked. She was ashamed to admit it but she liked the attention so she "went with it." Soon after that, he started becoming more forward and aggressive: texting her outside of class time, inviting her to hang out in private and perhaps most invasively, asking her personal questions about her marriage.

Her voice started shaking as she continued her story. I did my best to sit there and listen. I forced myself to look at her with kindness, even though my heart was bleeding. Moments matter … and this moment wasn't about my bleeding heart. It was about *hers.*

She told me that she felt like he had *chosen* her. He *knew* she would likely never come forward about his advances. Jeff was a huge player in the food service industry, mostly because of The Restaurant, so she felt forced to stay quiet about what was happening to her. Even though she *wanted* to tell someone, she feared it would burn bridges. This very fact was something Jeff had *calculated* and it made me sick. *I've fucking been here before.*

I'll admit that in that moment, I wanted to look away. I couldn't help it. This was almost *too* painful to go through. My heart was gushing like popping a cherry tomato in your mouth and having the guts run down your chin. But I dug deep. I dug deep because I didn't have the strength last time I was sitting there, hearing words like 'targeted,' 'fearmongering,' and 'repress.' I would stand up for Nancy because I was strong enough now. I wouldn't let this be another Sam or Rachel or Alisa.

Now was my chance.

I looked at Nancy, reached across the table and put my hand on hers. "I am so sorry that this happened to you," I said, meaning it with every fibre of my being. She responded the same way Sam had done, and Rachel had done, and how most women do: "I'm so sorry that I let it happen."

We sat there in a ping pong game of guilt and blame, shame and regret. She confessed to me that this secret she carried prevented us from ever being true friends.

"That ends now," I commanded bluntly. And I meant it too.

———

Every corner I turned there was another secret about him. There was another woman hiding a story about him, out of fear and shame. I wondered how many people in my life had secrets that they were afraid to share with me for fear of facing judgment. I wanted to hug them all, reach across the table, grab their hands and say, "This ends now."

I knew it would take time, patience, and a willingness to turn to them with an open heart and say, "It's okay. It's not your fault. I forgive you. I'm listening."

I *was* listening. I was listening now to all the red flags and all the signs and all the things that I should have seen before. It was my *duty*. There was a revolution stirring inside of me and seeing Nancy made it stir so viscerally that I couldn't calm it, even if I wanted to. Participating in that revolution meant accepting the hurt. Accepting the hurt gave me the power to stand up for these women who needed me. They needed me to be brave enough to hear their stories. They needed me to listen.

I tried not to waste time wondering if Nancy had told me back then, if I would have done the right thing, or if I would have reacted at all — it no longer mattered what I *would have* done then. It didn't matter if I was ready then. I was ready now. In that moment, with Nancy, in that coffee shop, I forgave myself for taking so long to get there. I decided, right then and there, to forgive myself for the time it took me to do the right thing.

Maybe it doesn't matter how long it takes you to do the right thing, just as long as *you do it* in the end.

That moment was the first time since the day I closed The Restaurant, that I didn't feel ashamed of my actions. Moments. Fucking. Matter. In that moment, I felt like I was living up to the person that I would have been proud of when I was a little girl.

When I told Nancy that I was sorry, she responded, "But you didn't do anything wrong …"

"I'm saying sorry to you because I know he never will." *I'm sorry. I forgive you. I love you. Thank you.*

———

I left the café and drove straight to Jeff's apartment. I knew I had to be strong and hang on to my power. I wanted to feel clear and steady, on four strong, sturdy legs. I wanted to keep doing the right thing. Being in his energy, and allowing him into mine, wouldn't allow my life to unfold in the way I knew I wanted it to. So, I knew that this had to be the last time I ever saw him. I also knew that meant saying goodbye to more than just him …

When Jeff came downstairs to meet me, I calmly explained that I wanted go for a walk with Gracie alone, and we agreed to meet back in his lobby in half an hour. I walked out the door with Gracie and fantasized about lifting her into my car, driving away and never speaking to him again.

Instead, Gracie and I just walked.

I walked her along the frosty hills of his apartment grounds. We played tug of war with a stick. I made a snow angel while she rolled around on her back, imitating me. I talked to her about Gnowee, about the house, about everything. When our time was up, I walked her back to his door, gave her one more belly scratch and a kiss on the snout, and said goodbye.

I haven't seen Gracie since that day. I don't know if she's alive, and I don't know if she's happy. But I know she misses me.

———

Nancy's story of Jeff's deviant behavior made me realize that I didn't have to *wonder* if there were *others*. I *knew* there were others. When I looked around at the women in my life, there wasn't a single one that hadn't been somehow affected by his misconduct. No one was safe around him. Not unless he took ownership for his actions and was committed to getting help.

Nancy's story also gave me the courage to finally reach out to Sam. We met for a coffee and heard each other out in person, for the first time. Like all the other difficult conversations I'd had that year, I wanted to run away from her truth. But I dug my heels in because it was the right thing to do. In the end it helped more than it hurt and I was happy I chose to be brave. Like Nancy, Sam and I ended up as good friends in the end.

There were many more times over the course of the next year (and beyond) that I sat across the table from strong, beautiful, innocent women and held their hands while they told me their stories about Jeff. One of the servers from my catering company came forward. Clients, friends and I even started getting messages from strangers. They all used words like 'preyed,' 'targeted,' 'harassed,' and 'predator.' They all said they were sorry. They all wished they would have told me sooner. Each and every time I heard someone's story, I apologized on Jeff's behalf, because I knew he never would.

Each and every time, I yearned for the truth and dreaded it, all in the same heartbeat.

Every one of their stories made me see things a little more clearly. Each story made me a little more adamant that he did not deserve my love. Each time it broke my heart; each time it made me stronger. Each time it fortified those four strong, sturdy legs. Each day, week, month and year I spent apart from him added another layer of that complicated but very real relief I felt, about cutting him out of my life for good.

But still, every time I heard his name, I could always taste salt and sour.

December was a month of firsts.

It was my first Christmas without Jeff so some of my friends banded together and threw a party called The Misfit's Christmas. We gathered at my friend's house and drank gin martinis all afternoon. We made vegan Irish cream while we played board games and did puzzles. We had a feast, got high and stayed up until the morning.

Instead of feeling lonely during the holidays, I was surrounded by people that loved me. It gave me the strength to conquer some other firsts: I took my first solo vacation in seven years, I drove on the highway for the first time in nearly a decade, I did my first poetry slam and I slept with one of my closest friends.

———

Lane and I had been friends for over 15 years. We met in grade 10 when he transferred to our school and was assigned the seat next to me in homeroom. We became fast friends. He was tall, goofy, sarcastic, funny and smart. We hung out after school every day and ate fast food burgers while smoking cigarettes in my car.

People sometimes assumed we were a couple, and we did have a connection that I'd never experienced with a boy before, but we remained platonic friends through the rest of high school. After graduation, we stayed in touch and when we bumped into each other at parties, we would always end up chain-smoking outside together while our significant others were inside. We had a unique bond and as time went on and we grew closer, I even started spending Christmas and Thanksgiving with his family, who welcomed me in with the most warmth.

When Jeff and I started dating, I stopped going to Lane's family Christmases and we slowly lost touch. I didn't realize how much I missed him until I saw him that night at my favourite pub.

245

We locked eyes and I felt it. Right away. That tingle. That spark. That connection. I swear, my heart stopped beating for a moment. No flutter, no racing … just a Full Stop.

I hadn't felt it with any of the other men or women who had entered my life fleetingly over the last several months, but this time I definitely, definitely felt it.

Lane had grown up! He was taller, broader and wore contacts lenses. I felt warm all the way to my toes when he walked over to me, picked me up and gave me a hug with all his might (which was a lot). He may have looked different but he was still the same goofball I cared for so deeply when I was a teenager. He was perhaps more serious, but as we caught up, I felt at ease as though no time had passed.

After many beers, we both decided we didn't want the night to end and since I lived closer and had the house to myself that night, I invited him over to my Dad's, where I was still living. In true teenage 'us' fashion, we ended up splitting a pack of cigarettes and drinking half a bottle of leftover Irish cream. As we talked about our high school days, I noticed he was looking at my lips as I spoke.

It could have been the booze or my sudden urge not to be alone, but as I watched his eyes staring at my lips, I decided I was going to kiss him.

I set down my drink, let the warmth of that moment move my body and straddled him on my couch. His lips were soft and his hands were big and I felt an avalanche take over my body. In that moment, I didn't care about the laws of the land. I didn't care that we were potentially messing up a 15 year friendship … maybe I should have. All I cared about was *this* feeling. This rush that I had been longing for since that night in the hotel room with Jeff before he flew to Halifax. I hadn't felt it since then. But now, here I was, and I felt like I *belonged* in Lane's arms.

We kissed on the couch to an entire Oasis song and then he lifted me up and carried me to my bedroom. He set me down and

I clumsily turned on a dim light near my bed and straightened the covers. I turned back around and we reached for each other. We both knew this was it.

———

That morning after, half sleeping and half cuddling, he rolled over and sheepishly asked me, "Are we still friends?" The daylight had sobered us both, but as we talked and he looked around my bedroom asking about my life, I felt connected to him and didn't want him to go. The spell was broken though when I realized that my Dad would be home soon, so after kissing me goodbye five or six times, he left and I was alone again. I lay naked in my bed and tried to rub my hangover out through my temples. I was rough around the edges, but I was *happy*.

It was something I hadn't felt in a long time, and I didn't give myself time to talk myself out of it. We talked on the phone later that night, and the next day I drove to his house over an hour away, for more. We continued to travel back and forth to each other for a few weeks. It was January now — the dead of Canadian winter, and although the trip was sometimes arduous, it was always worth it to spend a night in his arms, doing all the things you do with someone you've been longing to have, for 15 years.

He sometimes asked what happened at The Restaurant. He wanted to know that I was okay. I would always brush him off though, and he would eventually appease me by scooping me up and carrying me to his bed. I didn't want our time to be spent talking — I wanted to feel good. *Grant me this ... please.*

A few weeks into our love affair, we were lying around, tangled up in each other, making out, and he looked up at me and asked if I wanted children.

"Like... right now?" I asked, puzzled.

"Like ... with *me*," he replied, seriously.

A memory flashed in my mind. Jeff, on his knees, in our kitchen, hugging my waist, snotting into my t-shirt, telling me I'd make a good mother.

As I was pondering my long-winded answer about being unsure if I was maternal enough to be a good mother, Lane blurted out a confession. He was in love with me. That's what he said. He told me that he'd always loved me and that ever since the night we'd spent together, he wanted to buy the house across the street from his parents and he wanted me to live there with him and have family Christmas like we used to. He told me he would take care of me forever and that he wanted me to have his children. *I've. Been. Here. Before.* It was lemon trees in Costa Rica. It was babies on the beach. It was boys in bands and girls with strawberry lip chap. It was homemade chocolate cake and bouquets of roses drawn in handmade cards.

A disturbing thought crossed my mind — *If I would have known how much you loved me, I never would have slept with you.* It was only then, in that moment, that I realized how deep the mark Jeff made on me really was. It was only then that I realized how profound the trauma was, and how much healing I had left to do.

I didn't want things to end with Lane, but I knew I couldn't give him what he wanted in that moment. It would lead to all the things I wasn't ready for … so I said nothing.

He bore his soul and I said *nothing.*

I *wanted* to tell him that I loved him too. Because I did. I had loved him since I was a teenager. I wanted to strip off my stupid shield and throw it on the ground and smash it like a bag of potato chips. But I couldn't. I wasn't ready. I knew if I stayed there with him I'd eventually say the words, "Tell me who you need me to be, and I'll do it. Tell me who to be so you'll love me." It would have been so much easier in that moment to just tell him I loved him so we could run off into the sunset. We could have had such a *beautiful love story.*

But … I didn't want that life anymore. I knew that it would be impossible and unhealthy for me to build a life with someone who caused my heart to stop, every time I saw them.

I'd already been swept off my feet. I sought romance and grandeur and passion in Jeff and I wore those things like a badge of honour for six years. We slow danced in the lobby at the Waldorf Astoria. We slept in a bed of rose petals. We flew around the world, had sex on the beach and I watched him write my name in the sand. We walked through vineyards in the Tuscan sun, he serenaded me on the streets of Venice and read me poetry overlooking the Golden Gate Bridge.

I'd done all that and now I wanted *more*. I didn't want fireworks, for fireworks only last a few minutes. I wanted more than that … more than over the top gestures, love bombs or poetry. For once, I wanted to stay grounded, with my feet firmly planted below me, instead of being swept off them. I wanted to make damn sure that if there were any red flags, I would see them this time. I wasn't willing to fall in love if it meant being blind.

––––

A few days after rejecting Lane, I tried to explain to him the most compassionate version of my truth. *I'm sorry, please forgive me. I love you, thank you.* He didn't understand and I didn't blame him. It was complicated and messy. It was honest and ugly. Not everyone is ready for that.

I had no choice but to let him go and accept that if Lane walked into that bar that night to show me what I wasn't ready for, I was grateful even though it hurt like hell. For the next few nights, my loneliness nearly broke me. I stayed in bed for days and hugged my pillow. I wondered if I was doing the right thing. I missed Lane so viscerally, I would have sold my soul to not be alone in that moment.

It hurt so much to be so lost.

––––

It would take me almost two years and a handful of other relationships to realize that what happened with Lane wasn't actually about romance — it was about *worth*. In my heart, I didn't believe I was worthy of Lane's love. I didn't believe I was worthy of being a mother. Just like I didn't believe I was worthy of homemade cards or songs or a piece of goddamn chocolate cake.

Many people tried to show me over the next year or two. A few of them actually stuck around for a while, but my walls eventually wore them down. It would take me a long time to tire of hurting people and being hurt to finally be brave enough to sit with my loneliness, but, we'll get to that.

MISFIT'S CHRISTMAS IRISH CREAM (V) (GF)

MAKES A LARGE ENOUGH BATCH TO GET EVERYONE TIPSY AT CHRISTMAS

This recipe is a great gift to give to your friends in mason jars or serve on ice cubes at your holiday party (although it can of course be enjoyed year round!) It also goes great in coffee or Earl Grey tea, or drizzled on ice cream. You can store it in your fridge for up to 1 week, although in my experience, it never lasts that long!

To Make Irish Cream
6 cups (about 3 standard cans) coconut milk
½ cup brown sugar, packed
½ cup maple syrup
2 tbsp tapioca starch
6 tbsp cold water
2-3 shots of espresso (or ¾ cup really strong coffee) (or ¾ cup instant if it's Christmas Day and everything is closed!)
275 ml Irish whiskey
½ tsp salt

250

Misfit's Method

In a large pot, gently warm coconut milk on low heat. Once warm, whisk in sugars and turn up to medium-high heat. Let this mixture come to a soft boil, watching carefully and stirring often. When bubbling, combine tapioca starch with cold water and slowly whisk this mixture into the pot. Keep whisking until bubbles start, and then cook for 5 minutes on medium heat.

A trick to test readiness: Dip a wooden spoon into the liquid. When you pull the spoon out, use your finger to draw a line in the liquid on the spoon. Hold the spoon upside down, over the pot — if the line disappears, it needs more cooking time. Cook for an additional 3-5 minutes and test again. If the line remains for the count of 1, 2, 3… your Irish cream is done!

Remove from the heat and stir in espresso, whiskey and salt. If you'd like to make this non-alcoholic drinks, you can omit the booze here and add water instead. (You can always add the whiskey into each individual glass by pouring a virgin version of this recipe over 1-2 shots of your favourite whiskey or liqueur.) For best results, let it cool completely before serving or packaging.

"That poor girl. Someone should warn her."

It was an innocent text from a friend. She didn't know what stones it would turn or how much hurt it would cause. She was trying to empathize with me and protect someone. She thought she knew what was best for all of us.

At first, I didn't know what she was referring to. *What girl?* It didn't take long for me to put the pieces together. Jeff had posted a picture of himself and a beautiful brunette girl on his Instagram. The caption read something along the lines of, *"She's funny, beautiful... and she cooks!"*

In those next moments, I forgot *everything* I had learned. In yoga. In therapy. In meditation. I forgot all the mantras I thought I deeply understood, all the lessons I had under my belt and everything I knew about reacting, trauma and fight or flight. I forgot to breathe. I forgot it all and picked up my phone and dialed his number. We hadn't spoken since the day I said goodbye to Gracie.

"Who the fuck is this girl?!?" I exclaimed, not realizing how crazy I probably sounded.

"Calm down," Jeff barked.

"I. Will. Not. Calm. Down! Who the *fuck* is she?!?! Where do you get off rubbing that shit in my face?!?"

A moment of silence, or maybe a few moments of him defending himself. I don't fully remember. All I remember is him saying, "Everyone hates me, Yoda. *I hate me* ... for what I did to you. But then I found someone who made me feel less alone. Who made me feel like I wasn't broken anymore ..."

I hung up before he could finish and threw my phone on the ground, hoping it smashed to pieces along with his words. How was it fair that he got to live his life, without consequences, and I was over here, drowning? How was it fair that he found love and I was alone? How was it fair that he found someone to make him happy, and I couldn't even find someone to be with, for more than a few days before they stroked my wounds and all my trauma came pouring out?

I have to get out of here, I thought to myself.

I had recently been invited to be the chef at a technology-free retreat at an old ashram in a remote area. I originally turned down the offer since I wasn't interested in cooking right now, but now that I had broken up with my phone, and could obviously benefit from a social media detox, I decided to head to the retreat after all. I called the organizer, told her I'd changed my mind and away I went. *How hard could it be?* I wondered.

———

When I arrived at the retreat, my eyes burned from days of crying and I felt shaky and unnerved. I was reeling in pain from driving Lane away and the additional stress of seeing Jeff's new girlfriend was haunting me.

The retreat center was at the end of a long driveway, nestled amongst hundreds of pine trees that were dusted with snow. It was secluded and isolated from everything. *Perfect,* I thought.

There were quiet corners all over the ashram and hours of free time where I would curl up with a book by myself, sometimes annoyed if I was interrupted. But as time went on, I started talking openly with people which ended up in long conversations about topics that seemed too big for the outside world. The other women at the retreat all had their own stories and heartache to share. By the time the retreat was up, I'd spent time with all of them, talking about trauma, loss, healing and love. We formed deep bonds as we connected in a safe space over tea, beside an ancient fireplace. We all got up at 5 a.m. to do yoga and meditate together. We held hands and locked eyes. We laughed big, hearty, belly laughs. We chanted and sang. We went for walks in the snow at night and screamed at the top of our lungs in the woods. We talked about pain. We cried a lot.

"You might thank Jeff someday," one of the women said to me, as I told my story standing in the kitchen with big pots of soup and rice bubbling behind us. I of course scoffed at the idea and secretly held resentment to her for suggesting something so ridiculous.

One of the women at the retreat held a workshop on forgiveness. I didn't attend because the idea of forgiving Jeff felt so absurd. But I did ask her before I left, if she had any advice about how I could start moving on from Jeff, once I got back to the real world. I started telling her about the phone call we'd had, about his new girlfriend, about this and that. She eloquently interrupted me and said, "There's only one way, sweet girl. You've got to get him out of your system!"

I told her I'd already worked on getting him out of my life and started counting the ways when she stopped me, put her hand over my heart and motioned, "You've got to get him out of here." She patted my chest lightly, turned on her heel and walked away.

———

On the final evening of the retreat, I went to the kitchen to check out the supplies. There wasn't much left in the fridges or pantry, but there was an extensive supply of dry spices. I grabbed a frying pan and started toasting fennel, cardamom and coriander seeds. My eyes were still wet and my wounds were still fresh, so I allowed myself to get lost in the rhythm of the mortar and pestle I used to grind the spices. I let myself get lost in the coconut cream and the fresh chopped cilantro. I let some tears fall as I heated up the naan and stewed the lentils slowly.

Many retreat goers popped their heads in the kitchen to ask what I was making. I meekly responded and continued quietly prepping and simmering. I was warmed by their curiosity and compassion, and by the curry I created that day. It was the first

255

time I'd found joy in cooking (or eating, for that matter) in almost six months and it completely overwhelmed me.

As we ate my curry in silence that evening, I made eye contact with several of the women I'd met that weekend, including the girl I was angry at for predicting I'd thank Jeff someday. As I ripped off big chunks of naan and scooped curried lentils into my mouth, I let it all go. I let go of how Jeff was spending his life. I let go of forcing myself to be 'over' it. I let go of my imperfections, my lack of calm and the way I reacted. I let go and ate slowly, surrounded by women who were also letting go. *I'm sorry, I forgive you.*

I got up early the next day and cooked breakfast for everyone. I sang while I simmered steel cut oats and sliced bananas and mashed blueberries. I didn't realize it until much later that day, but I was smiling the whole time. *Thank you, I love you.*

———

When I returned home from the retreat, my phone was still sitting on my bedroom floor, where I had attempted to smash it a few days earlier. I picked it up and checked the screen, surprised to see it wasn't shattered by the force of my anger. I turned the screen on and scrolled to Jeff's name. I pressed 'Delete and Block,' as the first move to getting him out of my system. Next, I went back to his Instagram and deleted and blocked him there too. Next, I did the same thing with his family and any of his friends who knew the truth about him and hadn't acted on it.

There was no need for me to punish myself like this anymore. I had to continue to work on letting go, instead. It was a drastic, life-saving move and I never went back.

Although I slept better that night than I had in a while, my soul still warm from that curry, I still felt the need to escape. I was so broken from everything. From Jeff, from Lane, from all the others … I opened my laptop and started researching *ways to cleanse your soul.* I messaged a few close friends for advice. I picked up a few of my favourite memoirs and started leafing through the pages. Within an hour or two, I had decided. I booked a one way ticket to Europe.

I wasn't sure if I was going to Europe to celebrate, or to grieve, but if my favourite authors had taught me anything, it's that the moments that matter in life are almost always a combination of both.

SOUL-WARMING RETREAT CURRY(V) (GF)

SERVES 4 ENTRÉE PORTIONS (WITH LEFTOVERS)

This curry was one of the first things I made that I was really proud of. It wasn't a lot of work — in fact I almost forgot about it as it bubbled slowly on the back burner of the old stove, while my new friends and I talked of big things in the kitchen. But the flavour of this curry stuck with me and is something I make often at my kitchen at home. This recipe is rustic and it will likely taste a little different each time you make it. Serve it with rice, quinoa, naan bread or on its own.

For The Curry
1 tbsp coconut oil
2 tbsp olive or vegetable oil
2 medium onions, peeled and roughly chopped
4 cloves garlic, peeled and minced
1 thumb sized piece of ginger, peeled and minced
3 heaping tbsp curry powder (store-bought is fine, but to make your own, combine 1 tbsp each of ground, toasted cumin, turmeric and coriander seeds)
1 cup dry red lentils
1 cup dry brown or green lentils
Approximately 3 cups of your favourite hearty vegetables, chopped fine (I often use a combination of mushrooms, cauliflower, carrot, potato and celery and pulse them all in my food processor — but use whatever you have on hand)
1 cup crushed canned tomatoes (or 6-8 medium fresh tomatoes, chopped)
4 cups water or vegetable stock
2 cups coconut milk

257

1 tbsp salt

To Finish
1-2 cups of your favourite green vegetable (peas, green beans, chopped kale, spinach, broccoli, etc.)
Juice of 1-2 limes
1-2 tbsp sugar
Cilantro, chopped (optional)

Soul-Warming Retreat Method
Heat both oils in a large pot on medium heat and sauté onion, garlic and ginger for a few minutes until they are softened. Turn heat down to low and add curry powder, stirring often until your kitchen smells delicious (about 2 minutes.)

Next, add lentils, vegetables, tomatoes, stock, coconut milk and salt. Stir well. Place a lid on the curry and turn it to the lowest stove top setting, and set a timer for one hour. Treat this curry like you'd treat yourself at a yoga retreat — check in on it often, move softly and be gentle. Remove the lid at the one hour mark, stir, and cook for an additional 30 minutes on low with no lid.

Remove from the heat and stir in your favourite green vegetables. They will wilt from the heat of the curry. Add lime juice and sugar, to taste. Top with extra limes and cilantro.

This curry is even better the next day and in my experience, it's best served alongside some friendly strangers, with some naan bread and eaten with your hands!

I arrived at Schiphol airport in the early morning, exhausted from the long flight but feeling ready to conquer Europe. Memories of Jeff flooded my mind with each move I made, from gathering my luggage, to the moment I walked out of the airport for the first time and set foot into the streets. I was proud of myself for making it there. I knew that not everyone could do what I was about to do — spend six weeks in Europe, alone. I didn't think that made me better or worse, but I knew it made me *brave.*

The people in Amsterdam looked happy … everywhere I looked there were big, smiling faces! I spent my time writing poetry by the canal and people watching in dense, touristy streets. I drank lattes and wrote in my diary in cafés for hours on end. I giggled with glee when someone asked me for directions because although I'd only been in Europe for a short 12 hours, apparently I appeared to be a local. I ate pot brownies and stumbled the unknown streets at dusk. I had few plans after Amsterdam other than making it to Portugal eventually.

———

I arrived in Lisbon on the eve of my 30th birthday. I'd fled to Europe in bits and pieces, after spending the last several months counting my losses. I was determined, in my 30th year, to learn how to be lonely.

I made a short trip from the airport in Lisbon to a small town called Alfama. Its narrow cobblestone streets, secluded stairwells and dim-lit cafés reminded me of Venice. They reminded me to *Jeff.*

Hunger pains and jet lag both roared, so I ventured out of my room to find food and possibly a drink to take the edge of loneliness off. I left with only some cash in my pocket and my journal. I wandered around for a while, listening to melancholy men singing Fado — the music Portugal is famous for — in the streets. I found a seat outside a bustling, little bar where everyone smiled at me but no one spoke English. I sat there for a while with the unseasonably warm air blowing on my face and wrote a love letter to my 29-year-old self. I attempted to order some olives and wine, but struggled to communicate with the gruff Portuguese woman across the counter. A man sitting at a table nearby witnessed my struggle and offered his assistance. After he placed my order, I offered to buy him a glass of wine for his trouble. We spent the next hour or so, leisurely eating olives and drinking vinho verde until the hot, Portuguese sun faded behind the buildings.

Pedro informed me that he would be playing guitar at a bar at the top of the hill later that evening. He invited me to come see him play and when I told him it was the eve of my birthday, he clapped his hands and squealed with joy, insisting that I must come and let him buy me a drink.

Although I'd only known Pedro for less than a few hours, there was something about him that whispered he was safe. He had weathered, olive skin, a soft voice and small, delicate hands. I paid our bill and walked with him to his bar where he introduced me to all of his friends upon our arrival. They hugged me and kissed my cheeks, oozing hospitality and offering to share their wine and seafood. Almost instantly, Pedro's friends were my friends. It was the Portuguese way, I was finding out. We sat at a big, circular table near the window, occasionally tapping our cigarettes on the sill and exchanged travel stories. We talked about life and love and food and music as Pedro cooed 'La Vie En Rose.'

At the stroke of midnight, after far too much wine, I'd long forgotten that I was officially three decades old. Pedro hadn't forgotten though, and as the bar whirled around me with activity, I heard him start to softly sing "Happy Birthday to you, Happy Birthday to you …." He was standing in the middle of the stage, looking right at me with gentle eyes. I put my hand over my chest, closed my eyes, and breathed in that sweet, sweet moment — a broad, honest smile spreading across my face. Whistling and cheering came from all corners of the bar as I bowed and clapped. A platter of spiced cake with orange crema started making its way from table to table, each person pausing to smell it and then grabbing a piece with their fingers. Smoke filled the bar and the rumble of a motorbike mixed with cheers, from the bar next door.

When Pedro was finished his song, a French family I had met earlier that evening, starting singing 'Bonne Fête' to me in French. The table full of tourists next to them started singing to me in German. The next in Catalan. The next in Spanish. Before I knew it, every stranger in that bar had sung me 'Happy Birthday,' in every language I could imagine and I thought I was going to die with gratitude. Shots of ginjinha — a sickly sweet, fortified cherry wine — circled the room. I toasted with a group of Canadians as we hugged and left the threshold of the bar to dance and sing in the street.

My quest for learning how to be lonely could start the next day. For now, I was going to scatter the bits and pieces of myself that fled to Europe that winter all around the streets of Alfama, with those beautiful travellers, outside that perfect, little bar. They would be safe there, I knew.

Except for Pedro, I never saw any of my friends from that bar again — I left without even exchanging last names. Perhaps I would return to Portugal to find them someday. Or perhaps I would go to pick up the bits and pieces of myself that I left there that night.

———

I woke up on Pedro's couch. He was making breakfast in his kitchen and the smell of dark espresso and orange zest filled the air around me as I stirred. I dragged myself to a stool in his kitchen, rubbing my eyes in a hungover haze. When Pedro offered me a generous slice of orange cake, I shook my hand in front of my chest, rejecting his offer. He looked deflated and insisted. "My mother served us this cake when we were sick," he

261

explained, while nudging the plate closer to me with his hand. Not wanting to offend my host, I took a deep breath of air, choking back the feeling of vomit and sunk my teeth into the dense, slightly crumbly cake. The tanginess caught me off guard. As I closed my eyes, I let the cake soften in my mouth, tasting the subtle vanilla and feeling tiny bits of orange zest melting on my tongue. Pedro's mother was right — I instantly felt better. In fact, the small piece of cake I'd eaten had made me ravenous, so I picked up a pastry from a tray on the counter and quickly broke through to the pastry's cream filled centre. Custard now coated my fingers as I sucked on them, devouring every morsel of sweetness. Pedro gently pushed a plate of smoked sardines, mashed olives and soft cheese towards me. He tore a thick loaf of bread in half and we made sandwiches and ate cake until we were stuffed. The salt and smoke danced on my taste buds filling my soul as much as it cured my stomach lining. Next there was coffee which he made in an old French press that looked like it had made about a million pots in it over the years. He poured me a small cup and requested that I drink it slowly, allowing the grittiness of the undissolved sugar at the bottom to slowly melt, making each sip I took sweeter and sweeter.

My senses were overtaken, so I closed my eyes and smiled broadly. Pedro laughed — he seemed to understand what I was going through.

———

For the next several weeks, I ate everything I could get my hands on. Something had woken up inside of me since that breakfast with Pedro. I sat in restaurants by myself, with a glass of vino tinto and nothing else, and I just *ate*. I ate for joy. I ate for flavour. I ate for nourishment. I didn't bring my camera or take notes. I didn't depend on the comfort of my phone or a book beside me. I didn't need to talk about it with anyone or experience anything else during those moments other than the food. I ate enough salty oysters to feed all of Portugal. I gorged on chilled, lemony calamari salad at the Sunday market. I stopped dead in my tracks in the middle of a busy crosswalk once, after biting into a Pasti di Nata to exclaim (to no one other than myself), "God damn, that is good!!"

While I ate my way through Europe, I allowed myself to fall totally, fully, hopelessly in love — with olives. With sardines so salty from the sea all they needed was a squeeze of lemon and glug of oil. I fell in love with perfectly ripe tomatoes that reminded me of my childhood. With soft, stinky cheese. With Portugese buns — their tough, crunchy crust and airy innards. With bifana and piri piri. With francesinha. With vinho verde. With bocadillos de calamares. With olive oil so fresh it was bitter on your tongue. With butter so sweet it made you want to weep or eat the whole block.

I had fallen back in love with food, and I wanted to bask in how that felt. I wanted to bask in how grateful I felt to be there, travelling by myself, meeting beautiful people. I was grateful to have these stories. Stories of dancing on the beach and skinny dipping in the Mediterranean Sea. Stories of pub crawls in Porto. Stories of walking all day in the rain. Stories of sharing food with strangers who spoke no English, and how we somehow ended up spending hours together without words. Stories of nightclubs in Barcelona where I danced the night away with beautiful girls who smelled like spice and chocolate. Stories of people and romance and love and connection.

And finally, stories of food.

I was eternally grateful for Pedro — the mysterious guitar player who came to my rescue, gave me the best birthday I'd ever had, and made me feel something I hadn't felt in a very long time — *hungry.*

PEDRO'S ORANGE CAKE
SERVES 12 GENEROUS SLICES

This recipe was not easy to track down, but I eventually found Pedro and he was willing to give me his famous Orange Cake recipe. It had more sugar than I expected and I was surprised when he told me that he used to steep the orange peels in olive oil on his stove overnight! I've simplified his recipe for the purposes of this book, but I guarantee that this cake will heal whatever is plaguing you — the world's worst hangover, the flu or even a broken heart.

Start with "A bit of butter"

Then, Mix Your Dry Ingredients
1 cup almond meal/flour
2 cups flour
2 cups white sugar
2 tsp baking powder
1 tsp baking soda
1 tsp salt

Wet Mix
Zest from 2-3 oranges
¾ cup orange juice (or the juice from 2-3 large oranges, but it's best to measure this ingredients as it will affect your final outcome)
¾ cup good quality olive oil

1 Vanilla Bean
5 large eggs

To Finish
2-3 tbsp local honey
(Or a glaze made of icing sugar combined with orange juice)

Pedro's Method
Preheat oven to 350°. Coat a 12" bundt pan or a 10" spring form pan with "a bit of butter."

In a mixing bowl, combine dry ingredients.

In a measuring cup with a pour spout, combine olive oil, orange juice and zest.

In a large bowl or in your mixer, whisk eggs and vanilla bean pulp until they are frothy. Next, using a wooden spoon, you will incorporate the wet and dry ingredients to the eggs, in batches. Start by adding about a third of the dry mix, and half of the wet mixture. Continue adding, folding gently between each addition, ending with the dry ingredients. Be careful not to overmix.

Pour into your cake dish and bake for 35 minutes. At this point, the cake should be browned on top... but be careful not to disturb it too much or it will deflate! Turn heat down to 300° and bake for an additional 30 minutes (20 minutes if you're using a bundt pan.) Turn the oven off but leave the cake in, and set the timer for an additional 20 minutes.

After removing from the oven, let the cake cool for 10-15 minutes and then flip out onto a plate. If you wait too long, it might stick.

Once cool, drizzle with honey or combine some icing sugar with orange juice for a glaze, and serve, slightly warmed or room temperature. I have learned that this cake is even better the next day, dunked into sweetened Earl Grey tea.

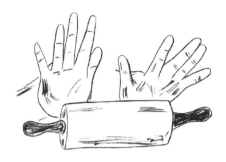

I wish I could say that my favourite meal was as life-changing as that bowl of spaghetti that Elizabeth Gilbert writes about in *'Eat Pray Love.'* But my favourite meal was purchased from an old man, with a cigarette dangling from his mouth and bucket full of oily lupini beans, by the beach. They weren't particularly special, other than the fact that they were covered in a thin layer of flaked salt and a few sliced chilies. The bag cost me less than one Euro and I hoped they didn't get covered in sand as I ate them straight from the bag while the sun set. (Although, I might have still finished them anyways.)

It was my last day in Europe, and as I sat there, me and my beans both warm from the sun, I thought about *food* for the first time in a long time. Shucking the last of those salty, spicy lupini beans between my teeth and throwing their outer husk in the growing pile on the sand, I thought about all the things I wanted to cook when I got home. I wanted to make my Dad patatas bravas — the modest fried potato dish, slathered in a spicy tomato sauce, sometimes with red pepper flakes or paprika. I'd eaten it over a dozen times since arriving in Spain and each time I ate it, I loved it more. I wanted to cook a big pan of paella over a fire, while my friends and I sat around listening for the mussel shells to steam open as the chicken thighs grew tender. I wanted to cook everything … which was a feeling I hadn't felt since closing The Restaurant.

What happened at The Restaurant had *taken* something from me — my passion extinguished along with all the memories we made there. But since coming to Europe, I saw food in a whole new light. The ability to travel, taste, cook and eat was a privilege and I'd been wasting it in my grief. Cooking had become a chore and nothing more than a job, but now I could feel it returning as my *passion.* It didn't matter if I was sitting alone in a café with a few olives, or if I was in a Michelin star restaurant — the experiences I'd had with food on this trip had brought me back to life. I hugged my legs towards me, sucked the salt and the chilies from my fingers, rested my cheek on my knee and thought to myself, *When I get home ... I'm going to cook again.* It was the third time in my life cooking would save me.

———

I stayed there on the beach, curled up in a ball, and I thought about my father. Like every time I thought about my Dad, a wide, involuntary smile spread across my cheeks — I had all the respect and admiration in the world for that man. I hoped silently that we would come to Europe together, someday.

I thought about my mother too, and how no matter who I was, she would always love me. Her unconditional love comforted me, even now, on that beach across the world, and would continue to do so for the rest of my life and all of my travels.

I thought about my closest friends. I thought about the ones I missed dearly and how the first thing I would tell them all when I got home, was how much I loved them. I thought about how grateful I was to them and to my sister, for lifting me back into the light. I thought about how beautiful it was to miss someone.

With those warm thoughts covering me like a blanket as I watched lovers and families all over that beach, I thought of Jeff. I missed him as a travel mate and as my fellow adventurer. I missed being intimate with him on beaches all over the world. Most of all though, I missed sharing food and wine with him, especially now on this trip, doing it all alone for my first time. We spent years dining side by side on bar stools, watching bustling kitchens and busy bartenders together. It was 'our thing.' And now I had to decide if I was going to let that part of my life slip away with him, or if I loved it enough to brave it on my own.

I had barely thought of him since the eve of my birthday — I suppose because I didn't want the memory of him clouding my time here. But now, as I sat on that beach, mourning the fact that he wasn't there with me, I promised myself that someday, I wouldn't waste another moment missing him. But for now, I gave myself permission to stay in that moment of longing. Moments matter, and I knew this moment was trying to teach me something. I didn't need to run from it — I was safe here. I just had to be brave enough to sit through it.

It was starting to get dark as the sun was hanging low over the beach. It was deep and red like the colour of Spanish tomato sauce; it had flecks of orange like the peaches on my Dad's tree. And where the sunset met the water, it was pale, golden yellow, like a slice of Pedro's Orange Cake. I took out my journal and started writing a poem about it — my words were coming back to me too, healing me a little more with each page.

I'd be flying home in less than 24 hours and I knew I needed to head back to my room to start packing. I hugged my arms around my knees a little tighter, not wanting to go, but feeling ready for whatever was next. I had *faith* that I'd be okay, and almost unwittingly, I started to say the 10 words that I had been repeating over and over since August. This time, I spoke to myself.

"I'm sorry for all the times I wasn't strong," I started. "I'm sorry for not choosing you. I'm sorry for what I put you through when I was trying to survive. I'm sorry for all the moments when I didn't love you enough. I'm sorry for taking so long to see the truth."

I took a deep breath and clutched my knees closer.

"I forgive you for actions that weren't only yours. I forgive you for giving away your power. I forgive you for not knowing better at the time. I forgive you if you have to live in your grief for a little while longer. I forgive you for being who you needed to be to withstand the trauma of finally leaving (and of staying).

I love you for being strong now. I love that you trusted yourself enough to take this adventure."

I wanted to get up because it was dark and I was cold and the next part felt too big to say, but I stayed until I could muster those last words.

"Thank you. Thank you for feeding me. For nourishing me. For being willing to sit in the quiet even when it hurts. For getting back to your words. For getting back to the stove. Thank you for breaking the patterns that no longer serve you.

Thank you for allowing yourself to miss him this one last time, and thank you … *thankyouthankyouthankyou* … for getting him out of your system."

———

I'll never forget the way I felt when I stepped off that plane and just *knew* that I could do this. I'll never forget my first beer in Amsterdam. I'll never forget those Spanish girls whose lips tasted like chocolate. I'll never forget the way Pedro's Orange Cake felt on my tongue. I'll never forget those salty lupini beans.

And I'll never forget the way I felt on the beach that night.

PORTUGUESE LUPINI BEANS (V) (GF)

SERVES SEVERAL PEOPLE AS AN APPETIZER IF YOU FEEL LIKE SHARING, OR IF YOU'RE ME, SERVES ONE

I'd never tasted lupini beans before I went to Portugal, but they are now a staple in my home and I put a dish of them out whenever I have people over.

These beans are special because they have an outer shell that needs to be removed — think of shucking a sunflower seed with your teeth! That's where all the flavour is — so marinate them for as long as you want to really enjoy that flavour. You can also eat them plain, with no seasonings, but I find they taste even better with a great marinade.

Simple Lupini Beans

About 2 cups cooked, rinsed lupini beans (I recommend buying these in glass jars from a specialty stores or deli, but canned beans will also work. Just make sure you rinse them first!)

1 tbsp really good olive oil
1-2 sundried tomatoes, chopped as finely as you can
Juice of ½ lemon
1 tsp balsamic vinegar
1-2 cloves of garlic, chopped as finely as you can
1 tsp dried oregano
Pinch of dried chili flakes
Pinch of salt

Method

Drain lupini beans.
Toss with remaining ingredients.
Serve chilled while watching the sun set.

PART FOUR

WHATEVER YOU DO,
DO IT WITH GRACE.

Whether you're in culinary school or self-taught, you quickly learn about the two most important ingredients in your kitchen — salt and acid.

Salt has many jobs in the kitchen. Its most basic and principal job is to sharpen and magnify flavours. It also assists in fermentation. It changes the colour of green vegetables and the texture of meat. It strengthens gluten and imparts important flavour to otherwise lifeless starches. Salt is so important, in fact, that there is rarely even a sweet recipe that does not contain at least a pinch of salt.

Salt is the first thing we reach for when our food doesn't taste quite right. Now, if you've added a bit of salt, and your recipe still isn't perfect, the next step is to try adding a dash of acidity. Sour ingredients cut through richness and tie flavours together. The tastiest cultures have the sour part of food down — In Thai cooking it is often tamarind; in Mexican cuisine, it's a dash of lime. Fish and chips beg for malt vinegar. Fresh baked Italian bread dipped in balsamic is heaven. A squeeze of lemon, as you'll note in most of my recipes, is often what ties a dish together — Aglio Olio just isn't the same without it.

Salt and sour is, simply put, *magic* on your tongue.

———

When I returned from Europe, with my love of cooking in tow, my first move was to take an unpaid *stage* at one of my favourite restaurants. Staging is an in-depth (often unpaid) opportunity for chefs to go into another kitchen and see how it operates, as well as learn new skills. It had been over six months since I'd stepped foot in a professional kitchen but I felt like I was ready. I spent a week in Ohio, learning everything I could, feeling like I was starting from the beginning again. It was so awkward and a bit scary to be in a new kitchen, taking out my knives, and feeling so lost.

I had been instructed to braise 40 pounds of sliced white onions for a French Onion Soup base. I thought I already knew how to make French Onion Soup, but since I was there to learn, I followed the recipe exactly. As instructed, I peeled and sliced the onions. Next I heated equal parts butter and olive oil in a pan just until it was melted. Then I added the onions and let them sizzle a while, adding a bit of salt, and then quickly turned it down to a low, low temperature … as low as the stove would go … and let them cook for the day.

The Chef came over later and asked me if I had tasted my onions. When I told him I had, he asked me if I thought they were seasoned properly. "They're delicious," I replied eagerly. Next, he emptied a box of kosher salt upside down into his palm and poured it into the pot. I yelped — I thought it was a prank! It was a *lot* of salt. He stirred the mass of onions and asked me to taste it again.

The flavour had been completely transformed.

He asked me again if I thought the dish was seasoned properly while he took the lid off a bottle of sherry vinegar. Without responding, I watched as he poured in about half the bottle — much more than I would have added if you asked me how much acidity the dish needed. As he stirred the large pot with a wooden spoon that was half my height, he hummed and told me about what acid does to salt. It brings it out, and mellows it at the same time.

I thought I already knew everything I needed to know about seasoning. I thought I understood the importance of salt and sour.

We cooked it down further and instead of making a soup, we served it as a chunky spread on thick cut slices of Italian sourdough, generously slathered with butter and then the onion mix and then a very large slice of Emmental cheese. Into the broiler it went for a minute or two, to let the cheese bubble and then onto a plate. I assumed it was for a VIP guest. "For you," Chef offered, sliding it towards me. As soon as I took my first bite, he asked, "Do you taste the salt?"

"Yes," I replied, my mouth full of food.

"Do you taste the sour?"

Another muffled, "Yes," as I wiped cheese and butter from my mouth with the back of my hand.

"What else?"

"Onions?" I answered haphazardly.

"Did you see what I added at the very end?" he inquired, his eyebrow raised, looking in the direction of the pot of onions. The pot was being cleaned by the prep cook but next to it, I saw the box of salt, the bottle of vinegar … and a bowl of brown sugar!

"You might think that the onions are sweet enough," Chef interjected, finishing my thought before I began to speak. I had learned in the fine-dining world that adding sugar to anything that is meant to be naturally caramelized, is 'cheating.' Chef continued, "But do you not agree — that after all the salt and sour — they deserve a little sweetness of their own?"

FRENCH ONION SPREAD

MAKES ABOUT 8 PIECES OF TOAST

4 tbsp butter or olive oil
2 kg (about 4 medium) onion, peeled and sliced thin
2 sprigs rosemary or thyme, chopped fine
1 tbsp flour
Healthy splash of any dry white wine or beer
½ cup vegetable, beef or chicken stock
Sprinkle of salt (use a bit more than you think you need)
Glug of sherry vinegar
2 tbsp brown sugar, packed

8 slices of your favourite bread (Italian baguette works well!)
8 sliced of your favourite melty cheese (Emmental works well!)

Method

Heat butter or oil in a large frying pan. When warm, add all of the onions and let it sizzle. Start on medium-high heat and once the onions are softened and slightly translucent, turn your heat down to low.

Keep stirring onions on low for 30-40 minutes, until they are deep, deep brown and soft. Turn the heat back up to medium-high and add herbs and flour and cook for 1-2 minutes. Next, add beer or wine and stir vigorously for a few minutes until it is absorbed. Next add stock, salt, vinegar and sugar. Cook for an additional 5 minutes or so and then remove from the heat.

Turn on your broiler and get a cookie sheet ready with 8 slices of bread. Toast the bread *lightly* for 1-2 minutes. Remove from the oven and spread the onion mixture evenly over the toast. Top each slice with cheese.

Place back in the broiler for 2-3 minutes, keeping a close eye. Once the cheese is bubbly, it's ready to come out. Serve warm with some more of that beer or wine, and an extra sprinkle of Maldon salt, if you have it. Accept any hugs or love you can expect from your guests.

When I returned from my stage, I continued re-establishing my business and trying to get it back to where it was before I left it. Within one week of returning home, I had relaunched my website, made a Facebook post telling everyone I was back and found a commercial kitchen to rent.

Relaunching my catering company wasn't about *survival* anymore — it was about love. I wasn't doing it because it was the smart thing to do, or because it was what made the most sense financially, I was choosing to do this because I *wanted* it. I wasn't sure if I'd have the support I needed to get back off the ground — my customers had been through a lot with me since I started. I'd opened three kitchens in five years; each time, my customers followed, but I questioned whether or not they would follow me yet again. Each time I allowed fear to creep in, I remembered that night on the beach. Some moments were harder than others to remember to put my faith over fear — but in those moments I made sure I had physical reminders to help me through. I made a list of things that I wanted in my life and pinned it to my mirror so I would see it every day. I covered my wall in post-it notes, in a kind of strange vision board fashion. I sat on my bed with my recipes and notebooks and started planning menus for events I wanted to host. I manifested. I made plans. I experimented at home in my kitchen for family and friends.

The post-it notes on my wall read: *"You started your first company with nothing." "Your life unfolds in proportion to your courage."* And finally, the message I really needed to hear: *"You deserve some sweetness of your own."*

I was back! And it felt fucking good.

I officially relaunched my business on Easter weekend of 2018. I put out an ad offering homemade Easter chocolates, expecting to receive a few orders over the next few days and be able to make a little money over the long weekend. When I opened my email the very next day, my inbox was completely full! I blinked ... I rubbed my eyes ... I pinched myself ... and I'm pretty sure I mumbled a few curse words in disbelief. I had received 64 orders overnight.

I worked day in and day out until I'd made over 1,000 egg-shaped chocolates by hand. My friends helped build boxes and twirl ribbons. Other friends offered to make deliveries for me. My Dad lent me his kitchen and cleared out his fridge to help me make the deadline. My sister labelled every box with handwritten cards.

I almost didn't have time to breathe during that whole weekend, but when I did, and I was looking at my little pile of cash that I'd made all by myself, and beaming with gratitude for everyone who helped, I couldn't help but feel so fucking proud of myself. It felt like the whole entire *world* was rooting for me in that moment.

I couldn't believe I ever told myself that I couldn't do this.

———

Now that I was back to work, I didn't want slip into old habits of using my busyness to distract myself from my healing. Self-care had been something I had struggled with for my whole life. As a child, I didn't want to sit still long enough to have a bath or let my mother brush oil through my ratty hair. I'd always found ways to resist rest, especially during my time as a business owner. It would take time to break those habits and patterns I'd built, especially when it was so easy, as a perfectionist, people-pleaser, to slide back into neglecting myself.

I started by doing simple things — like eating when I was hungry and resting when I was tired or sore. Self-care eventually grew to mean having good boundaries. It meant saying no to things that didn't serve me or the greater good. Sometimes it meant long, luxurious baths on a Sunday evening, but during that year, self-care became more to me that just a *#SelfCareSunday* post on Instagram. It couldn't be *gentle;* I had to fight for it. There was a fierce knowing, deep within me that I was worthy of my own time, love and attention. It took a long time to get there, but eventually I realized that self-care was actually how I took my power back. With that realization, it became natural and repetitive. It became guilt free and something I didn't need to justify or compare.

Self-care, for me, became long walks in the forest with my dog tagging along beside me. It was eating alone at restaurants with no books or phone, often sitting at the bar and watching the kitchen in action. It sometimes meant yoga and meditation, other times it meant blaring hip hop and screaming out of my sunroof with my girlfriends. Often it meant eating well, drinking lots of water and tea, and other times it meant chugging beer and eating burritos on a curb at 4 a.m. Self-care meant balance. It meant moderation. It meant breathing warm country air in my hammock with the sun on my face. It meant eating the whole damn cake again, refusing to settle for crumbs. It meant time with my family and the people who meant the most to me, and it meant time by myself to sit in the quiet and think. More than any of those things though, it meant continuing to write.

Words became my highest form of self-care. Reading memoirs written by strong women, going to poetry slams and open mic nights, listening to music, storytelling and writing every day. Self-care, for me, was working on this very book, day in and day out for months. It also meant taking breaks from it and not rushing the process. It was going through all my old diaries and every single word I'd ever recorded. It was reading my father's diaries from when he backpacked through Europe 40 years ago. It was writing letters to myself and then burning them. It was writing letters to people and then sending them. Self-care was about *words.*

All of these things enabled me to have a voice again. It didn't always feel like a big deal, but each time I handled situations independently, I gained a little more of that voice.

When a client of my mine, Judy, messaged me to tell me that she was unsatisfied with my food, my heart sank. I recalled the first time I'd ever dealt with a disgruntled client — it was shortly after I'd moved in with Jeff and I'd launched my catering business the first time. I had almost no customer service experience at all so when I received a complaint about one of my meals being too salty, I didn't know how to handle it. I remember how I let that single comment ruin my entire weekend. I paced and panicked and let it fester.

I asked Jeff for help in that situation, partially because he had customer service experience, but mostly because he *offered* to rescue me. Jeff crafted an email to that client using all the big words he'd learned in hospitality school. It cost me a few hundred dollars to try to appease him, and on Jeff's advice, I showed up at his house with a gift basket full of free food and a hand-written apology letter.

I still lost that client, but it wasn't losing that client that stuck with me — it was how I handled it … or rather, how I *failed* to handle it. I was so afraid of confrontation that I let Jeff deal with difficult situations for me.

This time around would *have* to be different. I had no one to lean on this time, so when I got that email from Judy, I took three deep breaths, waited an hour, and carefully crafted a response. I apologized sincerely, owning up to my mistake and offered a partial refund in good faith. She responded almost immediately saying how impressed she was with how professional I had been, and has been a client ever since.

I was proud of myself in that moment because I observed before I reacted. I remembered my breath, I was mindful and I remained calm. My voice did not waver as I spoke my new truth. As my confidence grew, I started public speaking and offering coaching to other entrepreneurs. With each new opportunity, I grew steadier and more certain.

——

As I was watching my life unfold before me, another gift would come my way, one that I never expected — *Mackenzie*.

COMEBACK CREAM EGGS (V) (GF)

MAKES 24 EGGS

These cream eggs are as decadent as they sound — they're almost pure sugar which is why I only make them once a year around Easter. Each year, I sell more than the year before...and now I'm sharing them with you!

The yolks aren't necessary for this recipe, but they do add a nice touch. You can also add other flavourings like peppermint or add a whole hazelnut to the middle for something different.

For The Filling
3 cups icing sugar
½ cup light corn syrup
¼ cup white shortening
1 tsp vanilla
Yellow food colouring (or turmeric)

For The Chocolate Coating
4 oz dark chocolate
2 tbsp coconut oil

Method
Sift the icing sugar into a large bowl and combine with corn syrup, shortening and vanilla until very well combined. You can use your stand mixer for this on very low with the paddle attachment, or by hand with some muscle and a wooden spoon. The mixture will resemble fondant and be *very* thick. The trick to this recipe is to work with

everything when it's cold, so it's a good idea to chill your fondant mixture before you get started on the next steps.

Prepare a cookie sheet with parchment paper. Remove a golf ball sized amount of the mixture and add a few drops of yellow colouring to it. This will be your "yolk." Form this mixture into 24 small balls. (To get even sized balls, first roll this into a thin log and then cut it in half, then in half again and so on until you have 24 even sized pieces.)

With the remaining white mixture, do the same thing to form 24 balls.

Here's where you get to have fun! Don't worry if your eggs end up not being perfectly egg shaped — a circle is just fine because everyone will appreciate the fact that you made these from scratch. Poke a hole in the white circle and try to put the yellow circle (yolk) as close to the middle as possible. Again, if this isn't perfect, don't sweat it! Form into a round egg shape and place on the parchment. When you have 24 "eggs," place them in the fridge or freezer for 10-20 minutes to chill.

In the meantime, slowly melt your dark chocolate and coconut oil in a small bowl over a pot of boiling water (or in the microwave).

Once chilled, dip each egg into the chocolate so the chocolate comes halfway up the egg. Place on back on cookie sheet and chill again. Once the chocolate is set, carefully dip the other half in the chocolate. If you work fast and everything is chilled, you shouldn't end up with a seam but if you do, just serve that side of the egg face down and no one will be the wiser!

Chill eggs completely before serving or packaging. These make a lovely Easter gift but are delicious any time of the year.

Mackenzie and I made plans to have tea, and as the day approached, I grew more nervous. I hadn't seen or spoken to her since the week The Restaurant closed and I had no idea why she was reaching out now, nearly a year later. I mentally prepared myself for what might be an awkward or unpleasant conversation. This was the textbook definition of a situation I would typically run from.

When Mackenzie arrived, we started by making small talk about work, boys and travels. I could tell she was feeling a little lost because I'd seen that look in her eyes in my own reflection, just a few months earlier. I wanted to soothe her discomfort like that peppermint tea on a cold spring morning ... but more than anything, I wanted to tell her, face to face, how proud of her I was for doing what she did last August.

So I did, and I hoped it might help.

I told her that when I was her age, starting out in kitchens, just wanting to belong, that I don't think I could have done what she did. I told her she was brave and I realized that no one had ever told her that before. I was breathing deeply as I spoke, using all the tools and lessons I'd learned to make it through this difficult conversation with her. I wouldn't run from her when she needed me to stay.

"I always thought that The Restaurant closing was *my* fault ..." she confessed.

"It's *not* your fault, Mackenzie. Just like it's not Rachel's fault or Frank's fault ... And you know what ... *It's not my fault either.* The Restaurant closed because of Jeff."

Those words. *My words.*

I didn't realize how powerful my words could be until I said them out loud just like I didn't realize how much she probably needed to hear them. I continued by saying, "Mackenzie … if you hadn't done what you did … who knows where we would all be right now. I really, truly believe that I might not be here to talk to you today."

I knew if nothing else came from the conversation, I at least had the chance to tell her she was responsible for saving my life.

Mackenzie told me that she had been bouncing around from job to job, because she couldn't find one that made her feel like she belonged, the way she did at The Restaurant. She told me that I made her feel like she was part of a *family*. "I know I came into The Restaurant at a time that was really hard for you," she stated, "but it was the best job I've ever had. *You* were the best boss I've ever had."

Those words.

Her words.

I didn't realize how much I needed to hear those words.

———

When Mackenzie left, I sat in the quiet thinking about our conversation and everything it meant to me. Mackenzie and I were more alike than either of us knew; but I understood it now. I was so grateful that the silence had been broken. It had been such a complex piece of the puzzle for half a year, and now that it felt like it was resolved, I wondered what healing could take place in the now empty space I'd been gripping onto for dear life.

What Mackenzie had said to me was more powerful than I realized. I needed to know, more than anything, that I had been a good boss. The giant gap in my story had now been filled — I had evidence — I *was* a good boss. I told my cooks every single night how much I appreciated them. I never let them leave without saying thank you. I paid them well. I showed them respect. I offered to help them even if it made me feel stretched thin. I wanted them to know how much they were loved. *I did my best.*

Even when things were at their absolute worst … I. Still. Did. My. Best. I tried until the very end and no one could take that away from me.

The truth is … I did remarkable things at The Restaurant. I created memories. I made people cry, real tears, with *food*. I *moved* people. I cultivated change in the food system. I was successful, and I had a box of trophies and a drawer full of 'thank you' cards to prove it. I didn't need proof though — because I could feel it in the depths of my marrow.

And now, this story could finally leave me.

This story I'd been creating in my mind that I wasn't allowed to be proud of what I accomplished at The Restaurant. The story I'd been creating that was made up almost completely of shame and regret. The story that didn't allow me to even mention The Restaurant's name without cringing; that caused me to avoid old clients and customers who might want to discuss it. The story that triggered me so viscerally I could barely drive or even walk past The Restaurant without turning away.

Now, there was just one more thing I had to do ….

———

I prepared myself by opening my emotional 'toolbox,' and taking out everything that might help. This included 30 minutes of yoga and intentional breathing before I left the house, and another 20 or so deep breaths in my car when I arrived. I parked a short two minute walk away and got out of my car, bracing myself, like I would for some kind of impact. *Loosen your jaw,* I reminded myself. *Relax your shoulders.* I had reached the steps of The Restaurant and it was time to either turn back, or be brave.

I put one foot in front of the other and walked up the five steps it took to reach the patio.

The flower pots were overflowing with dried tomato plants and remnants of the garden I'd planted but never got to harvest, last spring. There was a huge blank space above the front door where our old sign had been hanging, and there were wires and

287

scraps of wood hanging down, revealing its rushed removal. A lightbulb in the corner of the patio was broken, with exposed glass on the ground below it. I wanted to sweep it up, and was tempted to tend to the planter boxes, but I knew I couldn't stay.

I'd come here with purpose. I needed to come here to take three deep, intentional breaths and then walk away for good. I walked the perimeter of the patio and decided not to cup my hands around my eyes and press them up against the window to try to see inside. The 'For Sale' sign that had been outside the building since we left was gone and the windows were covered in paper. I was technically trespassing now, so I braced myself to do what I'd gone there to do.

My first breath was so deep, the cool, damp air made my eyes water and my throat constrict. I swallowed hard and took a second breath, this time even deeper. I closed my eyes and felt a rush of emotions and tears coming to the surface — I'd been avoiding this moment for six long months, and the last inhale felt surreal. Surreal and unfair, just like the first and the last time I'd stepped foot in The Restaurant.

But it was over now. I had survived. I could go now.

I opened my eyes, walked down the steps and back to my car. I felt oddly calm — I might have even smiled a bit.

I knew I wouldn't have been able to do this without Mackenzie. *I love you, thank you,* I whispered to her as I got in my car. We'd already said, "I'm sorry," "I forgive you," out loud.

————

The commercial kitchen I was renting was a few blocks away so I decided to go there instead of going home right away. I took out my knives and placed a damp kitchen towel under my cutting board, wrapped an apron around my waist and opened the fridge to inspect its contents. It was the end of the work week, so the fridge was pretty bare save for some butter, parsley and garlic. I immediately knew what I should make; my mouth starting to water already as I imagined the smell of pungent, hot garlic

288

married with olive oil and lots of butter, slowly sweetening in the pan.

Aglio Olio was, in the simplest form, noodles with garlic (*'aglio'*) and oil (*'olio'*). My mother always made it for me when I was young, calling it Garlic Noo Noos. This was long before I appreciated good food or knew what the dish was called in Italian. Garlic Noo Noos became one of the only meals in my repertoire as a teenager (long before that attempted Pot Roast, I could figure out this simple pasta dish). Chloe and I made it together often and it had become a staple of mine since college. Whenever I was sick, sad, starving or hungover, Garlic Noo Noos did the trick.

I gently slid a pan onto a burner and fired it up, adding a few knobs of butter … one more for good measure. As it melted and the smell started to fill the small kitchen, I peeled and sliced six cloves of garlic into micro thin slices. Collecting them with the edge of my knife into my palm, I emptied them into the pan, listening for that familiar sizzle. I lowered the heat a touch and shook the pan gently.

Next, I chopped the parsley, first running my blade over my steel. The sound and smells overwhelmed my senses so much that I wanted to cry. I got to work on roughly chopping the parsley instead, holding back my tears for now.

When the garlic was soft and browned on the edges, I turned off the heat and moved the pan over to the stainless steel counter. From the fridge, I pulled out a container of cold spaghetti I'd cooked a few days earlier. I considered adding half, but gave in and added the full container to the pan. I tossed it quickly with the hot, garlicky butter, added the parsley and a glug of olive oil nearby. Lastly, a generous squeeze of a dried up lemon half I'd salvaged from the bar. Just before it went into the bowl I added a large pinch of flaked salt and a few grinds of black pepper. One more toss and into the bowl it went.

I considered pouring myself a glass of wine and grating some good, expensive cheese on my noodles; I also thought about sitting in the dining room to eat my meal like a civilized person.

But instead I decided to eat it right then and there, alone, leaning the back of my legs against the cold counter top.

I wanted to eagerly shovel forkfuls of Aglio Olio into my mouth, but I knew I would enjoy it more if I slowed down, so I wrapped noodles around my fork and slowly chewed, allowing the salt and sour to coat my tongue. The caramelized garlic made the dish slightly sweet; the good quality olive oil made it slightly bitter; the lemon was sour and there was plenty of salt. The love I felt in that moment started at my taste buds and ended at my toes.

I ate the entire bowl of pasta as if I had been starved for years. I suppose, in a way, I had been starving.

But now I knew what it felt like to be full. Full of salty, sour Noo Noos, and full of love. I wasn't ever going back to feeling hungry for either of those.

———

Cooking had been my saviour, but it had also been my crutch over the years. Ever since I was a child, but especially since I started cooking professionally, I craved control. It was why cocaine had appealed to me so much and why it was so hard to give up. It was why I avoided being in situations that I could not control, why I had a fear of even the smallest height of a ferris wheel, and why I had turned down so many opportunities in my life.

The kitchen was a place where I could control my environment though — or at least that's what I believed for many years. This was one of the reasons I fit into the fine dining scene so well — cooking at that level required a certain level of control … of *preciseness*. It required perfectly cut carrot batons, all lined up in a perfectly sized insert on a perfectly cleaned counter that I had bleached so hard my hands stung. Being hyper organized was one of the reasons I excelled at catering and entrepreneurship, and why I had seen so much success in such a short time. Perfectionism and success went hand in hand in this industry, and although my willingness to do whatever it took for success was engrained in me, it had cost me a lot over the years, too. I had lost staff and friends over it, when my temper flared in moments of high stress. I had missed out on countless important family events. I had pushed friends away over time and sometimes being in a state of minimal control caused me to lash out. I had developed anxiety over things I could not control. Being in control was like being high, so naturally, it was hard to give up.

I knew if I was going to pick up where I left off and start from scratch, I was going to have to adjust some of those core beliefs. I was going to have to be *more* than just a chef in a white coat, in a clean kitchen, with perfectly cut carrots. I was going to have to develop coping mechanisms to counteract my perfectionist tendencies. I was going to have to let go of the idea that my self-worth was directly related to my professional success.

For a long time, I wholeheartedly believed that passion equalled sacrifice. Somewhere along the way, I adopted the belief that to be truly in love with something or someone, you had to give up huge parts of yourself to make it work or to attain your goal. I know this because I was able to read back on my whole life through my diaries, and I could see all my old patterns, and where those core beliefs began. I could also see how they hadn't served me — being imperfect was inevitable; being in control all the time, was impossible. Once I was able to see all of this clearly, I was able to see that I didn't want to live with that much anxiety anymore. I had to adjust and shift (which was no easy feat but not impossible).

I decided that I wanted to be a person who found success in my happiness, not in how many caterings I booked, how much money I made or how many followers I had. I decided to wear my happiness like a badge of honour, instead of my busy-ness. I started to actively reject the idea that loving something meant abandoning yourself. And eventually, I no longer believed that being passionate about something (a person, a place, a job, a hobby, art, food, love) required great sacrifice.

This way of life was, of course, not instant. There was a major detox of my ego taking place, as everyone in my little world, including strangers I only knew on the Internet, were *rooting* for me. They all wanted me to be successful, or at the very least, they wanted me to get back on my feet. Although their support was greatly appreciated, it was hard to admit that I didn't always feel like the success story that they wanted me to be. Sometimes I felt tired. Sometimes I felt defeated, scared and uncertain about my future.

I wasn't going to get anywhere without a bit of hustle, so on the days I wasn't tired or scared, I worked hard. But the main thing that made this time different was simple — I was unapologetically, defiantly, irrefutably *honest*. I turned down clients when I knew I needed a night off for self-care. I stayed in bed instead of working if my shoulder pain flared up. I only accepted catering jobs that I truly *wanted*. I spoke to clients honestly (while being professional) about my limitations. I set boundaries like a motherfucker.

In the process, I learned that my clients didn't want me to be perfect ... they wanted me to be *human*. And happy.

GARLIC NOO NOOS
FEEDS 1 HUNGRY HEART

In their most simple form, Garlic Noo Noos, or Aglio Olio, is just some boiled pasta, heated with some garlic and oil. This version has been eaten around the world by line cooks and service staff forever. In its fancy-form, it's served with chilies, lemon and really good cheese... sometimes a splash of wine, some cream or fresh herbs. You could even serve this with some chicken or garlic shrimp. My version of this dish has always been the most simple and this is what I eat when I'm hungover, sick, sad or feeling nostalgic.

I promise — if you cook this dish and eat it all, you will feel happy from the inside out.

For The Noo Noos

200 grams (about ½ a box) any kind of pasta you like (my favourite is spaghettini)

3 tbsp butter

6 cloves garlic, peeled and sliced thin (yes, use them all!)

Juice of half a lemon

1 small handful of chopped parsley, or a pinch of dried parsley

1 tsp salt

½ tsp black pepper

Parmesan cheese (optional)

Chili flakes (optional)

Method:

Cook noodles according to directions. For this, you need lots of boiling water and lots of salt. Be careful not to overcook. You want these noodles *al dente* ("to the bite," or, a little chewy). While your noodles are cooking, heat a large skillet, melt butter and oil on lowest setting. Add garlic and let cook for 5-7 minutes until fragrant. You're not looking to brown the garlic here — just flavour the oil and get everything happy. Add cooked noodles to the pan and increase to medium-high heat. Stir vigorously until pasta is sizzling, about 3 minutes. Remove from the heat and add lemon juice and parsley.

Season with salt and pepper (use more than you think you need) and pour into your favourite bowl. It will be slightly oily. Eat it slowly and send a prayer to people who don't eat carbs.

Toward the end of summer, I catered a 'high tea' event and decided to make a three tier Earl Grey Chiffon Cake with lavender vanilla-bean frosting. To make this elaborate cake, I sifted the pastry flour and sugar, carefully mixing it with chilled steeped Earl Grey tea concentrate and orange peel. I folded it gently and poured the batter into a meticulously lined cake pan. I watched the cake rise through the glass window of the oven door diligently for over an hour; being careful not to make any sudden moves or noises that might cause this high maintenance cake to fall. After carefully sliding it out of the pan and patiently waiting for it to cool so I could spread frosting on it, that cake crumbled to pieces.

I followed the recipe exactly. I double and triple checked the bake time and temperature. I consulted baking blogs and followed their instructions for testing my flour and baking soda's quality. In the end, there was no logical explanation for why that cake refused to hold together.

There was also no time to be frustrated or to start again. I had to be at the catering in a few hours so I did what any resourceful chef would do and started using icing as a 'glue' to form it back together. It was messy looking at first, but after going over it several times with a few extra layers and smoothing it out, that cake looked pretty good! No one would be the wiser — especially when chunks of cake were dunked into heaping cups of frothy coffee and black tea.

That cake got me thinking though — about my friendships that still needed a bit of icing to hold them together.

———

I had been focussing an awful lot of energy that year into carefully icing over the cracks that I'd made in my friendships. A lot of my relationships, especially with those involved at The Restaurant, felt more complicated than I could even find words for. A lot of my friendships felt like icing just wasn't going to do.

Mackenzie and I got together often. Watching her struggle to find her place in kitchens and in life, made me desperately want to just give her my recipe and show her, step-by-step, how to navigate through life and love and words and food. She would make it through eventually though — but she would do it in her own way. Instead of an elaborate Earl Grey chiffon cake she'd probably make some badass cupcakes with chocolate frosting and gold flakes. I tried to make sure she always knew she had a very special place in my heart and that there was always room for her at my table.

Sara moved away but we stayed in close contact and continued to get together whenever she came back to visit family. She promised to be first in line to buy this book and I believed her. Brandon and I became even closer friends and he continued to work for me at my catering company as my sous chef. Scarlett joined my front-of-house team too. It took almost three years for Marie to reach out, but eventually she did and we managed to keep in touch as well. These friendships felt innocent and transparent. Instead of icing over the cracks I'd made, I just let them be. These friendships had been crumbled and were slightly broken, but they were still edible and had sweet spots.

Rachel's store saw great success and she came to me often, to vent about her work related stress. I tried to give her my recipes for self-care, therapy, yoga ... but it turns out, sometimes these difficult lessons are things we must learn on our own. I could give her my cookbook, but I couldn't make the recipe for her. And I couldn't cheat and buy her a cake — she'd have to figure it out for herself. All I could do was be there for her until she did.

My friendship with Chloe became a complicated mess of crumbs and frosting, mashed up in a bowl with some screaming matches and tears. But we refused to abandon it and eventually made something beautiful with our mess. Cake pops, perhaps!

After some struggling, we figured things out and even booked a trip to Ireland together that summer. It was a road trip of a lifetime — messy at times, but wonderful. We laughed and cried and drank and danced. We fought and made up and told secrets and cast spells. We ate potatoes and fried fish almost every day.

I really wish I could say that all my friendships made it out of that tumultuous year, but the truth is, sometimes cakes just don't work out. Baking, as it turns out, is as fickle as the art of letting go.

My friendship with Frank, try as we may, never really went back to the way it was. I always knew I could call him if I ever needed him, but sometimes the distance he put between us shook the life out of me. Walls went up where I thought they wouldn't. I let my ego run wild at times, causing me to bounce between jealousy and resentment. Those heavy emotions sometimes caused me to doubt my worthiness instead of understanding the simple fact that wounds still hurt when they are poked.

Frank and I both tried to mend our friendship for a long time. We frosted all the cracks and kept layering it on with invitations to dinner parties and messages and phone calls. We tried and tried but I eventually realized that sometimes a broken cake is just that — broken. Realizing this created an intense, new grief inside of me that I couldn't even find words for. Over time, Frank and I drifted apart with heavy hearts. It happened as gracefully as it could and I believe we walked away with immense respect for one another. That was going to have to be enough for me.

———

In addition to making amends, I'd spent the last year desperately avoiding being alone. I either chose people who were entirely incompatible for me, or I chose people who wouldn't be crushed when I inevitably ran them out of my life. Even for the good ones (of which there were a few), I wasn't willing to put those love goggles back on. I tried to force companionship a few times in faraway place, with the girl next door, multiple first date

297

attempts and a brief stint on Tinder. None of those tactics will work, as I was learning, if you aren't willing to trust *yourself.*

I was still working on it, so I wore a ring on my left hand to remind me that I wanted to be on my own for a while. My friends affectionately called it my 'celibacy ring,' which in a lot of ways, it was. I had grown tired of breaking hearts, so abstinence seemed like a good idea. Some days I needed that ring more than others. Some days it felt easier to sit and flirt with a stranger for a few hours, but in those moments I would look down at my ring and rub it so many times that the tip of my thumb felt raw. It reminded me that although it would be easier to fall back into old patterns and relationships, it wasn't what was best for me. Some of those nights it took everything I had not to call one of the boys who got away, for a quick night of comfort, but I tried to honour what my ring symbolized.

I focused on myself, my work and my friendships instead of romance. I focused on yoga, daily meditation and healing work. I had conversations with that Little Girl who had spent the last six months mourning in her childhood home. That Little Girl who spoke to me in the pub that night with Monica. That Little Girl who reminds me when I need to rest. That Little Girl who sings in the grass, hugs strangers and loves with total abandon. That Little Girl who rides every ferris wheel she sees because she knows fear is just a part of life.

Life had made that Little Girl tired. Life had forced her to grow up too fast. I had allowed her to be hurt and tossed around and fucked so hard it hurt and then left behind. I allowed her to be overworked, stressed, stretched, forgotten about, tossed aside and as a result, I worried that she was jaded toward me.

So I was ready to spend some time with her. *She* was the one I needed to make amends with now. I was ready to show her I loved her, and ask for her forgiveness. She was my higher self after all; my greatest good. She was my best friend; my soulmate. She was the one who finished this book when it felt like I was too weak to go on. She was the one who got up on stage and whispered in my ear to be brave. She was the one who loved her friends endlessly. She was the one who kept going to therapy. She was the one who held my hand through it all.

Loving that Little Girl changed everything. (The celibacy ring helped too.)

————

My ring fell off a few months later. I lost it in the ocean on the coast of Ireland the day after I had a one night stand with an actor I'd met in a hostel in Galway. I was feeling liberated (and drunk) when my friends convinced me that it was perhaps time to explore the *fun* part of being single, instead of being so wrapped up in the healing process. The next day, while my friends and I drove our hungover, groggy bodies to the beach, I realized my ring was gone. I insisted we comb through the sand and pebbles looking for it, but eventually ended up in a fit of laughter with my friends at the irony of the cosmic joke.

We never found the ring and by the time I was home from Ireland, I'd given up the idea of replacing it. I didn't need the reminder anymore. I knew in my heart that was the last time I would be someone's 'Galway Girl.' I knew I was done being careless with whom I gave my midnights to. I knew that when I was ready to finally give my heart to someone new, that they would have to be a special person. I knew that I would have to trust myself fiercely before trusting another, so that I would never again say to someone, "Show me what you want me to be, so you'll love me," again. I knew that when I met the right person, I wouldn't need to explain that to them, but that they would just *know*.

I didn't need someone who could shift my world with their romantic gestures; I needed someone who shifted humanity with their love.

I didn't need someone to remind me that I was beautiful or that I was enough; I needed someone to remind me if I ever forgot about "Self!"

I didn't need someone who would tell me I was doing great; I needed someone to tell me that it was okay if I wasn't okay.

I didn't need someone to hold my hand as I walked through life; I needed someone who held me with an open palm.

I didn't need someone who would love me despite my story; I needed someone who loved me *because* of my story.

I didn't need someone to take me to all the best restaurants or fly me across the world; I needed to be with someone who understood I could do that all on my own, and wanted to join me when I was ready.

I didn't need someone who was eager for me to be their whole family or to be my best friend; I needed someone who placed immense, deep-rooted value in their own family, whether it was the one they were born into or the one they had built.

I didn't need someone who found me inspiring; I needed someone who was already inspired.

I didn't need someone to lie next to, to keep me warm at night; I needed someone who made me feel warm from the inside out.

I didn't need someone to make me a better person; I needed someone who tried their hardest to make the world a better place for me, for our children and for themselves.

I didn't need someone to be my guardian; I needed someone to be my witness.

I didn't need someone to love me; because I loved me.

I didn't need to feel like I was on a rollercoaster. Instead, I wanted the kind of love that makes you feel like you're on the beach with crystal clear waves caressing your skin and a bright, blue sky of possibilities overhead. When I fell in love again, I wanted the kind of love makes me feel the way I do when I'm eating overflowing bowls of Aglio Olio. I want a love that makes me feel the way I do when I'm backpacking the world, eating Pedro's Orange Cake, stepping off a plane in a new place and dancing in the moonlight. I want a love that makes me feel like

I've arrived and one that makes me feel like I'm going home. I want a love that feels safe and wild. I want a love that makes me feel like I'm at a big table, laughing with friends, cooking beautiful food. I want a love that makes me feel the way I do when I tell stories.

For this special person, I was willing to *wait.* I was going to be patient and not go searching. I would continue to live my very best life, work on my memoir, go to therapy and heal. I would do it all while travelling the world, cooking my heart out and becoming more of the girl I saw in the mirror every day and told, "I'm sorry. I forgive you. I love you. Thank you."

I was willing to wait for him or her for the first time since I was 16 years old.

COLCANNON (GF)

SERVES 8 SIDES OR 4 MAINS (BECAUSE YES, SOME PEOPLE EAT A BOWL OF MASHED POTATOES AND CALL IT DINNER.) (THERE'S KALE IN IT, OKAY!?!)

I had the choice here to include my Earl Grey chiffon cake recipe, or this recipe for Colcannon that I picked up in Ireland. When I started to think about how I would rather spend my time in the kitchen, buttery mashed potatoes took the lead pretty quickly!

I can't count the amount of times I ate this dish while travelling in Ireland — Colcannon is basically the best mashed potato you've ever had in your life. I did some research and experimenting, and this is as close as I could get to the way it tasted in Ireland. Basically it's butter, with a side of mash!

For The Butter
1 cup (2 sticks) butter or margarine
1 small white onion, finely diced
4 cloves garlic, sliced
2 sprigs rosemary, minced

301

For The Potatoes
1 kg potatoes (8-10 medium sized) peeled and roughly chopped
Packed ½ cup kale, sliced very thin
1 tbsp Dijon mustard
1 ½ tsp salt
½ tsp black pepper
Dash nutmeg

Method
In a small pot, melt butter and add garlic, onion and rosemary. Let this mixture steep on very low for about one hour. This may require you to move it on and off the burner — just be careful not to let this golden nectar burn!!

Meanwhile, put potatoes in cold, salted water and bring to a boil. Boil until cooked well — you should be able to break one easily with a fork (about 30-40 minutes on medium-high heat). Strain potatoes and while hot, add the butter mixture, sliced kale and remaining ingredients. Mash while controlling drool. Adjust seasonings and serve immediately. Don't be ashamed to add an extra dab of butter to the top.

Bonus points for turning any leftovers into delicious fried potato pancakes. Just mix in a few pinches of flour and a few tablespoons of egg with remaining potatoes, form into patties and fry in a cast iron skillet on medium heat with lots of oil.

As the anniversary of the day we closed The Restaurant approached, there was a mix of volatile emotions that came with it. It had been the most intense year of my life, without a doubt, and although there were parts of me that were still blistered and broken, I was also very proud of everything I'd accomplished. But as the year mark approached, I began to feel anxious, as if something was stirring. There was this *feeling* bubbling up inside me. A feeling of ... unfinished business, as if something needed to be said (or screamed). The more I tried to calm it down, the more it pushed itself up in my throat, until one day, as I was driving home from grocery shopping, the feeling crept up on me so furiously I had to pull my car over, thinking I was going to be sick. I was close to home — I could actually see the grapevines in my Dad's yard from where I was parked. I turned the car back on thinking that it was probably nothing ... perhaps I was low on sugar and just needed to get home. My body began shaking and a real threat of projectile vomiting ensued, so I took my keys out of the ignition once more, and held them in my lap. I sat there, alone in my car, surrounded by bags of groceries, feeling sick to my stomach and light in the head, and not entirely sure why. I started talking to myself in an effort to calm myself down, and I was completely shocked by the words that flowed out of me.

"I know it's easier for people if I'm doing well. And I am......... doing well," I began. "I know it feels better when I just try to be happy. And I am........... trying........" I trailed off, my tear ducts swelling.

So much of my energy had been spent trying to forget him and get him out of my system, I sometimes forgot that, for a time, he was the person who I imagined myself spending the rest of my life with. It felt somehow wrong to mourn the loss of him, and there was shame attached to the idea of missing him at all.

I rubbed the centre of my chest and continued, "I gave him this huge piece of me that I wasn't ready to give. I just handed it over to him … willingly … with no cost or conditions or boundaries. I gave him this huge, huge piece of myself and I didn't even miss her." I looked at myself in the mirror. *Was I really the one I needed to talk to right now?* By the time I started speaking again, I was yelling. Screaming into the air that surrounded me in my car. Screaming at *him.*

"… She's been missing since the day I met you and I want her back. I want her back, Jeff!!!!"

I was grasping at my steering wheel and had started shaking. I had gone from having a seemingly quiet revelation in my car surrounded by the ingredients to make mushroom soup, to having a full blown, imaginary conversation with Jeff. I hadn't spoken to him in months, but my sub-conscious had decided it was finally time. It was finally time to tell him how angry I was, how hard the last year had been and how much I missed him.

And, it was time to admit to myself what I'd been avoiding — that when we truly love who we are, we don't tend to give up huge pieces of ourselves to others, without thinking twice.

"It's easier for people if I'm angry at you …" I trailed off not wanting to say it out loud. I stared out the window and wondered what would happen if I just started my car and forgot this conversation ever happened and went on my way and just drove. If I didn't make myself go through what I was about to say out loud. If I kept myself safe from whatever pain this moment was going to stir up inside of me. I thought back to the last time I ran from a moment that mattered because it felt like it was going to be too hard. I thought about that girl sitting in that pub across from Monica. I thought about wanting to run from conversations with Rachel and Nancy and all the others. I realized that this moment wasn't so different from those, and I wondered if it was possible

304

to give myself the same time, space and love that I gave to them, in those moments.

I dug my heels in. I braced myself. I took three of the deepest breaths my lungs would allow. In my head, I could hear the words of all the brave women who had come before me, all the women who loved me, my mother, Ruby, my soul sisters, Di, my favourite authors and storytellers and healers. I could hear them saying, *"Those moments didn't wreck you and this one won't either. Be strong. Say it."*

"Life is easier if I hate you," I began. "Hating you is the only way I can make sense of what happened. To do this, I've had to dig up evidence from our six years together. I've forced myself to believe that you are sick and deranged and a terrible person, because it's the only way I could have made it through the worst year of my life. If I believe you are sick, that means that you might have still loved me through all of this. But here's the thing: if you aren't mentally ill or a sociopath or a sexual predator, then what?" A pause. Another three deep breaths. "Then ... what??!?" I was shouting now. "... You just ... didn't love me?!?!" Snot dripped from my nose.

"You. Didn't. Love. Me." I repeated it again and again, holding myself and rocking back and forth until my voice trailed off again. I contorted in my chair. I felt like poorly microwaved food with hot spots all over but my insides were cold. That's when it came.

The rebellion ceased and the truth was right there in front of me. All I had to do was reach out and grab it, if I was brave enough.

I dug my heels in again and concluded, "If you didn't love me, that has nothing to do with me."

It had nothing to do with my worthiness. It had nothing to do with being enough. It had nothing to do with my personality, my actions, my problems, my weight, my freckles, my words, my tastes, my temper, my talent, my family or any of the other things

305

that made me, me. Perhaps since day one, he *wanted* to love me. When we fell hard for each other that night on his couch, he might have believed he loved me as much as I believed I loved him. But the fact that Jeff couldn't love me had absolutely nothing to do with me.

All I could control was how much I loved myself, and how much I loved others. But I could not control how much Jeff loved, or failed to love me. I had tried for years, doing everything I could think of, for him to think I was worthy enough for his love. For him to want to marry me. For him to finally step up and be a good man. All those years I spent feeling like I wasn't enough, doing whatever I could to be loved were crashing down before me. Those years had worn me out. They'd buckled me, weathered me, and jaded me.

I'd spent the last year trying to *unbuckle* myself. Contorting and clawing and sprouting out of the space I was in after he was gone. Over what had almost been a full year, I'd examined the situation forwards and backwards, sideways and inside out, and no matter what I conjured up, I could never quite feel settled on any given explanation. I realized in that moment in my car, that there *was* no explanation for why he did what he did. His childhood wounds were not an excuse for his poor behavior — plenty of people have tough upbringings (much tougher than his), and they don't act out the way he did.

So, I decided right then and there, for the first time in a year, that I wasn't going to make excuses for him anymore. That didn't mean that I couldn't show him mercy or grace. What it meant was that I could finally stop seeking answers. I could let go of all of those unanswerable questions I'd been carting around with me for a whole year because I understood the biggest truth of them all — that he must have been in *so much* pain to do what he did. I dried my eyes in my mirror. Another three deep breaths; decidedly calmer now.

The next words that came out of my mouth were perhaps some of the most important words I'd ever said to him, even though it was only in my imagination. "How could you have loved me, when you didn't love yourself?" I repeated the question several times.

There is no way someone who loved themselves would act that badly. There is no way someone who loved themselves could be so cruel and careless with someone else's heart. Jeff did not love himself despite his best efforts to show the world that he did. And the reason I knew this was explicitly true, was because I recognized that truth in myself. Hurt people hurt people. And when you walk this world knowing that you are incapable of love, because you do not and cannot love yourself, it creates the distinct kind of pain that enables narcissists and people like Jeff to do the horrible things that he did.

A lot of things that happened that year were Jeff's fault. I don't need to list them here just like I didn't need to list them that moment in my car. As I looked at my own eyes in my mirror that day, I knew things were going to be different from here on out. I can't explain it; it was just a knowing. I was now in possession of a truth I couldn't ignore. A truth so powerful it could guide me to being able to say those 10 words to Jeff someday. A truth so powerful it could allow me to close my eyes and feel peaceful the next time I heard his name.

As these thoughts rolled around in my chaotic brain, a flashback occurred. Jeff. Kneeling in our kitchen. Holding my waist. Begging me to go with him.

Rejecting that offer to flee had been the first time, since the day I met him that I had chosen myself over *him*. I had been chiselling off little pieces of myself to give to him for six years because I was desperately looking for something in myself that I hadn't found yet. Belonging. True Love. Family. I thought I'd found it when I found him ... but the truth is, I had gotten farther away from myself with each day and each year and each moment that passed.

That part wasn't his fault.

A lot of things were his fault. But the fact that I didn't love myself, that was on me.

This lead to an even bigger question which I also repeated out loud to myself several times, "How could I have loved *him* all that time, when I didn't love *myself?*"

———

Without fully realizing it, I was standing now. I was in the ditch beside my car, my feet planted firmly on the ground as I rooted down and clenched my fists. I was quietly repeating my revelation to myself, *"You must have been in so much pain to do what you did ..."* But I wasn't only speaking to Jeff when I said it. I was also speaking to Louis. I was speaking to my mother. I was speaking to Doug. I was speaking to my friends who had chosen to leave this world too soon.

I was speaking to myself now, too. I was in so much pain the day I asked those girls to sign those contracts; the day I fired Frank. I was in so much pain the day I decided to open our doors for one last weekend. I was in so much pain when I asked Sam not to tell anyone what happened to her. My most shameful actions had been born from my loudest pain. *You must have been in so much pain ...* It wasn't an excuse for either of us, but I kept saying it over and over as I started walking from the ditch across the field to the forest that was behind my Dad's house.

There was a pebble covered, dirt pathway from the road to the edge of the field. It would only take 10 minutes or so to walk the few hundred metres through the field to the edge of the forest. Directly on the other side of the forest was my Dad's yard. I'd walked through that forest more times than I could count. Every spring, my Dad and I went foraging for wild leeks. In the winter, I took my dog on long walks through the untouched, snowy forest floor, watching her play and laughing as her snout was covered in a mix of pure white snow and deep brown earth. I took Mackenzie there to show her the old abandoned tree house I loved when I was a girl. *I've been here before,* I said to myself as I walked across the field, now at a frantic pace, finally arriving at the crest of the forest.

I looked back at my car, far in the distance now, and considered going back. But my legs had brought me here and I was ready to learn whatever lessons the forest had to give me. I walked several metres into the uber green forest; trees with leaves as lush as they would get. I clenched my fists and pushed them down to the ground. Finally standing still, I lifted my shoulders, filled my lungs with more air than they should hold, bent over slightly and let out a solid, searing scream. I screamed until my throat hurt, my stomach muscles clenched and my face was red and hot with tears. I let it all go in that forest where I grew up and where I'd spent the last year mourning and healing and talking and changing. I let go of spending another moment wondering why Jeff did what he did. I let go of the idea that he might get help someday. I let go of thinking about his new girlfriend, of wondering if he'd ever be a good man. I let go of blame and spite and resentment. I let go of all that hate wrapped around my heart.

I let it all go as I fell to my knees in a fury of words and silence. Sometimes you have to keep your sorrow in the woods, for she is the only one still enough to hold it. Trust me when I tell you that she can, and she will.

I lay on the ground for a few minutes, calmer now, grounded by the dampness of the leaves and twigs pressing against the backs of my knees. I was overtaken by that same feeling I had when I left the pub after talking to Monica and seeing the truth for all that it was. That feeling of being eerily tranquil despite the storm that had just erupted. That moment had changed my life; this one did too. Moments matter.

I spoke once more, but much softer now. I spoke directly from the very middle part of my heart which at that time, felt so exposed it could have been hanging down by my knees, covered in gooseberries and dried leaves, resting limply on the forest floor with the rest of me.

"… It's okay that we leapt," I began. My throat was sore from screaming so I spoke even quieter now, no longer speaking out of anger or resentment, but from *grace*. The woods held me as I continued, "It's okay that you robbed me of myself when I didn't fight to keep her. It's okay that you took so much of what I gave so blindly. And it's okay that we broke apart."

One more deep breath — the deepest yet. I exhaled fully while I brought my hand to my chest and my eyes to the sky. Truth and trust. Love and fear. Honest and ugly. Salt and sour.

"It's okay if we let go now …"

Shortly after my declaration, I picked myself up and walked out of those woods. I walked in the direction of my Dad's house instead of to my car, knowing it could remain there for the day and I could pick it up tomorrow. What I needed now was rest. I crossed the field and found my way to my Dad's front door, where I knew I needed to be. I collapsed on the porch before I made it to the chair, but it didn't matter, I was safe here. I'd always been safe here.

———

This moment was the start of something new. The peace it would allow into my life would not unfold for almost another full year. But that's the thing about big moments and forests — they take a long time to grow into their fullness.

FOREST SOUP (GF)

SERVES 8 APPETIZER SERVINGS OR 4 ENTREES

This recipe is best when made with wild mushrooms and ramps. The season for these is short, so I always make a double or triple batch and freeze it, and use any leftover leek greens for pesto. This soup symbolizes the beginning of my favourite season — foraging season! You can of course make this soup from store-bought mushrooms and leeks — it is hearty and delicious either way.

For The Soup
2 tbsp butter or olive oil
2 kg mushrooms, cleaned well, sliced thin
200 grams wild leeks (or 2 large regular leeks) cleaned well and sliced thin
1 tbsp garlic, minced
2 sprigs rosemary or thyme, chopped fine
Healthy splash of any dry white wine (optional)
4 medium potatoes, peeled and medium diced
4 cups vegetable or chicken stock
2 packed cups spinach or kale, roughly chopped
½ cup heavy cream
Juice of half a lemon
Dash of hot sauce or pepper, plus salt to taste

Method
First, clean the leeks and mushrooms very well, especially if using wild ones! There's all kinds of dirt and possibly critters living within those leaves, so soak them in a sink full of cold water 1-3 times until the water runs clear. Dry them well on towels before cooking.

Heat butter and oil in a heavy bottom, large pot. Sauté mushrooms first, stirring often and letting them brown. Next add garlic, herbs and leeks and let them soften on medium-high heat for 5 minutes or so. Next, giving yourself some space to avoid any steam, add a healthy splash of white wine, stirring well and cooking on high for about 2 minutes. Next, add potatoes, stock and seasonings. Let simmer with a lid on, on medium-high for 25-30 minutes, until potatoes are tender.

Remove from heat and add spinach or kale. Take half the soup from the pot and add it to a blender. Purée with cream until smooth and add back to the pot. This soup is best when half blended, and half left chunky... but use your own discretion here. Season with lemon and hot sauce and reheat gently.

Serve warm with big chunks of bread or crackers.

311

I woke up a few hours later on my Dad's porch. I stayed outside to absorb what was left of that gorgeous, late summer day. My experience in the woods had both invigorated and exhausted me, so I spent the rest of the day in my hammock for as long as the sun would allow.

In a few days, the anniversary of The Restaurant's closure would arrive. On that day, I decided to gather my friends and decorated a huge table with homemade food and did one of the bravest things I've ever done. My legs shook beneath me as I read a chapter from this book to them aloud. As my knees and voice shook, I heard that Little Girl remind me, *"This is the life you are fighting for."* These are the things I could now safely bring to the table. Food and words. My cookbook memoir.

———

It had been a full year of lessons and losses; a year of learning and healing. It was the year I made a beautiful life from scratch.

In that year, I'd lost my grown-up house but gained a new appreciation for my childhood home. I conquered so many fears that year including banishing my fear of heights (which I cured by riding every single ferris wheel I saw that year — county fair time was coming up again!) I had written almost an entire book. I became a public speaker, a poet and a world traveller. I made friends; I lost friends. I spent time being both celibate and explored my sexuality. I was productive and I rested. I demolished core beliefs that had been with me since I was a child and I built stronger ones that were fueled by love instead of fear. I made amends. And I officially filed for bankruptcy.

Bankruptcy stung. It created a lot of resentment knowing that Jeff didn't have to face the same consequences I did. But after some time and healing, I realized that filing for bankruptcy was actually a *privilege*. It was my way of breaking free from him. It certainly was not easy to accept and the process was grueling and sometimes humiliating, but as time went on, I allowed it to sting less and less. I changed my language from, "I have to file for bankruptcy," to, "I *can* file for bankruptcy." This was the price for my freedom and it is a price much less than some people pay for theirs.

More importantly than all of that though, the thing that impacted me most about the one-year-mark was that *I survived.* One year. Thirteen moon cycles. Twelve months; four seasons. Seven countries; thirteen plane rides. Fifteen ferris wheels. 75,000 words. Close to 100 therapy sessions and 365 Ho'oponopono prayers.

It was time for the next adventure, so I decided to pack up the few things I had and moved to the city.

——

After a brief search, I was lucky to find a rental property that was not only close to my family but was also relatively affordable. It also didn't require a credit check which was helpful because although my finances were starting to get back on track, it was going to be a while before I was free from bankruptcy. (That day did come, the following summer, and I celebrated it with close friends and a bottle of Dom Pérignon!)

Starting from scratch is never easy but my new home was never empty and my fridge was never bare. Friends gave me their old couches and dressers, my Dad helped me build a bed, my mother bought me plush towels and my sister helped me decorate. My new home was modest, but it was my own. I manifested what I wanted my home to be like using chalk on my living room wall. I used words like 'safe,' 'warm,' and 'calm.' The kitchen was small but it was there that I made Pedro's Orange Cake on Sundays. I made Aglio Olio in huge batches when friends came

314

over — noodles and garlic were inexpensive so I splurged on real butter and good olive oil. The antique kitchen tools that hung in the entranceway of The Restaurant now hung on my dining room wall. They hung there as I threw dinner parties for friends, when I hosted my first Thanksgiving with my family and as I spread out my first manuscript on the dining room table.

In my hallway, I hung a picture of The Restaurant to serve as a reminder of a difficult time, but of something I achieved none the less. It made me feel brave every time I looked at it. I covered a new wall with new post-its, goals, dreams and reminders. This time, I included my desire to go back to school, do a TED talk, finish my manuscript and run a marathon.

I found a trail nearby for me and my dog to hike along. I explored my new neighbourhood but brought her back to my Dad's home often, partly for her, partly for me, and partly for him. I visited him every week and called him often when my thermostat wasn't setting right or when there was a leaky pipe in the basement. I never stopped needing my father.

I spent evenings in my bathtub reading memoirs. Most mornings, I meditated in my office where there was a patch on the floor that felt warm to the touch, if I got there early enough. That home became my sanctuary and where all the things I was afraid of became possible.

I even bought myself a lemon tree.

———

The gaping wound that was left from Jeff and The Restaurant was now covered in a thick layer of love. It had been stitched up tightly by my girlfriends who had loved me back to life. It had been disinfected by my parents and my sister, constantly rinsing the wound and tending to me. The scar was smoothed over by travel, adventures with strangers, living in hostels and standing on my own two feet. It had been healed by learning how to cook again and falling in love with my words.

Walking past the site of what was The Restaurant still felt challenging. For over a year, the windows were boarded up and it all felt very symbolic. The day it reopened as a sandwich shop might have been a difficult day, but honestly, that felt symbolic too. The same way I was coming back to life, so was that beautiful, old building.

There were tiny sprinkles of salt and sour every now and then that made their way into my wound. Although the wound was scabbing over, there were things that triggered me over the next year that caused an instant sting. I was left out of an article about Strong Female Chefs, by my city's most popular culinary publication, because of the big black X Jeff had left on my reputation. I still drove an extra 15 minutes to a grocery store on the other side of town because the thought of running into Jeff still sent me into a slight panic. I had to decide how I was going to navigate friendships with people who were still associated with Jeff — which was so much more complicated than I ever imagined it would be. I was constantly approached by customers of The Restaurant, some of them still quite disgruntled 18 months after we closed, who demanded I reimburse them for gift certificates.

Sometimes triggers came in the form of phrases like, *"When you went out of business,"* or *"Restaurant life isn't for everyone."* Sometimes, I felt impatient by a stranger's ignorance, but I was able to show them kindness, more often than not. I understood what true compassion looked like, after all, because I gave it to myself on such a regular basis.

Sprinkles of salt and sour might always sting. But I try my best to use the tools I've learned about in therapy and yoga. I try my best to stay calm and integrated, which is of course easier when it's just a papercut. Sometimes big wounds opened, like when we found out my sister's tumour came back, when Ruby passed away or when my landlords decided to sell my new home and I was forced to move out.

316

No matter how big the sting, a little sweetness always helped. Salt and sour became opportunities to show grace.

———

I haven't seen Jeff in person since the day I said goodbye to Gracie. I received a belated 'happy birthday' email from him in 2018, but haven't spoken to him otherwise. I don't know what he's up to and I don't plan on ever speaking to him again. This is the choice I've made for myself.

I *wish* I could report that I've moved on completely and I never give him a second thought but the truth is, I work hard every day to understand my feelings of resentment, mixed with hope and forgiveness. I had to dig deep to even give myself permission to *mourn* him. What I realized in that process is that *loss is loss*. Yes, sometimes I was angry. And yes, I was relieved to have him out of my life.

But that doesn't mean I did not mourn the loss of him.

I loved him. With everything I had. Until the very end.

I'm going to say that again because it's one of the deepest truths I know and one of the hardest ones to admit or understand. But that's why it must be said. As much as this is a story with heavy themes and heartbreak, it is just as much a story about love.

Jeff and I didn't *fall out of love*. We didn't lose the spark (not that this would have been easier if we did). But the act of losing him and still loving him through all of the aftermath, is one of the most difficult things I've ever done in my life. And the thing I'm most proud of.

Of all the brave things I've ever done — travelling alone, quitting my job to start my own business, zip lining through dodgy ropes in the rainforest, getting over my fear of heights, reading my book in public … the bravest thing I've ever done was *actively choosing* to be without him. It's the part of my story that has enabled me to be more of the person that I want to be.

317

This doesn't mean that *you* have to forgive him. But it does mean that it feels safe for me to turn that page now.

———

Part of turning that page means sharing this story, and believe me when I say, I thought long and hard about *not* publishing this book. Once it was all written down, I thought about just keeping it close to me when I slept each night and then eventually moving it into the closet with the stack of diaries I've kept since I was 10 years old. There was a huge piece of me that wanted to forget this ever happened. I wanted to be one of those happy, free people who just, 'Got Over It.' Unscathed. Unscarred.

But I've lived in the world of Untrue. And I wasn't willing to go back there. To live in my truth, I had to acknowledge how much this experience changed me. (And also, how grateful I was that it did.)

And yet, there are times when I feel pulled by both sides. I feel drawn in by my own demons to be angry and to pity myself. That person often finds solace with those who are also angry; those people in my life who would love to see me be a little petty, or at least get even. But that version of myself is not a happy person. She's not moving on. She's doesn't love herself. So I keep her at bay and choose grace over vengeance. I retreat to my yoga mat instead of retaliating. I look inside myself for answers and sometimes I ask God. And each time I've asked for answers, I've been shown again and again that this story is supposed to leave me. I lived it because it is meant to be told. So in the end, I've chosen to share it.

For a while, I wrote in fear about what Jeff, or Jeff's family, might do should any of them ever read this book. But I realized, once I finished writing, how very important this story is to tell and I have held that in my heart through the entire writing and publishing process. It has enabled me to choose love for myself and my story, over fear for the unknown.

Love over fear. Always.

I may have to face the consequences of publishing this book, but I now know that I will have the strength to make it through anything that comes from this. If I don't sell a single copy, I know I was brave because *I did this*. I lived through it, and I survived. If there are just two words that I've put together that helps one woman see that she is in a bad situation, then I will be even more proud.

If all this book does is help one, single person, I'm fine with that.

Even if that single person is me.

10 words had saved
me that year.

I'm sorry.

I forgive you.

I love you.

Thank you.

As I worked on, and struggled with, the ending of this book, I kept coming back to those 10 little (big) words. Ho'oponopono (or my version of it), is not a new concept. The technique of saying difficult things out loud, writing them down and reviewing them often had obviously worked wonders for me in the last year. But one of those 10 little (big) words left me with a disturbing feeling that lurked in the background of every interaction and every time I spoke, until I was willing to face it.

As this went on for months and months, and I sat and shared the mixed feelings I had with close friends and Di, that icky word *forgiveness* kept popping up. I'd heard the word in therapy over and over. I'd read it in almost every book that inhabited the mountain beside my bed. I'd watched the powerful women I respected talk about it on the TED stage, I heard about it in podcasts and read poetry about it. But *forgiveness*, as it turns out, is actually a very long and complicated word.

Months had passed since that day in the woods when I screamed it all out and thought I had let it all go, but there was this little piece still lingering. This piece that hurt when I thought about it because a part of me believed I would never actually get there. How does one forgive the unforgivable, I wondered.

"Practise," Di told me.

So, I practised. I started by listing all the hurt.

"It hurts that it wasn't one girl, one time. It hurts that I stayed around for so much bullshit..." I listed hurt for days on end. *"It*

hurt when you took Nick's sweet letter and made it into something bitter." "It hurt that you didn't have it in you to support me through my sister's surgery." "It hurt that I had to walk away from The Restaurant and leave it all behind."

The more hurt I listed, the more that one, single word made my stomach turn. The more I worked on this very chapter of this book, the more my skin crawled. That one, 11-letter-word haunted me for months and months. But there was still one more person on my journey that needed forgiveness. So, I *practised.*

On days when I had the strength to do it, I listed all the times he'd hurt me on paper and burned them over and over again. Whenever I prayed, I included a prayer for his healing. When I wrote about him, I tried to do it with as much grace as possible. If I was ever angry at him, I tried to release it in constructive ways and move on from it. It felt redundant but each time I did it, I felt a little better.

Any love I sent him didn't subtract from the love I gave myself each day. The love I sent him didn't make me weak. The love I sent him didn't mitigate the love I felt for my friends or family. The love I sent him didn't negate the romantic love I felt for others along the way. The love I sent him didn't cause me to grow bitter.

All it did was set me free.

That's what forgiveness became to me. It did not mean, for a single minute, that I excused any of his actions. All it meant was that I chose to believe that good people can do bad things, and that even bad people can do bad things and not be bad forever. I couldn't waste time hoping for that, and I wouldn't wait for an apology because these things were out of my control, I knew. But what I *could* control was how I chose to feel about him now.

Walking in this world is hard enough. Being *human* is hard enough. I'd seen first-hand the damage that could be caused due to a lack of love. Once I recognized that, I knew it wasn't fair to put myself through that for a moment longer … I loved myself too much for that now.

———

By the time this book was finished, I still wasn't ready to say those 10 words to Jeff, and I had to accept that it might never happen. I was however able to say them and mean them, to every single significant person in my life, and maybe most importantly, to myself.

Surprisingly, my healing journey did lead me to finding gratitude for Jeff. There was a difference between giving him credit for anything I had attained on my own, and thanking him, wholeheartedly, for the gifts that were able to transpire in his absence. *This was my work now* — and I decided to lean into it, instead of running away. The day I was able to lean into it fully and authentically, and say *Thank You* to Jeff, was the day I finished this book.

I started by listing the tangible gifts I could see that were brought about because of him and his actions — my new home, which brought me so much joy and freedom, may never have come to be, had I not have been so violently uprooted. Once I found one reason, others followed quickly and swiftly. My favourite example was my dog Gnowee, since Jeff was the one who pushed me to adopt her. I started with being thankful for those two things — my home and my dog — and then slowly but surely, all the more profound, subtle gifts which had come into my life because of him, became clear.

I silently thanked Jeff for the years we spent travelling and the memories we made, which regardless of what I knew now, felt real and precious at the time. What I'd seen of the world in his company, I decided to keep and not let be tainted, because it had given me the tenacity it required to travel this big, bright, scary world alone. Proving I could travel alone became paramount after him, but I had no idea how deeply I would fall in love with unknown places. I had no idea how richly I could connect with strangers, which led me to one of my greatest love stories (but you'll have to wait for my next book to hear that one)! Either way, my sense of adventure had become a part of my constitution so I thanked him for leading me to that part of myself.

I thanked him too for uprooting my career path in such a way that it made me appreciate catering on an entirely new level. Finding my way back to the stove was a *gift.* One that I wouldn't ever take for granted. I felt like I owed the limitless possibilities I felt now to my time at The Restaurant, so I thanked Jeff for putting me on that path. No matter how arduous that chapter of my life was, I was certain that my time spent there gave me the stamina and emotional fortitude I needed to make it through whatever challenges I might face for the rest of my life. My experience there led me to a new way of dealing with conflict and showed me how important it is to leave any situation, no matter how insurmountable it feels, with my character intact.

I thanked Jeff often for the elementary act of staying out of my life. I certainly wouldn't call it a *clean break,* but after witnessing what so many women go through when they decide they need to find a Way Out, I felt incredibly grateful to him for leaving me alone when I asked him to. Bankruptcy and material loss are nothing compared to what some women have to go through and I knew I was one of the lucky ones. At first, it hurt so much when I realized he wasn't going to fight for us, but now with some time and space, I realized it had been one of his greatest gifts to me.

I thanked him for showing me his true colours early in our relationship. Those red flags in the beginning forced me to see that I needed to set some money aside if things with him didn't work out. I don't know where I'd be now without those gut feelings or that stash of cash. Cleaning up his mess led me to some of the greatest friendships I have ever known, and somehow gave me the ability to connect with everyone I cross paths with on a much deeper level. This eventually led me to a consulting business, public speaking, podcasting and even going back to school. I gave myself permission, often and freely, to be grateful for that.

Even though it hurt more to say this than everything else combined, I thanked him for not having children with me. The deep grief that came with the certainty that I would not bear his children and that he might have children with someone else, devastated me daily. I also had to acknowledge and work through the realization that I may never be a mother in a traditional sense. It broke my heart and somehow, in the same breath, I knew it was in my greatest good. It was an insidious grief that I couldn't write about or speak about for a long time. But I believe that deep down, Jeff *knew* that he would never be a good husband or father, so I thanked him for not putting me through that.

Knowing men like Jeff just *existed* in this world, sometimes without consequences, made me cautious in a way that I wasn't, when we met. I was still navigating what it might look like to let myself fall in love again, but all I knew was meeting him made me beware of shiny objects for the rest of my life. Whether this would save or stifle me had yet to be seen. Either way, I thanked him for the awareness.

I thanked Jeff often, and wished for his healing. Each time it allowed me to let go a little more. The obvious reward for letting go — my freedom — was sweet. But the bounty that followed was sweeter. Relief. Sanctuary. Vulnerability. Hope. Sobriety. A gentleness I didn't know I had. My next great love story. The knowing that I belonged to myself. *This book.*

I'm not sure if I felt him actually *leave* my heart, but I knew it viscerally when he was gone. I knew that because of him displacing me, I had to learn my place. Because of losing the life I knew, I had to learn how to be lost. Because of the chaos he created, I had to learn stillness.

I wasn't strong then. But I am strong now.

That is because of you. *Thank you.*

———

Each day that I thanked Jeff I loosened the rope I was tethered to, a little more. Each day that I got closer to forgiveness, I felt myself becoming more liberated. I feel certain that someday, I will be able to release the anger and grief that still resides deep in my bones, and that when I am ready, I will be brave enough to cut the last cord and finally be free. Until that day comes, I choose to be patient and kind to myself, and believe that I'll get to forgiveness *someday*. And maybe, just maybe, the simple act of letting go daily, with passionate fury, and writing about it, could help someone else see that it's possible. What a gift I could give just by showing up and being myself.

Having the *will* to forgive has been the difference between *wanting* to be happy, and actually *being* happy. I owe it to myself because I've lived with hate for long enough. Hate for myself. Grief for my losses. Shame for my actions. Guilt for my story. I spent a whole year making amends and healing myself in increments. There was a slow rhythm to it that I grew to appreciate. Just like caramelizing onions, I had to be patient. I had to keep going. But now, I was ready for some softness and sweetness.

———

I wanted this book to be filled with recipes passed down from my family so I wrote a cookbook. I followed my stomach growls and cooked everything I could until I narrowed it down the recipes you've found here. It was one of the most beautiful, challenging, heartwarming, meaningful experiences of my life so far. To complete this collection, I had to track down Pedro (a man with no computer, internet connection and no permanent address). I had the opportunity to sit with my mother and talk about the food of our childhoods. I discovered one of my oldest friends kept a recipe I gave her nearly a decade ago, framed it, and hung it in her living room. I watched as my father tracked down his family's ancient pierogi recipe, and made it with my aunts and cousins. I cooked dishes from my time at The Restaurant that brought up trauma and elevated my healing all in the same bite. Most importantly though, the recipes in this book have enabled me to sweeten a chapter of my life that I thought would always taste sour.

I wanted this book to be more than just a collection of recipes — I wanted it to be about the *stories* that led me here. Writing this memoir has enabled me to see the whole picture and when I read back on all the moments that have mattered, I still feel a little shocked as to how *small* most of those moments were — a 30 second phone call that I was never meant to hear, one cup of tea with a friend, one miscalculation. I operated in those teeny, tiny moments for so long … right up until I decided to leave. Once I decided to leave though, I realized I couldn't do it in tiny steps anymore. It would have to be a giant leap. I needed to be willing to face that plummet, even if it took me all the way to rock bottom. It was a burning bridge over a gaping hole. No. Turning. Back. There was no other Way Out for me.

But the most profound lesson I have uncovered from that incredibly daunting, painful, seemingly impossible process is that sometimes the Way Out is really the Way In.

In my darkest hours, I found power and faith and friendship.

Later, I found mercy and humility and gratitude spilling out of my pores.

Even later still, I found adventure, passion, balance and tenderness.

And eventually, I found forgiveness. Which has led me to love in more ways than I could ever imagine: Platonic love, sister love, romantic love, doggy love and finally, "Self!" love.

———

For the first time since I started writing this book, and perhaps for the first time in my life, I no longer feel the need to perfectly wrap up my story, with a sparkly, golden bow. It doesn't need to be a fairy tale. It doesn't need to be clean or shiny. It can be black and bitter and burnt, as long as it's true. If I can live every moment of my life moving forward in a way that is both honest and kind, I will be happy.

Whether you finish this book in a day or a year; whether you take it all in or take what you need, I want this book to bring you

327

hope. I want you to find a message within the mess of this story. If this book makes you want to ugly cry, let it out and tell a friend. If this book makes you want to yell or scream — do it. Get mad. Dig deep. Go into the woods and scream as loud as you can — you might be surprised with what comes out. If this book makes you want to tell your own story, I'm here to remind you that you *are* brave enough. Take up space — you're big enough. You. Are. Important. Enough. You don't have to earn it or work for it. You are already, in every way, in every sense of the word, *enough.*

You are worthy of your words, so don't be afraid to speak your truth. We can all find our truths, and help others find theirs — just by using the voices we've been given.

My own truth, as it turns out, is that I never wanted a *simple* life. Sure, the promise of lemons in Costa Rica sounds magical, but I want *more* than that. What I want now is bigger than the love from another. It's bigger than belonging. What I want now is the same thing I begged and pleaded for on that Tuesday in August and in that church pew. I want truth. Big, bad, dark, scary, honest, ugly, salty, sour truth.

The truth is that I no longer have to choose between the loves of my life — food and words. Instead, they both exist as luminous, vivid flares in my heart, bringing people together and making me feel alive.

The other truth, which took longer to uncover and even longer still to accept, is that I no longer have to choose between my happiness and his. And I promise, *neither do you.*

———

I know this story is hard to read; I know because it was hard to write. But I also know that my life is better for it happening and perhaps your life is better now too, after reading or listening. All I know is that where there was once just a boy and a restaurant and some plaques on the wall, there is now a life full of love and meaning. Where there was once a broken-hearted girl mistaking intensity for love and negotiating with her intuition, there is now

328

a girl who and is careful with people's hearts (and her own). Where there was once a girl determined to belong, desperate for control and chasing perfection, there is now a girl made of boundaries, growth, grace and grit. Where there was once a 'Before' and an 'After,' there is now The Present Moment. Moments matter and *this one* matters most.

My days were once made of struggle and doubt, and those things are still in there, but *love* is there too. There's teaspoons of hustle and heaping spoons of gratitude. There are sprigs of prana, dashes of possibility, full litres of sunshine and scant cups of sadness. There's sticky bits, burnt bits, crumbled cake and lots of gravy. There's family gently folded in, in the form of Mom's Pot Roast and Dad's Pizza. There's comfort in Pedro's Orange Cake and adventure in Colcannon. There's grief in Santa Barbara Brussel Sprouts and relief in Sara's Gazpacho. There's salt. There's sour. There's *so much* sweetness. They are all part of my story, so they're all included in the recipe.

My recipe.

My recipe for starting over.

WITH GRATITUDE

I thank Spirit for sending me love notes in the form of people, every single day. Those people, in no particular order are:

Dad: I've been nervous to write this because I feel like there is no possible way I could even begin to acknowledge how much I appreciate and admire you. Not a day goes by that I do not realize how lucky I was to share 2018 with you. You are a constant source of support and joy in my life and you've been an amazing friend and father. Thank you for *everything.*

Mom: Every time I travel, I bring a roll of loonies and give them to people who need them. You taught me that. Thank you for supporting this book and giving me your pot roast recipe. Thank you for fiercely loving me, for showing me how to be generous and kind, for always being just a phone call away and for teaching me how to cook from scratch.

Sister: Thank you for dropping everything to be by my side when I needed you. Thank you for letting me use your house as my second home and storage unit, and for helping me, always. You're the best sister I could ever imagine.

Thank you, to my entire family including my Omi & Opi and all my aunts, uncles and cousins who have shown interest and support for this book. And thank you to my chosen family — especially Ruby and Doug — for a love that is without conditions.

"Chloe:" Thank you first and foremost for being my friend. Thank you for telling me a truth that wasn't easy. You were the first person who saw my first manuscript and I have to thank you for believing in every crazy idea I've ever had, including this book. Thank you also for answering every question I've ever sent you on spelling and grammar! (Grammer?! I'll never figure it out! Glad I have you!)

To my oldest, closest friends: Rochelle, Emily Anne, Laura, Jessa and Shannon. You have been through the ups and downs of life with me, and the events mentioned in this book are no exception. Being able to talk openly and honestly with all of you about my struggles and triumphs has helped me heal in unfathomable ways. You have helped me move (some of you more than once), let me cry on your shoulder (literally or on the phone from far away), held my pain and kept my secrets. You are the definition of what true friendship looks like. Special shout out to my oldest, dearest friend Jason who is a fellow traveller, chef and writer. I hope to share stories, food and adventures with you for decades to come.

To the circle of women who came into my life during the third section of this book, either at home or abroad, for a minute or for a lifetime, I thank each and every one of you, but especially: Carlen, Amber, Karissa, Chantelle, Brooklyn, Noelle, Jordan and Jenna. I don't know where or who I would be without my soul sisters. Your work and words and hugs and love have meant so much to me. Thank you from the bottom of my heart. Special thank you to Emma for being my healer, confidant and hiking buddy. Also, you were right. ;)

A special nod of gratitude and love to my LSC Girls: Roks, Nic and Desi. I look up to all of you, am proud to stand beside you and I want to be like you when I grow up!

Thank you to Louis and all the boys from my hometown, who taught me about growing up in all kinds of ways.

To those who have shared my pain, brought me joy, been exceptionally kind and been my friend: Sarah Beauchamp, Amanda Fell, Erin Harris, Kim Saunders, Tracy Little, Stephanie Brewster, Andrew Wolwowicz, Martina Biljan, Julie Walsh, Carla Calderon Perez, Kandice Trickett, Shannon Kamins, Lisa McClelland, Chad Hull, Kelly Edwards, Abby and Cam McCuaig, Simon Thorel, Kirsten Mould, Paul Abeleira, Devon

332

Slack, Scott and Becca Baechler, Joey!, Chantal Gauthier, Dean Myserscough, Ashleigh Ross, Mariam Waliji, Matt Marsh, Aaron Bolohan, the Coughlins, Steph Berube, Richard Placzek, Pam Scharback, Katie Sullivan, Peter Barlow, Chelsea Stewart, Chad Stewart, Nick and Sheila Erratt, Sylvie and Andy Roth, Mindy and Marty Menard, Jane and Chuck Magri, Tabitha Switzer, Kate St. Laurent, Mariah Fisher, Greg Wight, Julie Bouchard, Heather Taylor, Becky Stephenson, Stephanie Williams, Lauren Wilk, Ashley and Matt Rubenhagen, Alex Connon, Danielle Guetter, Cheryl Wituik, Nika Duda, Rhonda Fabian and the team at Farber, Laura Pitman, Jessica Taillieu, Emma Richard, Peggy Malone, Jess Merucci and Jenny Thompson, Kylie Agniso, Margaret Coons, Krista Ewer, Jess Ireland, Rhonda Bernardi and Vanessa Warren. I could thank so many of you in various places throughout these acknowledgments — y'all are amazing! If I've missed you, please know I appreciate you deeply!

Thank you to all the patrons of The Restaurant and supporters of my business since then. Thank you to all the clients who have become friends, especially Jen and Gerry Finck, Katie and Kyle, Gavin and Loraina and The Haneys. Thank you to all of you who have welcomed me into your kitchens and made me feel like family — Brad and Debbie... I'm lookin' at you!

To everyone involved in this project... someone give me a rooftop so I can shout off of it how grateful I am to all of you! To Krista Kankula, my incredibly patient and talented copywriter, and my dear, dear friend. Our coffee dates and deep conversations have been some of the highlights of this process. Sue Campbell — the best proofreader in the world and an incredibly generous person! Thank you for being meticulous and patient, and for hours of hard work. Thank you to my web designer Amanda Devries and to Roman Hidalgo for a super fun photo shoot! Thank you to my incredible illustrator, Andres Garzon, for making my vision come to life and for your incredible talent and beautiful art. Thank you to Katelyn Landry for creating the book cover that I didn't even know I wanted — to say you exceeded all my expectations and wildest dreams is an understatement. Thank you also to Nicole Osbourne for her support in that art.

A special THANK YOU goes out to my editor Genevieve Georget, who doubles as one of my favourite authors and humans. You brought this book into its wholeness. Your perspective and sage advice has meant more than you know and I am so incredibly honoured for your guidance, editing and friendship.

Thank you to anyone who lent recipes or experiences to this story, and a special thank you goes out to my Recipe Taste Testers! This book would never have made it to the hands of whomever is reading it now, without all of you. Thank you to those who let me into their lives for fact checking and to everyone who gave honest feedback along the way. Thank you to Allyson Proulx for letting me use and adapt her quote, "Rise is a long word." Thank you Jennifer Broxterman for beta reading this book, and to Heather Marshall for her hours of counsel and for answering every single email and late night text.

To the core team at The Restaurant: "Brandon," "Marie," "Scarlet" and "Sara" — thank you for sharing your stories and memories with me, for being brave until the very end and for all your love since the day we met. Thank you especially to "Rachel," "Frank" and "Mackenzie" — I might not be here without you. Thank you to the rest of The Restaurant family for your service and kindness.

To my mentors, chefs and colleagues over the years: Thank you for your continued support and for seeing me as the person I want to be. Thank you to all the chefs who reached out and made me feel less alone. Special shout out to my friend, 'Kitchenaide Kelly,' and to Ashton and Tommy.

To my healers: Candice Melrose, Jill Lauren, Sheilha, Angie Wiseman and Lisa Lopes — the work you do is so important and special. Thank you to my therapist, Di, for your life-changing advice and guidance. Thank you also to all the souls in my life who have helped heal me through yoga, wild writing, singing bowl sessions, given me crystals because we believed it would help, offered reiki and touched me with the intent of relieving pain.

To my friends Amy, Austen and Mark who left this world too soon: I miss you.

Thank you to Jocelyn and Wayne for creating the best pizza in the world and a safe space to speak and share. Thank you to Ellie and Jeff and the entire team at The Root Cellar for not only making such a positive impact in our food system, but also for being my second home and letting me park at the bar for hours on end while I finished this book. (Kale Caesar Salad for the win!)

To my dog, Gnowee: who I know can't read this but I will feed you infinity treats and love you forever!! She was by my feet as I poured everything out on paper, by my side when I woke up and nuzzling my face during those really hard moments. A girl and her dog, I tell ya!

To the authors and artists out there who have shaped my experience and helped me through these big life things. Thank you to everyone who is making honest art, authentic media and truth-telling podcasts.

Thank you everyone in my life who believed in this book, followed me on my journey and is with me now. Thank you to everyone who gave me a chance to talk about my book — through public readings, open mics, podcasts and interviews. Thank you for promoting this story and supporting my soul-cry.

Thank you to "Lane," JW, Chaten, Chelsea, The Poet and anyone else who has taught me valuable lessons in love.

Last but not least, thank you to my guardian angel, "Monica." I am forever in your debt.

———

I consider these pages to be some of the most important pieces of work I've ever written. And I consider you to be the most important people I'll ever know.

ABOUT THE AUTHOR

Yoda Olinyk is a chef and a first-time author. She lives in Southwestern Ontario with her dog Gnowee, where she operates her small (but mighty) catering company. Her future plans include travelling, studying psychology and getting started on her second book.

Manufactured by Amazon.ca
Bolton, ON